AN INDEX

TO

NORTH CAROLINA NEWSPAPERS,

1784-1789

AN INDEX

TO

NORTH CAROLINA NEWSPAPERS,

1784-1789

Alan D. Watson

ISBN 0-86526-253-5

CONTENTS

Foreword...vii

North Carolina Newspapers, 1784-1789 ix

Newspapers Indexed...xxvi

Index...1

Appendix 1: Advertisements in North Carolina Newspapers, 1784-1789 67

Appendix 2: The Speed with Which News Was Reported
  in North Carolina Newspapers, 1784-1789 68

FOREWORD

During the observance of the bicentennial of the federal Constitution, the Historical Publications Section undertook a number of joint publication projects with the North Carolina Commission on the Bicentennial of the United States Constitution. In 1988 the section issued *North Carolina Votes on the Constitution: A Roster of Delegates to the State Ratification Conventions of 1788 and 1789*, by Stephen E. Massengill. In 1989 John C. Cavanagh's *Decision at Fayetteville: The North Carolina Ratification Convention and General Assembly of 1789* appeared. With the publication of *An Index to North Carolina Newspapers, 1784-1789* by Alan D. Watson, the series "North Carolina and the Constitution" comes to an end.

The North Carolina Commission on the Bicentennial of the United States Constitution expired on December 31, 1989. Before its termination, however, it made a grant of $5,000 to the Historical Publications Section to assure the publication of this index to North Carolina newspapers. In particular Rob Sikorski and Earle Blue, formerly of the commission's staff, deserve special mention for shepherding the grant through the state budget office.

The index was compiled and edited by Alan D. Watson, one of the state's leading scholars on colonial and Revolutionary North Carolina. Dr. Watson is professor of history at the University of North Carolina at Wilmington. He is the author of numerous books, articles, and essays on North Carolina history. His special insight into the historical contours of the era makes this index especially valuable to a wide variety of researchers interested in the social, economic, political, and genealogical heritage of the state.

Several members of the section's staff made important contributions to the publication of this index. E. T. Malone, Jr., saw the manuscript through press. Alisa F. Richardson, formerly a member of the section's staff, prepared the index on a computer for typesetting, and Lisa D. Bailey assisted with the proofreading. Their work is gratefully acknowledged.

Jeffrey J. Crow
Historical Publications Administrator

February, 1992

North Carolina Newspapers, 1784-1789

Two centuries ago David Ramsay presaged a common maxim when he wrote that the pen and press bore equal merit with the sword in the realization of American independence. Contemporaries as well as later historians have agreed substantially with Ramsay's assessment. In 1776 John Holt of the *New-York Journal* declared, "It was by means of News papers that we receiv'd & spread the Notice of the tyrannical Designs formed against America and kindled a Spirit that has been sufficient to repel them." A more objective commentator in the twentieth century, Arthur M. Schlesinger, concurred when writing that the Revolutionary movement "could hardly have succeeded without an ever alert and dedicated press." Whether as vehicles of propaganda, as asserted by the Progressive historians of the early twentieth century, or media that helped to spawn and refine republican ideas generating an ideological impetus toward revolution, American newspapers had an inestimable impact on the course of events that culminated in independence.[1]

In the Revolutionary struggle, however, North Carolina newspapers played a far less prominent role than did those in most of the colonies, and North Carolina was one of the last to obtain printing presses. James Davis inaugurated the *North Carolina Gazette*, the province's first newspaper, in 1751 in New Bern. Davis, a Virginia emigré, probably learned the printing trade under William Parks, printer of the *Maryland Gazette* and then the *Virginia Gazette*. Davis published his *Gazette* intermittently over the course of a decade, replacing the paper in 1764 with the *North Carolina Magazine; or, Universal Intelligencer*. In its large size and consecutive pagination the *North Carolina Magazine* resembled a magazine, but in content and format it remained a newspaper. After approximately four years Davis quit the *North Carolina Magazine* to resume the *North Carolina Gazette*, the last issue of which appeared in 1778.[2]

The only other town in prerevolutionary North Carolina to enjoy the advantage of a newspaper was Wilmington. Andrew Steuart, an Irish-born Philadelphia printer who came to North Carolina in expectation of becoming the public printer of the colony, launched the *North Carolina Gazette and Weekly Post Boy* in 1764. He ceased its publication in 1767, apparently due to financial stringency. At Steuart's death two years later, Adam Boyd, a clergyman of Pennsylvania birth and "a gentleman of fine literary and classical attainments," purchased Steuart's old press and three sets of type. He commenced the *Cape-Fear Mercury* in October, 1769. Boyd subsequently warmed to the patriot cause, offered his paper as an organ of the Wilmington-New Hanover Committee of Safety, and permanently suspended its publication upon enlisting in the First North Carolina Battalion on January 4, 1776.[3]

---

[1]David Ramsay, *The History of the American Revolution* (New York: Russell & Russell, 2 volumes, 1968 [1789]), II, 319; Arthur M. Schlesinger, *Prelude to Independence: The Newspaper War on Britain, 1764-1776* (New York: Alfred A. Knopf and Random House, 1965), 284, 285, hereinafter cited as Schlesinger, *Prelude to Independence*; Philip Davidson, *Propaganda and the American Revolution, 1763-1775* (Chapel Hill: University of North Carolina Press, 1941); H. Trevor Colbourn, *The Lamp of Experience: Whig History and the Intellectual Origins of the American Revolution* (New York: W. W. Norton, 1974).

[2]Robert N. Elliott, Jr., "James Davis and the Beginning of the Newspaper in North Carolina," *North Carolina Historical Review*, XLII (January, 1965), 3-4, 7-11, 14-18, hereinafter cited as Elliott, "James Davis and the Beginning of the Newspaper in North Carolina"; Stephen B. Weeks, *The Press of North Carolina in the Eighteenth Century* (Brooklyn: Historical Printing Club, 1891), 9-10, 17-18, 21-23, hereinafter cited as Weeks, *Press of North Carolina in the Eighteenth Century*; William S. Powell (ed.), *Dictionary of North Carolina Biography* (Chapel Hill: University of North Carolina Press, projected multivolume series, 1979—), II, 34-35, hereinafter cited as Powell, *DNCB*; Lawrence C. Wroth, *The Colonial Printer* (Charlottesville: Dominion Books, 1964; New York: Grolier Club, 1931), 41-43, hereinafter cited as Wroth, *Colonial Printer*.

[3]Weeks, *Press of North Carolina in the Eighteenth Century*, 32; George Washington Paschal, *A History of Printing in North Carolina* (Raleigh: Edwards & Broughton, 1946), 15, hereinafter cited as Paschal, *History of Printing in North Carolina*; Durwood T. Stokes, "Adam Boyd, Publisher, Preacher, and Patriot," *North Carolina Historical Review*, XLIX (January, 1972), 1-21; quotation from Catherine DeRosset Meares, *Annals of the DeRosset Family: Huguenot Immigrants to the Province of North Carolina, Early in the Eighteenth Century* (Columbia, S.C.: R.L. Bryan, 1906), 61.

The overwhelmingly rural character of colonial North Carolina largely explains the absence of news sheets. Newspapers appeared in towns in order to take advantage of the potential of an aggregate market. North Carolina's lack of urbanization, however, militated from the beginning against the successful introduction of newspapers. The first town, Bath, arose a half century after the settlement of the colony. Yet it and most other towns were little more than villages or crossroads communities, important commercially but woefully small. On the eve of the Revolution the ports of Wilmington, New Bern, and Edenton exhibited the greatest size, but none contained more than a thousand residents. Altogether, probably no more than two percent of North Carolina's population lived in towns on the eve of the Revolution, a figure that changed little during the ensuing five decades.[4]

After the hiatus caused by the Revolution the newspaper reappeared in the state in the 1780s. At least eight were printed in six towns—New Bern, Edenton, Wilmington, Fayetteville, Halifax, and Hillsborough—before the end of the decade. The Revolution accelerated the growth of New Bern, the first capital of the state. Nicely situated on the confluence of the Neuse and Trent rivers, New Bern took advantage of ocean traffic via the Pamlico Sound and served as an *entrepôt* for the hinterland trade. Travelers reacted ambivalently to the town. Johann Schoepf called New Bern "small, not yet rich." Francisco de Miranda found the houses "only so-so, and small for the most part"; but J. F. D. Smyth and William Attmore praised the quality and size of the residential structures. Smyth in 1784 believed that New Bern was larger than Wilmington. Certainly by the beginning of the nineteenth century New Bern had emerged as the state's largest town, containing 2,467 residents according to the census of 1800.[5]

Distantly following New Bern in the census tally were Wilmington, 1,689, Fayetteville, 1,656, and Edenton, 1,302. Wilmington, the colony's major deep-water port, was located on the Cape Fear River, the only river in the state that flowed directly into the Atlantic Ocean. The town also evoked conflicting feelings among its visitors. Miranda described its location as advantageous and pleasant, its buildings comfortable, clean, and generally better than those of New Bern, and its residents "more sociable, more generous, and better dressed." Schoepf also thought that Wilmington's 150 framed residences made a "good appearance." Contrarily, Smyth dismissed Wilmington as "nothing better than a village." And a young merchant from London in 1786 described Wilmington as "without exception . . . the most disagreeable, sandy, barren town I have visited on the continent. . . ." Still, by virtue of its location Wilmington continued and expanded its commercial preeminence after the Revolution.[6]

---

[4]H. Roy Merrens, *Colonial North Carolina in the Eighteenth Century: A Study in Historical Geography* (Chapel Hill: University of North Carolina Press, 1964), 142, hereinafter cited as Merrens, *Colonial North Carolina in the Eighteenth Century*; Alan D. Watson, *Society in Colonial North Carolina* (Raleigh: North Carolina Department of Cultural Resources, Division of Archives and History, 1975), 75-87; Guion G. Johnson, *Ante-Bellum North Carolina: A Social History* (Chapel Hill: University of North Carolina Press, 1937), 114-119, hereinafter cited as Johnson, *Ante-Bellum North Carolina*.

[5]Johann David Schoepf, *Travels in the Confederation [1783-1784]*, translated and edited by Alfred J. Morrison (New York: Burt Franklin, 2 volumes, 1968; Philadelphia: William J. Campbell, 1911), II, 128-129, hereinafter cited as Schoepf, *Travels in the Confederation*; Francisco de Miranda, *The New Democracy in America: Travels of Francisco de Miranda in the United States, 1783-1784*, translated by Judson P. Wood, edited by John S. Ezell (Norman: Oklahoma University Press, 1963), 6, hereinafter cited as Miranda, *New Democracy in America*; J. F. D. Smyth, *A Tour in the United States of America* (New York: Arno Press, 2 volumes, 1968; London: Printed for G. Robinson, J. Robson, and J. Sewell, 1784), II, 89, hereinafter cited as Smyth, *Tour in the United States*; Lida Tunstall Rodman (ed.), *Journal of a Tour to North Carolina by William Attmore, 1787* (Chapel Hill: University of North Carolina Press, 1922), 45-46; Alonzo Thomas Dill, Jr., "Eighteenth Century New Bern. A History of the Town and Craven County, 1700-1800, Part VIII. New Bern at the Century's End," *North Carolina Historical Review*, XXIII (October, 1946), 515, hereinafter cited as Dill, "Eighteenth Century New Bern." A correspondent to the *North Carolina Gazette* in 1799 believed that the number of inhabitants in New Bern had doubled during the past decade and a half. *North Carolina Gazette*, January 12, 1799.

[6]Miranda, *New Democracy in America*, 14; Schoepf, *Travels in the Confederation*, II, 145; Smyth, *Tour in the United States*, II, 87; Louis B. Wright and Marion Tinling (eds.), *Quebec to Carolina in 1785-1786: Being the Travel Diary and Observations of Robert Hunter, Jr., A Young Merchant of London* (San Marino, Calif.: Huntington Library, 1943), 280, 287, hereinafter cited as Wright and Tinling, *Quebec to Carolina*.

Edenton, the seat of Chowan County, was located on the northwestern end of Albemarle sound. Geographically isolated from the rest of the state and located some distance from the ocean, Edenton seemed destined to remain a small town. As a port, it specialized in coastal and West Indian commerce, but the Revolution seemed to sap the town's spirit of enterprise. Trade began to bypass Edenton for Halifax and small ports along the rivers that fed the Albemarle Sound. By most accounts postwar Edenton was uninviting. Containing about 100 "very indifferent" frame houses (though including an elegant brick courthouse) in the mid-1780s, the town was described as a "dull disagreeable place" and "sickly," and indicted for its indolent populace, both black and white. On the other hand, Smyth found Edenton "by far the most pleasant and beautiful town in North Carolina. . . ."[7]

Fayetteville, on the upper Cape Fear, evolved from the village of Cross Creek, which arose just after mid-eighteenth century in an effort to divert North Carolina's backcountry trade from South Carolina to Wilmington. Cross Creek's rivalry with a nearby settlement ended in 1778, when the two were united as Campbellton, renamed Fayetteville in 1783. Strong economic ties linked Wilmington to Fayetteville which brokeraged commerce between Wilmington and the western part of the state. On his famed Southern tour in 1791, President George Washington reported that six thousand hogsheads of tobacco and three thousand hogheads of flaxseed had been sent to Fayetteville during the previous year. A principal, though unsuccessful, contender for the site of the permanent capital of the state, Fayetteville continued to rank as one of the fastest growing towns in North Carolina during the late eighteenth century.[8]

North of Fayetteville, Halifax and Hillsborough, the seats of Halifax and Orange counties respectively, were two of the state's largest urban communities. Halifax, located on the Roanoke River about fifteen miles from the North Carolina-Virginia border, contained about fifty houses in 1774, and exhibited an "active trade" ten years later. A center of horseracing and boasting "many handsome buildings" according to a traveler in the 1780s, Halifax was a seat of backcountry aristocracy. Hillsborough, like Halifax, was a locus of backcountry commerce. According to a visitor in 1784, it was "a healthy spot, enjoys a good share of commerce for an inland town, and is in a very promising state of improvement." The next year a Hillsborough resident agreed that the village "begins to thrive." At that time it contained some forty houses, a church, a courthouse, and a promising academy. The "advanced state of agricultural improvement" in the area as well as the "very genteel society" of Hillsborough impressed another observer, Elkanah Watson.[9]

North Carolina's first postwar newspaper appeared in New Bern when *The North Carolina Gazette, or Impartial Intelligencer and Weekly General Advertiser* emerged from the press in September, 1783. Printed by Robert Keith and Company for Thomas Davis, son of James Davis, the *Gazette* survives in two extant issues, the last of which is dated September 2, 1784. The Keith paper was followed by *The State Gazette of North-Carolina*, printed by Abraham Hodge and Andrew Blanchard, and later by Hodge and Silas W. Arnett, and then by Hodge and Henry Wills. Publication of the *State Gazette of North-Carolina* in New Bern extended from

---

[7]Thomas C. Parramore, *Cradle of the Colony: The History of Chowan County and Edenton, North Carolina* (N. p.: Edenton Chamber of Commerce, 1967), 38-39; Elkanah Watson, *Men and Times of the Revolution; or, Memoirs of Elkanah Watson . . .* , edited by Winslow C. Watson (New York: Dana, 1856), 37, hereinafter cited as Watson, *Men and Times of the Revolution*; Wright and Tinling, *Quebec to Carolina*, 266; Smyth, *Tour in the United States*, II, 93; Schoepf, *Travels in the Confederation*, II, 111, 115-116.

[8]Merrens, *Colonial North Carolina in the Eighteenth Century*, 157-160; Walter Clark (ed.), *The State Records of North Carolina* (Winston and Goldsboro: State of North Carolina, 16 volumes [numbered XI-XXVI], 1895-1906), XXIV, 513-517; XXV, 470-472, hereinafter cited as Clark, *State Records*; John A. Oates, *The Story of Fayetteville and the Upper Cape Fear* (Charlotte: Dowd Press, 1950), 159-178, 259-261; Donald Jackson and Dorothy Twohig (eds.), *The Diaries of George Washington* (Charlottesville: University Press of Virginia, 6 volumes, 1976-1979), VI, 119.

[9]Smyth, *Tour of the United States*, I, 84-88, 160-161; Schoepf, *Travels in the Confederation*, II; Griffeth J. McRee (ed.), *Life and Correspondence of James Iredell* (New York: Peter Smith, 2 volumes, 1949; New York: D. Appleton, 1857), II, 98, 104-106, 126, hereinafter cited as McRee, *Iredell*; Watson, *Men and Times of the Revolution*, 253.

November, 1785, to July, 1788. At that time Hodge and Wills moved their business to Edenton, where they resumed the *State Gazette* in September and continued its operation into the 1790s.[10]

The *State Gazette* encountered competition both in New Bern and in Edenton. In the former town Francois X. Martin brought out his *North-Carolina Gazette, or New-Bern Advertiser*, later *Martin's North-Carolina Gazette*, on January 4, 1785, and continued the paper under various titles (mainly the *North-Carolina Gazette*) to 1798. Maurice Murphy published the first number of *The North-Carolina Gazette; or the Edenton Intelligencer*, probably in October, 1787, and continued that paper (as *The Edenton Intelligencer*) at least through July of the following year.[11]

Wilmington and its upcountry trading partner, Fayetteville, tardily acquired news sheets. Caleb D. Howard and a man named Bowen established *The Wilmington Centinel, and General Advertiser* in March, 1788. The operation quickly disbanded, for Howard soon departed, going to Fayetteville. There he entered into a partnership with John Silbey to publish the *Fayetteville Gazette*, the first issue of which appeared on August 24, 1789. The name changed in 1790 to *The North Carolina Chronicle; or, Fayetteville Gazette*, whose publication ceased in 1791.[12]

North of Fayetteville, papers were published briefly in Halifax and Hillsborough, the result of the endeavors of Thomas Davis. Early in 1784 Davis probably transferred his press from New Bern to Halifax, fulfilling a two-year design to move to that town. No extant issues survive of the Halifax paper which was begun in March and apparently enjoyed a brief lifetime. Davis switched his operation to Hillsborough by July, 1785, where Robert Ferguson printed *The North Carolina Gazette* for him. The first of five extant issues is dated October 6, 1785; the last, February 23, 1786. The paper had been discontinued by July, 1786.[13]

The North Carolina printers were a diverse, mobile lot, mostly obscure immigrants to the state. But that was true of most such men, especially south of New England, before the Revolution and during the early days of the republic. Thomas Davis seems to have been the only North Carolina-bred printer, learning the trade in his father's shop and inheriting the press and type at James Davis's death in 1783. Abraham Hodge, born in New York in 1755, served with George Washington at Valley Forge before coming to North Carolina in the mid-1780s. With the exception of Francois X. Martin, little is known of the other printers.[14]

Francois X. Martin, born in Marseilles, France, in 1762 to a prosperous merchant family, became one of the most illustrious citizens of the state and nation in the late eighteenth and early nineteenth centuries. He possessed a classical education in preparation for the priesthood. Shunning that profession, Martin sailed to the West Indies while in his teens, made his way to Virginia to fight as a volunteer in that state's militia during the Revolution, and finally appeared in New Bern in 1783. Prior to printing the *North-Carolina Gazette*, Martin taught French, delivered the mail, and worked as a typesetter, probably for Robert Keith. After instituting his newspaper, Martin read law and was admitted to the bar. He prospered from his

[10]Clarence S. Brigham, *History and Bibliography of American Newspapers, 1690-1720* (Westport, Conn.: Greenwood Press, 2 volumes, 1976; Worcester, Mass.: American Antiquarian Society, 1947), 760, 771, 772, hereinafter cited as Brigham, *History and Bibliography of American Newspapers*; Weeks, *Press of North Carolina in the Eighteenth Century*, 37; McRee, *Iredell*, II, 231n; *State Gazette of North-Carolina* (New Bern), March 27, 1788; *State Gazette of North-Carolina* (Edenton), September 8, 1788.

[11]Brigham, *History and Bibliography of American Newspapers*, 759, 771-772; Weeks, *Press of North Carolina in the Eighteenth Century*, 39.

[12]Brigham, *History and Bibliography of American Newspapers*, 762-763, 780; Weeks, *Press of North Carolina in the Eighteenth Century*, 44-46; *Fayetteville Gazette*, August 24, 1789.

[13]McRee, *Iredell*, II, 96, 142; Clark, *State Records*, XVII, 91, 504; Brigham, *History and Bibliography of American Newspapers*, 766.

[14]Stephen Botein, "'Meer Mechanics' and an Open Press: the Business and Political Strategies of the Colonial American Printers," *Perspectives in American History*, IX (1975), 151, 157, hereinafter cited as Botein, "'Meer Mechanics' and an Open Press"; Clark, *State Records*, XIII, 259-260; Weeks, *Press of North Carolina in the Eighteenth Century*, 26-30, 36, 39, 41, 43; Powell, *DNCB*, II, 40-41.

printing and legal endeavors, eventually concluding his career as an eminent and wealthy jurist in the Gulf Coast states.[15]

Whatever their pretensions or education, and despite an increasing demand for their trade, printers remained mere artisans or mechanics in the estimation of society. Moreover, their nomadic ways rarely allowed them to establish roots in a town from which they might wield an influential voice in local affairs. Those who achieved notoriety, like Benjamin Franklin or Francois Martin, transcended the printing business. Only after abandoning the *North Carolina Gazette* about 1798 was Martin fully admitted to New Bern society, allowed entrée to the inner sanctum of town politics, and able to realize the prospect of promotion in the judicial system.[16]

Inaugurating a newspaper was no easy task. Sibley and Howard launched the *Fayetteville Gazette* only "after experiencing a variety of disappointments and unforeseen causes of delay … ." After distributing a prospectus of their undertaking, they blamed a deficient transportation system and a busy summer season for a delayed public response. Sibley and Howard also felt that their venture was jeopardized by the past failures of prospective publishers who could not fulfill their promises. When moving to Halifax, Thomas Davis intimated that previous efforts to establish a paper there had been unavailing.[17]

In fact, while Sibley and Howard trusted their future to an uncertain public response, many publishers established papers on the basis of promised patronage. Abraham Hodge reportedly was induced to come to North Carolina in 1784 or 1785 by some prominent citizens, presumably from New Bern, but James Iredell soon lured him to Edenton with promises of printing assignments. In Wilmington, Archibald Maclaine and friends were disillusioned soon after they helped to underwrite Bowen and Howard's *Wilmington Centinel* to serve as a mouthpiece for the Federalists in the area. With seeming ingratitude, Howard defected to the Antifederalists; Bowen became a touring exhibitor of waxwork figures. Although Bowen returned somewhat contritely, neither he nor Howard provided the abject apology demanded by Maclaine, who with his friends determined to seek another printer. Without patronage the paper folded, explaining Howard's move to Fayetteville.[18]

The newspaper publisher realized a pecuniary return primarily from subscriptions and advertisements. A considerable disparity existed among the subscription prices quoted by the sheets for which there are figures: 40 shillings per year for the *Wilmington Centinel*; 25 shillings per year for the *State Gazette of North Carolina*; 3 Spanish milled dollars (£1.4.0) for Keith's *North Carolina Gazette*.[19] Newspaper circulation is impossible to determine, most difficult even to approximate. None of the North Carolina towns had as many as twelve hundred white inhabitants before 1790. With a population of 2,467 in 1800, New Bern could not have contained more than two-thirds that number, or approximately 1,600, in 1790, and slaves,

[15]W.B. Yearns, "Francois X. Martin and His *History of North Carolina*," *North Carolina Historical Review*, XXXVI (January, 1959), 17-19; Weeks, *Press of North Carolina in the Eighteenth Century*, 37-39; Samuel A. Ashe (ed.), *Biographical History of North Carolina* (Greensboro: Charles L. Van Noppen, 8 volumes, 1905-1917), IV, 306-314.

[16]Botein, "'Meer Mechanics' and an Open Press," 150-160.

[17]*Fayetteville Gazette*, August 24, 1789; Clark, *State Records*, XVI, 195-196.

[18]Weeks, *Press of North Carolina in the Eighteenth Century*, 41; McRee, *Iredell*, II, 231, 239-240, 243. Adam Boyd in 1775 successfully sought financial support from the Wilmington-New Hanover Safety Committee for his *Cape Fear Mercury*. Leora H. McEachern and Isabel M. Williams (eds.), *Wilmington-New Hanover Safety Committee Minutes, 1774-1776* (Wilmington: Wilmington-New Hanover American Revolution Bi-centennial Association, 1974), 14-15. James Carey, who founded *The Wilmington Chronicle: and North Carolina Weekly Advertiser* without any predetermined support, found his financial position precarious in less than six months. *The Wilmington Chronicle: and North-Carolina Weekly Advertiser*, July 3, October 8, 1795.

[19]*Wilmington Centinel*, June 18, 1788; *State Gazette of North-Carolina* (Edenton), September 3, 1789; *North Carolina Gazette, or Impartial Intelligencer*, July 29, 1784. The Spanish milled dollar was worth ninety pence in Pennsylvania in the 1780s and ninety-six pence in North Carolina according to legislation in 1785. Rollo G. Silver, "Aprons Instead of Uniforms: The Practice of Printing, 1776-1787," *Proceedings of the American Antiquarian Society*, LXXXVII, Part 1 (1977), 168, hereinafter cited as Silver, "Aprons Instead of Uniforms"; Clark, *State Records*, XXIV, 723. The North Carolina figure will be used in subsequent calculations.

prominent in all eastern towns, probably accounted for half or more of that total. Edenton in 1786 counted 1,112 residents, 480 of whom were white. Four years later there were but 180 free families in the town, 281 in Fayetteville, and 40 in Hillsborough.[20]

Beyond the towns in which the sheets were published, the geographic extent of newspaper subscriptions is conjectural. Adam Boyd in November, 1772, circulated the *Cape Fear Mercury* in Granville, Guilford, and Chatham counties. During the summer of 1787 Francois X. Martin published essays by "Horatio" from Long Island on Holston in present Tennessee and by "A Yeoman" from "Westfields" near Salisbury. By December, 1787, Martin forwarded his paper regularly to subscribers in Kinston, Greenville, Tarboro, Halifax, Warrenton, Louisburg, Oxford, Williamsburg, Harrisburg, Edenton, Washington, and Wilmington. In setting up the *Fayetteville Gazette*, Sibley and Howard apparently circulated their prospectus over an extensive area.[21]

According to Charles Christopher Crittenden the largest circulation of any North Carolina newspaper before 1790 probably did not exceed 150. The average was 100, perhaps an understatement. After all, the circulation of the *Philadelphia Gazette* and the *Virginia Gazette* before the Revolution may have reached three thousand and eight hundred respectively. At any rate, gauging paid circulation of the North Carolina papers at one hundred copies per annum, income would have been £200 for the *Wilmington Centinel*, £125 for the *State Gazette*, and £120 for Keith's *North Carolina Gazette*.[22]

The printers never realized those sums however. Subscribers were notably tardy in meeting their obligations, and the printers were reluctant to alienate them. Besides, the scattered population and small sums involved rendered legal prosecutions impractical. James Davis in 1778, "once more" called upon his "old customers long in arrear . . . to make payment." Martin and the publishers of the *Wilmington Centinel* issued similar pleas. After a year's publication in Edenton, Hodge and Wills of the *State Gazette* announced that "nothing but a *punctual discharge of the last year's subscription*, can ensure a continuation" of the paper. And the *Fayetteville Gazette* shut down its press in 1791 due to "the extreme want of punctuality in so large a number" of its subscribers.[23]

Revenue from advertising doubtless helped but also proves difficult to ascertain. The *Wilmington Centinel* and *State Gazette of North-Carolina* charged eight shillings per advertisement for the first week and four shillings per week thereafter. Keith required one dollar (eight shillings) for the first three weeks and a quarter of a dollar (two shillings) per week thereafter; Davis, in Hillsborough, five shillings for the first week and three shillings for each subsequent week. However, in the case of the *Gazette* in Hillsborough, failure to send payment with the advertisement resulted in a doubling of the charge.[24]

The average number of advertisements as seen by the sample in Table 1 varied widely, from

[20]See note 5; Clark, *State Records*, XVIII, 434; *Heads of Families at the First Census of the United States Taken in the Year 1790: North Carolina* (Baltimore: Genealogical Publishing Company, 1966), 9.

[21]William L. Saunders (ed.), *The Colonial Records of North Carolina* (Raleigh: State of North Carolina, 10 volumes, 1886-1890), IX, 356, hereinafter cited as Saunders, *Colonial Records*: *Martin's North-Carolina Gazette*, July 11, August 15, December 19, 1787; *Fayetteville Gazette*, August 24, 1789.

[22]Charles Christopher Crittenden, *North Carolina Newspapers before 1790* (Chapel Hill: University of North Carolina Press, 1928), 19, hereinafter cited as Crittenden, *North Carolina Newspapers*; Botein, "'Meer Mechanics' and an Open Press," 148-149; Robert M. Weir, "The Role of the Newspaper Press in the Southern Colonies on the Eve of the Revolution: An Interpretation," in *The Press & the American Revolution*, edited by Bernard Bailyn and John B. Hench (Worcester: American Antiquarian Society, 1980), 112-113, hereinafter cited as Weir, "Role of the Newspaper Press."

[23]Botein, "'Meer Mechanics' and an Open Press," 150-151; *North Carolina Gazette* (New Bern), April 3, 1778; *Martin's North-Carolina Gazette*, August 1, 1787; *Wilmington Centinel*, December 18, 1788; *State Gazette of North-Carolina* (Edenton), September 3, 1789; *The North Carolina Chronicle; or Fayetteville Gazette*, March 7, 1791. For a printer whose patrons were $3,000 in arrears see the *Wilmington Gazette*, April 30, 1805.

[24]*Wilmington Centinel*, June 18, 1788; *State Gazette of North-Carolina* (Edenton), September 3, 1789; *North Carolina Gazette, or Impartial Intelligencer*, July 29, 1784; *North Carolina Gazette* (Hillsborough), February 23, 1786.

13 per issue for Keith's *North Carolina Gazette* to 4.7 for the *Edenton Intelligencer*. Davis's *North Carolina Gazette* in Hillsborough, the *Wilmington Centinel*, and *State Gazette* carried 10.6, 10.9, and 6.7 respectively. If each advertiser retained his notice for four weeks, the *Centinel* and *State Gazette* would have realized £141.14.0 and £87.2.0 respectively on an *annual* basis. Keith would have been paid only £84.10.0, and Davis, £96.9.2. Thus the North Carolina publishers probably realized less from advertisements than from subscriptions.[25]

Because the newspaper business offered at best a minimal income, economic success for the newspaper printer rested upon a combination of activities that included job printing and retailing paper products. Silbey and Howard of the *Fayetteville Gazette* announced their intention of carrying "into effect every Branch of Printing. . . ." Most of the newspaper printers advertised "Blanks" of all kinds, which for Keith's *North Carolina Gazette* included bills of lading, seamen's journals, indentures, powers of attorney, letters of administration, administration bonds, guardian bonds, superior court writs, county court writs, sheriffs' bail bonds, jurors' tickets, and bonds and conveyance to soldiers' lands. Printers also offered sundry articles of paper supplies and writing implements such as wrapping paper, writing papers, pasteboard for bonnets, ink powder, ink stands, and sealing wax.[26]

Bookselling and bookbinding offered printers opportunities to augment their income. Robert Keith maintained a bookstore in conjunction with his printshop, selling Bibles, testaments, prayer books, spellers, and primers. Among other works Bowen and Howard sold *The Chorister's Companion* and the *American Singing-Book*. In addition to publishing a new edition of James Davis's *The Office and Authority of a Justice of the Peace* among other works, Francois Martin combined his printing operation and legal acumen to write or edit and publish law books, case books, and statutes. Martin as well as Hodge and Wills of the *State Gazette of North-Carolina* printed pamphlets for adversaries during the controversy over the ratification of the federal Constitution. Hodge and Wills also proposed to publish an edition of the *Laws of the State of North-Carolina* (by James Iredell) and an edition of David Ramsay's *The History of the American Revolution*. In addition to popular almanacs and spellers they sold a Masonic discourse delivered before St. John's Lodge in New Bern, a comedy entitled *The Politician Outwitted*, *The Defence of Count Cagliostro*, and military regulations for the cavalry of the Halifax District.[27]

The printer, however, found that the market for his skills was limited to a relatively small number of customers who had the ability, funds, and leisure to take advantage of the printed word. This restricted demand not only confined printers to towns but also rendered it difficult for them to subsist for any length of time outside the larger urban areas. Essentially the success or longevity of the newspaper depended upon a reliable source of income for the printer beyond his dependence upon the open market. This might consist of a supplemental profession, such as the bar for Francois X. Martin, or a public printing contract from the government.

Employment by the government as public printer offered a lucrative source of funding. The office of public printer, filled by appointment of the General Assembly, entailed the printing of session laws, legislative journals, gubernatorial proclamations and messages, and money. During the war James Davis became the first state printer, continuing in the position to which he had

---

[25]By way of comparison advertisements in the prerevolutionary *Maryland Gazette* and *Virginia Gazette* averaged 42 to 55 per issue; in the New York dailies in 1795, 350 insertions per issue. Advertisements in the prerevolutionary *Pennsylvania Gazette* generated only one-third of the revenue realized by subscriptions. Weir, "Role of the Newspaper Press," 111, note 23; Allan R. Pred, *Urban Growth and the Circulation of Information: The United States System of Cities, 1790-1840* (Cambridge, Mass.: Harvard University Press, 1973), 23, hereinafter cited as Pred, *Urban Growth and the Circulation of Information*.

[26]*Fayetteville Gazette*, August 24, 1789; *North Carolina Gazette, or Impartial Intelligencer*, July 29, 1784; *Wilmington Centinel*, December 3, 1788; Botein, " 'Meer Mechanics' and an Open Press," 143-145.

[27]Weeks, *Press of North Carolina in the Eighteenth Century*, 36; *Wilmington Centinel*, January 8, 1789; *Martin's North-Carolina Gazette*, July 11, 1787; *State Gazette of North-Carolina* (Edenton), October 6, 1788; January 8, October 22, 1789. *See also* Paschal, *History of Printing in North Carolina*, 14.

been appointed by the colony in 1752, and retiring in 1782. The General Assembly selected his son, Thomas, to succeed him as state printer. In fact, the father may have even received an implicit promise that the mantle of state printer would fall to his son. Thomas received a salary of £600 per year exclusive of the cost of paper.[28]

Thomas Davis remained the state printer for three years, though the office became more competitive as the number of printers and presses in the state increased. In September, 1783, two prominent politicians, Benjamin Hawkins and Hugh Williamson, criticized Davis for failing to produce the laws and resolutions of the Assembly, pointedly observing that several other printers sought employment by the state. Legislation in 1784 reappointed Davis to the position of printer, but when he sought to change the basis of his salary from a fixed sum to cost plus, a legislative committee reported adversely on his petition. The state terminated Davis's contract in 1785, replacing him as the public printer with the New Bern firm of Arnett and Hodge. Hodge and his successive partners served as the printers for the state through 1797.[29]

Thus a reliable source of funding beyond a dependence upon subscriptions and advertisements seemed mandatory to the success of newspaper publication. Bookselling and job work were not the answer. No doubt the public printing contract enjoyed by James Davis, Thomas Davis, and Hodge and associates not only helps to explain their decision to venture into newspaper publication but also more especially the longevity of their sheets, particularly in the cases of James Davis and Hodge. On the other hand the deprivation of the printing contract may well have accounted for the collapse of Thomas Davis's *North Carolina Gazette* in Hillsborough in 1786. Martin's legal work doubtlessly helped to keep his sheet afloat. In fact, other than Martin's *North-Carolina Gazette* the only papers that were not subsidized privately or in which the publisher did not have the state printing contract were the *Edenton Intelligencer* and the *Fayetteville Gazette.*

Publishing a newspaper was a tedious, time-consuming, labor-intensive task, reflecting generally the temper of life in the eighteenth century. The publisher-printers sometimes shouldered the burden; otherwise, like Silbey and Howard, they employed a journeyman printer. In turn the printers or journeymen utilized the help of a "devil," or apprentice, to set the type. Robert Keith, for example, advertised for a "couple of lads, fourteen or fifteen years of age," to serve as apprentices in his printing shop. Instead, he probably settled for Francois X. Martin, who used his training to establish his own printing business and newspaper. Hodge and Wills in 1789 sought a good compositor who could occasionally work the press as well as set type—doubtless a rarity in a town of Edenton's size.[30]

The press, lead type, and printing appurtenances were not only expensive but scarce during and after the Revolution. Americans had only begun to experiment with the manufacture of presses and type at the advent of the conflict with England. The great bulk of their printing equipment came from the mother country, however, and the wartime disruption of trade, inflation, and speculation curtailed the printing trade. The cessation of hostilities made the press and other equipment easier to obtain but hardly lowered their price. James Davis, who had lost all his equipment during a hurricane in 1769, doubtlessly obtained a new press and type from England, all of which he bequeathed at his death in 1783 to his son Thomas. The other

---

[28]Mary Lindsay Thornton, "Public Printing in North Carolina, 1749-1815," *North Carolina Historical Review*, XXI (July, 1944), 184-191, hereinafter cited as Thornton, "Public Printing in North Carolina." Andrew Steuart apparently came to North Carolina in 1764 with the expectation of becoming the public printer. His cause precipitated a battle between the House of Commons on the one hand and the governor and Council on the other. The Commons emerged victorious and James Davis retained the contract. Jack P. Greene, *The Quest for Power: The Lower Houses of Assembly in the Southern Royal Colonies, 1689-1776* (New York: W. W. Norton, 1972), 291-295.

[29]Thornton, "Public Printing in North Carolina," 196.

[30]Elliott, "James Davis and the Beginning of the Newspaper," 5; Johnson, *Ante-Bellum North Carolina*, 775; Worth, *Colonial Printer*, Chapter III; McRee, *Iredell*, II, 243; Weeks, *Press of North Carolina in the Eighteenth Century*, 36-38; *State Gazette of North-Carolina* (Edenton), January 8, 1789.

printers in the state probably brought used equipment with them from the northern states as they immigrated to North Carolina.[31]

Inhibiting newspaper publication and all modes of printing throughout the eighteenth and early nineteenth centuries was the irregular supply of paper. During the Revolution a short-lived paper mill operation was started in the vicinity of Hillsborough. In 1789 Gottlieb Schober announced his intention to erect a paper mill in Wachovia; two years later the manufactory was operational. In the meantime Thomas Davis ran out of paper for his Hillsborough printing establishment, and the expectation of Sibley and Howard of the *Fayetteville Gazette* to print "on paper of their own manufacture" seemed fanciful. North Carolinians remained dependent upon unreliable importations of paper.[32]

The content of the papers represented a mélange that ranged from foreign, national, and local news to political disquisitions, literary essays, poetry, marine lists, and advertisements. Allan Nevins appropriately observed that the files consisted of a "superabundance of jumbled, disparate and mainly trivial details" that imposed "on the writer a burden of assortment and synthesis under which most men break down." Lacking a formal newsgathering agency, the printers took copy from every available source, often subject to the vagaries of the weather and human frailties in their receipt of information. In fact, newspaper composition was a haphazard process caused by a reliance upon undependable sources of information that left the printers grasping to fill space, even in the four-page sheets of North Carolina.[33]

Reporting the news constituted a primary function of the newspaper. The speed with which news traveled bore important consequences. During the antebellum era there seemed to be a positive correlation between the flow of information and the ability of urban areas to maintain and expand their influence. The sheets slighted local news in favor of international and national information. Not only did the printers lack a reportorial staff; they also assumed that local news was reasonably familiar, particularly by the time it might appear in the weekly news sheet. Still they bestirred themselves to include marriage and death notices, marine arrivals and departures, and sometimes other bits of local color.[34]

Although the time of Atlantic ocean transit steadily decreased during the eighteenth century, and the regularity and dependability of travel improved, Table 2 shows that news from the British Isles required three months or more to reach North Carolina; that from the Continent, four months. London remained the principal provenance of European news, directly and indirectly from the continent, as it had during the colonial era. Occasional datelines included Dublin, and, on the continent, Paris, Warsaw, St. Petersburg, Vienna, Frankfort, Berlin, Amsterdam, Stockholm, Lisbon, and The Hague. The *Fayetteville Gazette* carried datelines for Malta (185 days) and Calcutta (284 days). The *State Gazette* proudly announced copy from the *Madras Courier*, taken from a Boston paper, said to be the first time that news from India had been seen in North Carolina.[35]

---

[31]Silver, "Aprons Instead of Uniforms," 164-174; Worth, *Colonial Printer*, Chapters V and VI; Elliott, "James Davis and the Beginning of the Newspaper," 5-6; Weeks, *Press of North Carolina in the Eighteenth Century*, 26; *State Gazette of North-Carolina* (Edenton), September 3, 1789.

[32]*North Carolina Gazette* (New Bern), November 28, 1777; Saunders, *Colonial Records*, X, 217-218; Clark, *State Records*, XII, 413, 812, 875; McRee, *Iredell*, II, 142; Adelaide L. Fries et al (eds.), *Records of the Moravians in North Carolina* (Raleigh: State Department of Archives and History, 11 volumes, 1922-1969), V, 2269, 2271, 2279, 2303, 2304, 2321, 2326, hereinafter cited as Fries, *Records of the Moravians; Fayetteville Gazette*, August 24, September 14, 1789; Silver, "Aprons Instead of Uniforms," 174-176; Worth, *Colonial Printer*, 169-171; *North Carolina Gazette* (Hillsborough), October 6, 1785.

[33]Allan Nevins, "American Journalism and Its Historical Treatment," *Journalism Quarterly*, XXXVI (Fall, 1959), 413.

[34]Weir, "Role of the Newspaper Press in the Southern Colonies," 126-127; Pred, *Urban Growth and the Circulation of Information*, passim; Johnson, *Ante-Bellum North Carolina*, 783.

[35]Ian K. Steele, "Beyond the 'Imperial School' or The Significance of the Atlantic Ocean in Early American History," paper presented at the American Historical Association meeting, December 1984; Al Hester, Susan Parker Humes, and Christopher Bickers, "Foreign News in Colonial North American Newspapers, 1764-1775," *Journalism*

The state remained relatively isolated from Europe, receiving its foreign news much later than the larger, busier north Atlantic ports which traded extensively with the British Isles and continent. In fact, it took from two to four times as long for information of European origin to reach North Carolina as it did for communication from any of the states along the Atlantic coast. By and large the delay experienced by North Carolina in securing European news was occasioned by the printers' dependence upon communications from the ports of New York and Philadelphia. Since the time lag in 1790 for Philadelphia's receipt of news from England was over two months and for continental Europe, almost three months, North Carolinians necessarily read dated dispatches.[36]

Within the United States the datelines indicate that North Carolina printers relied principally upon New York and Philadelphia (followed distantly by Boston and Baltimore) for national as well as international news. The affinity for New York and Philadelphia, the first two capitals of the nation, had arisen during the colonial era when the towns became efficient distributors of news throughout the provinces. North Carolina's contact with neighboring states was slight. Even after the *State Gazette* moved to Edenton, only 7 of the 15 issues sampled contained Virginia datelines (Petersburg, 2; Richmond, 2; Norfolk, Winchester, Fredericksburg), and two weeks passed before North Carolinians were informed of the happenings. Ties with South Carolina were also tenuous. Only one-third of the issues of the *Wilmington Centinel* contained Charleston datelines, which were a week and a half dated. Georgia and the West Indies were infrequently mentioned, surprisingly in the latter instance given the extensive commerce that was conducted between North Carolina and the islands.

The printers obtained news beyond their immediate locale principally from published materials—particularly newspapers and to a lesser extent magazines, supplemented by private communications. Postage-free printers' exchanges by which newspapers circulated gratis among the printers, a policy instituted in the colonial era by deputy postmasters Benjamin Franklin and William Hunter, was continued by the United States. During the course of the debate over the Constitution, Postmaster Ebenezer Hazard was erroneously accused of revoking the privilege of the postage-free exchange because it would favor those who supported the new government. The printers' exchange remained the primary means by which printers secured information before the advent of the telegraph in the nineteenth century.[37]

The means by which the printers secured newspapers and letters varied from ship and private rider to the post. Although postal service early became a vital artery in the communications network of the American colonies, North Carolina was the last of the thirteen to obtain it. Not until January, 1771, did Governor William Tryon inform the General Assembly of the province that a post had been established through North Carolina via Edenton, Bath, New Bern, and Wilmington to connect Suffolk, Virginia, and Georgetown, South Carolina. By 1774 a branch route linked Fayetteville (Cross Creek) and Wilmington. At that time consideration was given to an alternate route through the province from Suffolk to Halifax and then to New Bern, which would have avoided long, dangerous ferries over the Albemarle Sound and the Neuse River. However, that route never materialized, and the post remained slow, unreliable, and expensive.[38]

Quarterly, LVII (Spring, 1980), 22, 44, hereinafter cited as Hester, Humes, and Bickers, "Foreign News in Colonial North American Newspapers"; *Fayetteville Gazette*, October 12, 1789; *State Gazette of North-Carolina* (Edenton), July 2, 1789. Of course some time elapsed between the receipt of the news and its printing. Thus the figures exaggerate the time differential. *See* Weir, "Role of the Newspaper Press in the Southern Colonies," 127-128.

[36]Weir, "Role of the Newspaper Press in the Southern Colonies," 129-130; Pred, *Urban Growth and Circulation of Information*, 26; Hester, Humes, and Bickers, "Foreign News in Colonial North American Newspapers," 22.

[37]Richard B. Kielbowicz, "The Press, Post Office, and Flow of News in the Early Republic," *Journal of the Early Republic*, III (Fall, 1983), 256, hereinafter cited as Kielbowicz, "Press, Post Office, and Flow of News"; Wesley E. Rich, *The History of the United States Post Office to the Year 1829* (Cambridge, Mass.: Harvard University Press, 1924), 63-66, hereinafter cited as Rich, *History of the United States Post Office*.

[38]Charles C. Crittenden, "Means of Communication in North Carolina, 1763-1789," *North Carolina Historical*

After the collapse of royal government, the Americans reinstituted the post. North Carolina was part of the Southern District that extended from Annapolis, Maryland, to Savannah, Georgia. The disruption of communication seemed more immediately severe in North Carolina than in most states. Yet by 1777-1778, the post was operable in North Carolina, though only along one road—the coastal road—in the state. A congressional ordinance in 1782, which placed the postal system on a firm foundation, remained the basic law for the postal department of the country until 1792. It established or confirmed routes, set fees, and determined the duties of postmasters.[39]

Postmaster General Hazard, who had suggested the postal legislation of 1782, actively sought to improve postal service in the 1780s by utilizing stage lines to carry the mail and by establishing branch or cross routes. Stages appeared in North Carolina in the middle of the decade, though a traveler in 1786 remarked that such transportation was as yet unreliable. However, in 1787 Congress made that form of mail carriage virtually mandatory, at least along the major mail route that hugged the coast from Maine to Georgia. In North Carolina stage transport of the mail (as well as freight and passengers) had become routinized by 1789.[40]

The branch route from Wilmington to Fayetteville lapsed during the Revolution, and Hazard was aware of the need to provide better service to the interior of the state. In 1787 Congress authorized the establishment of a number of cross routes to link the coast with the western regions. The General Post-Office advertised contracts for the minor runs in September, 1788, and included a route from Wilmington to Fayetteville via Elizabeth Town, and another from Fayetteville to Camden, South Carolina, and from thence to Charleston. Nonetheless, the contracts remained unfulfilled before North Carolina entered the United States. In 1789, of the 75 post offices and 2,400 miles of post roads in the nation, North Carolina boasted only four post offices—Edenton, Washington, New Bern, and Wilmington—along that single coastal route of approximately 380 miles that Tryon had instituted two decades earlier.[41]

Not surprisingly the newspaper printers were in the vanguard of those who sought to improve postal facilities. In some cases they supplemented the public mail system with private carriers. Recently arrived in the state from Pennsylvania, Robert Keith recognized the need for a regular post from the east to the interior of the province. Francois Martin served as the postmaster in New Bern during the 1780s, and utilized a rider in 1787 to deliver his paper to the western parts of the state. During the sitting of the General Assembly in the western town of Hillsborough in 1788, Hodge and Wills in Edenton proposed to undertake a private post from Hillsborough via New Bern and Washington and which would return by way of Tarboro. In July, 1788, Bowen and Howard of the *Wilmington Centinel* established a weekly post, underwritten by private subscription, from Wilmington to Fayetteville, a service that continued into 1789.[42]

During the 1780s the printers rarely committed themselves editorially. Instead they opened their papers to the public, announcing that "Articles of Intelligence and Essays will be gratefully

---

Review, VIII (October, 1931), 376-378, hereinafter cited as Crittenden, "Means of Communication in North Carolina"; Hugh Finlay, *Journal kept by Hugh Finlay, Surveyor of the Post Roads on the Continent of North America* . . . . (Brooklyn: Frank R. Norton, 1867), 65-88, hereinafter cited as Finlay, *Journal kept by Hugh Finlay*; *Cape Fear Mercury* (Wilmington), May 11, 1774.

[39]Rich, *History of the United States Post Office*, 51, 56; Hugh B. Johnston (ed.), "The Journal of Ebenezer Hazard in North Carolina, 1777 and 1778," *North Carolina Historical Review*, XXXVI (July, 1959), 358-381.

[40]Rich, *History of the United States Post Office*, 60, 62; Wright and Tinling, *Quebec to Carolina*, 263, 274-275, 283-284; *State Gazette of North-Carolina* (Edenton), January 8, 1789. For the summer 1786 stage route from Suffolk, Virginia, to New Bern see *State Gazette* (New Bern), July 6, 1786.

[41]Rich, *History of the United States Post Office*, 62; *State Gazette of North-Carolina* (Edenton), October 20, 1788; Kielbowicz, "Press, Post Office, and Flow of News," 257; Arthur Hecht, "Postal History of North Carolina, 1789-1795," *North Carolina Historical Review*, XXV (April, 1958), 126-127, hereinafter cited as Hecht, "Postal History of North Carolina"; Finlay, *Journal Kept by Hugh Finlay*, 88; Wright and Tinling, *Quebec to Carolina*, 263; Watson, *Men and Times of the Revolution*, 41.

[42]Weeks, *Press of North Carolina in the Eighteenth Century*, 36; *Martin's North-Carolina Gazette*, December 19, 1787; *State Gazette* (Edenton), October 27, 1788; *Wilmington Centinel*, July 2, 30, 1788; February 5, 1789. John M. Whitney in

received." However, the *North Carolina Gazette* at Hillsborough contained editorial criticism of the General Assembly's paper money policy and treatment of loyalists. In his *North Carolina Gazette*, Martin condemned the secret proceedings of the Constitutional Convention in Philadelphia. Hodge and Wills of the *State Gazette of North-Carolina* added a "Laus Deo" after the report of North Carolina's ratification of the federal Constitution and followed with an obviously appreciative summary of the celebration in Edenton. They also condemned card playing and commented favorably on the progress of North Carolina's burgeoning number of academies. But by and large harsh, controversial editorial opinion and subsequent violent confrontations between editors awaited the nineteenth century.[43]

Although little editorial commentary dotted the papers, the printers indirectly expressed their sentiments when deciding what to include in their sheets. A prime criterion was utility. Not only did the printers seek to bring the "Freshest Advices" or news to their readers, they carried material in their "Miscellany" and "Anecdote" departments that was directed toward the moral and cultural improvement of the populace: "Hints for Young Married Women" and "Maxims for the Conduct of Young Gentlemen." On the other hand Martin rejected one submission of poetry, claiming "the only touchstone by which we try the literary favours of our correspondents" is that "there should be sense." Likewise, Silbey and Howard refused to bring a poetic offering because "any particular benefit resulting from it to society cannot be discovered—utility we ought not lose sight of."[44]

The arrangement of press materials exhibited little consistency. Foreign news dominated the front and part of the second page, followed by reports of developments in the states. Advertisements occasionally appeared on page one. When available, letters to the editor always filled the front page columns of Martin's *Gazette*, and they often appeared in a similar position in most other papers. Pages two and three contained continuations of letters, news, marine lists in the cases of the ports, and advertisements. The last (fourth) page invariably housed the "Poet's Corner," or space devoted to literary compositions, "Anecdotes," and additional advertisements.

Whatever the arrangement of materials, the press in the eighteenth century was elitist. Literacy levels dictated readership, and Kenneth Lockridge's discovery of limited literacy in eighteenth century Virginia must certainly apply to North Carolina. Educational opportunities were severely restricted; further, the more agrarian oriented societies of the southern colonies and states did not require the skill or literacy levels of the more complex economies of the northern colonies. In addition, most news could only appeal to those of broad geographic perspective, while polemical essays studded with Latin quotations and allusions to ancient history required a classical education for proper appreciation.[45]

Advertisements also reflected upper-class use and readership of the papers. Not only did the expense of advertising place that means of public notice beyond the average citizen but the advertisements revealed an elitist orientation. Of the sampling of 371 advertisements from seven papers, shown in Table 1, almost two-thirds involved the sale or rental of land, lots, and houses; slaves; the sale of merchandise; the establishment, movement, or dissolution of businesses; notices by administrators or executors of estates; positions (apprentice or supervisor

---

1786 tried to organize a stage line from Fayetteville to Wilmington via Elizabethtown, estimating that he would need at least seven passengers and thirty-five letters per week to cover expenses. *North Carolina Gazette* (Hillsborough), January 19, 1786.

[43]*North Carolina Gazette* (Hillsborough), February 16, 1786; *Martin's North-Carolina Gazette*, July 11, 1787; *State Gazette of North Carolina* (Edenton), October 22, December 3, 1789; Johnson, *Ante-Bellum North Carolina*, 786-794.

[44]*Wilmington Centinel*, June 18, 1788; *State Gazette of North-Carolina* (Edenton), February 5, 1789; *Martin's North-Carolina Gazette*, July 11, 1787; *Fayetteville Gazette*, September 21, 1789.

[45]Weir, "Role of the Newspaper Press in the Southern Colonies," 131-132; Kenneth Lockridge, *Literacy in Colonial New England: An Inquiry into the Social Context of Literacy in the Early Modern West* (New York: W. W. Norton, 1974), 21-23, 136-138, note 55.

of a sawmill) or goods wanted; schools; and ships sailing, for sale, or for hire.

The desire on the part of the elite to gain access to the outside world was almost pathological. It helped to underpin the famed notion of southern hospitality. Visitors of proper station were not only welcomed as house guests but beseeched to remain for protracted sojourns while their hosts pumped them for every possible tidbit of information. Printed matter offered the other principal window to the outside world. Archibald Maclaine chastised George Hooper for "never think[ing] of sending me any new publication, though you know how much I like such things. . . ." And William Hooper in Hillsborough complained to James Iredell in Edenton, "I have not seen a paper or magazine since I came hither. We hold no more intercourse with the public and political world than if we were no part of it. When opportunity offers, pray send us all you can spare." It was a plea often repeated.[46]

The attitude of the upper class did not reflect merely an academic exercise to enlarge their fund of knowledge. Superior knowledge confers status, or at least reinforces customary authority, which helped to explain the avidity for any news, even the seemingly trivial or irrelevant affairs of the European courts that seemed to absorb so much space in the papers. Additionally the elite expected and were expected to illumine the less fortunate members of society. When Archibald Maclaine of Wilmington considered the propriety of a second ratifying convention in 1788 to ratify the federal Constitution, he wrote, "It would be in vain to attempt petitions in this, and the neighboring counties, unless persons of some degree of popularity would undertake to forward the business." On the other hand the well-to-do felt the threatening pressure of the egalitarian spirit of the Revolution, reinforced as it was by the evangelical movement of the mid- to late-eighteenth century. Thus the small number of newspapers in North Carolina rendered access to them all the more important, especially in a traditional society greatly dependent upon the oral transmission of information.[47]

If the determination of a subscription list proves guesswork, secondary readership of the papers is altogether speculative. Access to papers was gravely limited in North Carolina by a scattered population, paucity of towns, and difficulties of transportation. Although copies may have been available where people congregated regularly—county courts, churches, militia musters, taverns, stores, the ability or desire to take advantage of the sheets was problematical. Limited literacy reinforced by poor lighting and worn type militated against prolonged reading. So did the content of the papers, which was obviously oriented toward the wealthy in a state widely noted for its relative poverty. When farmers gathered to escape the drudgery of everyday life, perusing a newspaper, if it was available, must have ranked low on their list of priorities.

Though the newspapers may not have been widely read, they certainly had an impact beyond their primary audience. According to recent studies, the process known as the "two-step flow" of communications provides a nexus between the mass media and the general populace. The first level involves those individuals directly affected by the mass media; the second, the interpersonal transmission of news by the first group to the general populace. The "two-step flow" of communication becomes more important for traditional societies in which access to media such as newspapers is more limited than for highly developed societies. In developing societies where there are a few acknowledged leaders, the "two-step flow" of communication may well be not only the most common but the most effective means of diffusing information.[48]

---

[46]Clark, *State Records*, XVII, 128; McRee, *Iredell*, II, 90. See also McRee, *Iredell*, II, 96, 239. Social stratification continues to influence greatly media-reading habits and attitudes. Frederick Williams and Howard Lindsay, "Ethnic and Social Class Differences in Communication Habits and Attitudes," *Journalism Quarterly*, XLVIII (Winter, 1971), 672-678.

[47]McRee, *Iredell*, II, 243; Weir, "Role of the Newspaper Press in the Southern Colonies," 145; Wilbur Schramm, "Communication Development and the Development Process," in Lucian W. Pye (ed.), *Communications and Political Development* (Princeton, N. J.: Princeton University Press, 1963), 53, hereinafter cited as Pye, *Communications and Political Development*.

[48]Pye, *Communications and Political Development*, 25-28; Elihu Katz, "The Two-Step Flow of Communications; An

During the Revolutionary era the newspapers had profoundly affected the opinion-making process in the colonies. They had stirred popular resentment, imputed base motives to British actions, and proclaimed to varying degrees the provincial right of autonomy. During the 1780s the opportunity for the North Carolina press to manipulate and mold the public mind reemerged amid the controversies surrounding the conduct of the state judges and the putative unconstitutional usurpation of power by the state legislature. Those questions were quickly followed and overshadowed by the contest over the ratification of the federal Constitution.

The Articles of Confederation, which instituted in 1781 the first formal national government for the revolutionary states, proved a short-lived experiment. The Articles represented the American reaction to English rule and reflected the democratic forces unleased by the Revolution. It provided a framework in which relatively powerful state governments dominated a weak central structure that lacked the power to tax and regulate commerce. Fear of executive influence led to a government dominated by the legislature, which in turn exercised executive functions. As the term implied, the union was a loose alliance of independent states broadly controlled by a national authority.

A growing dissatisfaction with the inability of the national government to cope with foreign and domestic exigencies resulted in the drafting of the federal Constitution at Philadelphia in 1787. After the submission of the Constitution to the states for ratification, proponents of the new government, called Federalists, and their opposition, styled Antifederalists, waged a heated campaign. In North Carolina's first state convention at Hillsborough in 1788, the Antifederalists easily defeated a move to ratify the federal Constitution. Rather than accept the new document, they called for a series of amendments to define more clearly the powers of the government and to protect explicitly the civil liberties of its citizenry. After the institution of the United States in 1789 (without North Carolina and Rhode Island), the Federalists in the state redoubled their efforts, secured a call for a second convention to meet in Fayetteville in November 1789, conducted a vigorous educational-propagandistic battle, and obtained an overwhelming vote for ratification.[49]

Jackson T. Main ascribes the ultimate victory of the Federalists in the country in part to the fact that most newspapers supported the ratification of the Constitution. While Federalists' sheets comprised a vast majority throughout the states, they barely held their own in North Carolina, a factor which may have accounted for, but more probably reflected, the majoritarian Antifederalist sentiment in the state. Before Howard became a "rank anti-federalist," the *Wilmington Centinel*, patronized by arch-Federalist Archibald Maclaine and his friends, dutifully trumpeted the Federalist cause. Readers were apprised of the ratification proceedings in Virginia, New Hampshire, and New York, and were informed of a joyous Wilmington celebration following the news of New York's approval of the Constitution. In July 1788 the *Centinel* reprinted a letter written by George Washington which praised Maryland's ratification; in January 1789, the paper carried a letter from a Rhode Island Federalist who commended North Carolina's seeming repentance of its "anti-federal conduct."[50]

Likewise the sheets in Edenton, a stronghold of Federalism, advanced the cause of the Constitution. Both in New Bern and in Edenton to which it moved at the instigation of James Iredell and the Federalist coterie there, the *State Gazette of North-Carolina* supported the new

---

Up-to-Date Report on the Hypothesis," *Public Opinion Quarterly*, XXI (Spring, 1957), 61-78; Lloyd R. Bostian, "The Two-Step Flow Theory: Cross-Cultural Implications," *Journalism Quarterly*, XLVII (Spring, 1970), 109-117; Pred, *Urban Growth and the Circulation of Information*, 17.

[49]Penelope Sue Smith, "Creation of an American State: Politics in North Carolina, 1765-1789" (unpublished doctoral dissertation, Rice University, 1980), 487-491, 507-508, hereinafter cited as Smith, "Creation of an American State"; Blackwell P. Robinson, *William R. Davie* (Chapel Hill: University of North Carolina Press, 1957), 160-169, 175-176, hereinafter cited as Robinson, *William R. Davie*; *Martin's North Carolina Gazette*, August 15, 1787.

[50]Jackson T. Main, *The Antifederalists: Critics of the Constitution, 1781-1788* (Chicago: Quadrangle Books, 1964), 250-252; *Wilmington Centinel*, July 16, 1788; January 22, 1789.

government. The other Edenton paper, the *Intelligencer*, which was published at least during 1787-1788, appeared also to be a vehicle for Federalism. Its contributors included Elkanah Watson, who was born in Plymouth, Massachusetts, traveled widely in America and Europe, and settled in Chowan County in 1787 to pursue a mercantile-shipping trade. Though Watson's communiques do not appear in the few extant issues of the *Intelligencer*, he left a Commonplace Book containing several letters that he had penned for publication in that paper.[51]

The Antifederalists countered with Martin's *North-Carolina Gazette* and the *Fayetteville Gazette*. New Bern was an enclave of Federalism in the overwhelmingly Antifederalist Craven County. But Martin managed to survive in the hostile atmosphere of the town, perhaps because his paper enjoyed a widespread circulation throughout the county and state, particularly in the backcountry. After Howard abandoned his Federalism and in turn was eschewed by Maclaine, he moved to Fayetteville to start the *Fayetteville Gazette* with Sibley.

Pamphlets supplemented the newspaper fare. The different formats of the two media commended them to different audiences. Newspapers provided a quicker, more direct, less expensive means of reaching a wide audience. Pamphlets, offering an opportunity to develop extensive arguments, obviously were aimed at a more limited, usually more knowledgeable readership. They were designed mainly to unify party or factional leadership.[52]

Despite their differences, the newspapers and pamphlets could be used interchangeably. The first of several pamphlets published in North Carolina during the ratification controversy, bearing the date of January 8, 1788, written by James Iredell, and printed by Hodge and Wills of the *State Gazette* in New Bern, was *Answers to Mr. Mason's Objections to the New Constitution recommended by the late Convention at Philadelphia*. It was printed first in serial form in the *State Gazette* before being collected and published as a pamphlet. On the other hand, *To the People of the State of North-Carolina*, written by "A Citizen of North-Carolina" and published by Hodge and Wills in August 1788, was subsequently reprinted piecemeal in the *State Gazette* and in the *Norfolk and Portsmouth Gazette* in Virginia.[53]

Historians have traditionally associated the Federalists with the upper stratum of society, the genteel, who conducted a more restrained, dispassionate, learned approach in the ratification debate. However, in both the pamphlets and in newspaper essays the Federalists stooped to name calling, traded insults with Antifederalists, and resorted to arguments ad hominem. One of the more acrimonious newspaper exchanges was conducted via the *State Gazette of North-Carolina*, centering on five essays by "Aratus," who championed the Constitution and in the process evoked several angry replies. While Louise I. Trenholme contends that part of the newspaper warfare may have hindered the Federalist cause, a more recent student feels that the "Aratus" episode "blunted the Anti-federalist attack, diverting it to ineffective polemic." For example, responses to "Aratus" essays in the *State Gazette of North-Carolina* "degenerated into a disordered series of personal insults," leading to the conclusion "that it was the Anti-federalists who were bested by the exchange. . . ."[54]

---

[51]Louise I. Trenholme, *The Ratification of the Federal Constitution in North Carolina* (New York: AMS Press, 1967; New York: Columbia University Press, 1932), 124, hereinafter cited as Trenholme, *Ratification of the Federal Constitution in North Carolina*; Thomas C. Parramore, "A Year in Hertford County with Elkanah Watson," *North Carolina Historical Review*, XLI (October, 1964), 452-458, hereinafter cited as Parramore, "A Year in Hertford County."

[52]See Bernard Bailyn (ed.), *Pamphlets of the American Revolution* (Cambridge, Mass.: Belknap Press of the Harvard University Press, 2 volumes, 1965), I, esp. 3-8; Schlesinger, *Prelude to Independence*, 44; Frank Luther Mott, *American Journalism: A History of Newspapers in the United States Through 250 Years, 1690-1940* (New York: MacMillan, 1945), 54-55.

[53]Smith, "Creation of an American State," 616-617; Robinson, *William R. Davie*, 194, 211-212; Trenholme, *Ratification of the Federal Constitution in North Carolina*, 121-124, 201-202; McRee, *Iredell*, II, 186-215; Hugh T. Lefler (ed.), *A Plea for Federal Union: A Reprint of Two Pamphlets* (Charlottesville: Tracy W. McGregor Library, 1947), 12-16, 21-38, hereinafter cited as Lefler, *A Plea for Federal Union*.

[54]Robinson, *William R. Davie*, 196; Smith, "Creation of an American State," 616-617, 625-626, quotation on 626;

The ratification struggle was significant for the press in North Carolina and the nation. Revolutionary Americans not only understood the importance of the newspaper in the confrontation with the mother country but cherished the conviction that liberty of the press was inviolate. The North Carolina printers reflected the Revolutionary settlement. Whereas the motto of the *Edenton Intelligencer* declared, "Where LIBERTY dwells there is my COUNTRY," Thomas Davis tried to define the privilege more clearly: "Influenced by all parties, but restrained by none." Most of the newly constituted states drafted constitutions that contained provisions similar to that of the North Carolina Declaration of Rights: "That the freedom of the press is one of the greatest bulwarks of liberty; and therefore ought never to be restrained."[55]

The members of the Philadelphia Convention in 1787 failed to include a safeguard for the press in their document, believing it unnecessary in light of the division of powers between the state and the national government. Furthermore, according to Alexander Hamilton in *Federalist No. 84*, protection for the press would stand or fall on the wishes of the people, whatever the form of government. In similar vein, Sibley and Howard of the *Fayetteville Gazette* appealed for support to the "candid public, upon whose patronage and protection we rely. . . ." But the Antifederalists viewed with alarm the failure of the Constitution to protect the liberty of the press among other civil liberties, and, under pressure, in its first session in 1789, Congress formulated a Bill of Rights that contained the injunction that Congress "shall make no law . . . abridging the freedom . . . of the press."[56]

Among the many explanations for North Carolina's reluctance to embrace the Constitution must be counted the dearth of media communications. As North Carolina joined the Union in 1789, it remained, even more than the nation, in "a pronounced state of public information isolation." Only three towns—New Bern, Edenton, and Fayetteville—had newspapers, and those sheets were but pitiful imitations of those found in the cities of the northern states and in Charleston, South Carolina. The postal system had advanced little beyond that of the colonial era. Transportation remained in a rudimentary state. Roads and bridges had not improved materially during the past half century; ferriage was still unreliable, expensive, and frequently dangerous. Public accommodations were barely tolerable beyond the principal towns, and even there compared unfavorably with arrangements to the north. The absence of a satisfactory communications network in part produced an isolation, parochialism, and internal political fragmentation that proved difficult to overcome.[57]

Access to the media, or the lack thereof, greatly influenced the political process. The paucity of alternative information sources exaggerated the importance of local leadership. In the communities where there was little competition among politicians or news from the outside world, few opportunities existed to examine or consider alternative models of action. Political skill centered not upon issues and problem-solving but upon tapping public emotions.

Parramore, "A Year in Hertford County," 452-458; Trenholme, *Ratification of the Federal Constitution in North Carolina*, 209; Crittenden, *North Carolina Newspapers*, 67-69, 72-83; Charles Pettigrew to the Edenton Printers, July 16, 1789, *The Pettigrew Papers*, edited by Sarah M. Lemmon (Raleigh: State Department of Archives and History, projected multivolume series, 1971—), I, 71-73; Lefler, *A Plea for Federal Union*, 16, 39-73. The exaggerated statements of both sides likely made an impact. Manipulating the endpoints of a reference scale, or emphasizing the extremes as did the Federalists and Antifederalists, may well alter perceptional evaluations of the center. *See* Eleanor L. Norris, "Perspective as a Determinant of Attitude Formation and Change," *Journalism Quarterly*, L (Spring, 1973), 11-16.

[55]John L. Cheney, Jr. (ed.), *North Carolina Government, 1589-1979: A Narrative and Statistical History* (Raleigh: North Carolina Department of the Secretary of State, 1981), 810.

[56]Clinton Rossiter (ed.), *The Federalist Papers* (New York: New American Library, 1961), 514; *Fayetteville Gazette*, August 24, 1789; Cecelia M. Kenyon, "Men of Little Faith: The Anti-Federalists on the Nature of Representative Government," *William and Mary Quarterly*, 3rd Series, XII (January, 1955), 3-43; Irving Brant, *The Bill of Rights: Its Origins and Meaning* (New York: New American Library, 1965), 20.

[57]Pred, *Urban Growth and the Circulation of Information*, 13, 37, 39; Wright and Tinling, *Quebec to Carolina*, 265-287; Crittenden, "Means of Communication," 383.

Demagoguery held sway as the populace sought satisfaction from identifying emotionally with those in power, whether planters, politicians, or preachers.[58]

The future promised improvement. The federal Constitution envisioned a more powerful central government that made immediate, positive changes in the postal system. North Carolina reflected those alterations as the number of post offices and miles of post roads increased dramatically in the 1790s. The transportation "revolution" of the nineteenth century, encompassing turnpikes, canals, and the adaptation of steam to land and water vehicles, was encouraging. Advancements in educational opportunities, particularly the academy movement in North Carolina, were modest but portended a more literate populace. Perhaps most important was the political partisanship generated by the emerging party system of the early republic. The contending factions supported the newspaper press as organs for their respective positions.[59]

However, these factors little redounded to the immediate benefit of the newspaper press in North Carolina. The state remained rural, provincial, poor, and ignorant, achieving an undesirable reputation for its torpidity and cultural barrenness. According to one authority, the state was a "vast burial ground of dead newspapers" in the first half of the nineteenth century.[60] With few exceptions the available newspapers, short-lived and restricted in their circulation, were almost an embarrassment. Not until the second quarter of the nineteenth century was serious consideration given to internal improvements and public education in North Carolina; not until the eve of the Civil War might the state boast a mildly flourishing newspaper press.

---

[58]See Pye, *Communications and Political Development*, 58-63.

[59]Hecht, "Postal History of North Carolina"; Johnson, *Ante-Bellum North Carolina*, 20-31, 764-774. For the impact of literacy, including its link to modernity, see Daniel Lerner, "Toward a Communication Theory of Modernization: A Set of Considerations," 341, in Pye, *Communications and Political Development*.

[60]Johnson, *Ante-Bellum North Carolina*, 764.

NEWSPAPERS INDEXED

The North Carolina Gazette, or, Impartial Intelligencer, and Weekly General Advertiser. New Bern. Printed for R. Keith and Company.

July 29, 1784
September 2, 1784

The N. Carolina Gazette. New Bern. Printed for Thomas Davis.

December 9, 1784
January 6, 1785

The Noth-Carolina Gazette, or New-Bern Advertiser. Printed for Martin & Co.

November 3, [1785]
March 29, [1786] *(The North Carolina Gazette)*
July 11, 1787   *(Martin's North-Carolina Gazette)*
August 1, 1787
August 15, 1787
December 19, 1787

The North Carolina Gazette. Hillsborough. Printed by Robert Ferguson for Thomas Davis.

October 6, 1785
January 19, 1786
February 2, 1786
February 16, 1786
February 23, 1786

The North-Carolina Gazette; or the Edenton Intelligencer. Printed by Maurice Murphy.

December 19 (missing pp. 3,4), 1787
April 9, 1788 *(The Edenton Intelligencer)*
June 4, 1788

The State Gazette of North-Carolina. New Bern. Printed by Arnett & Hodge.

January 12, 1786
February 23, 1786
July 6, 1786 (Printed by Hodge & Blanchard)
January 18, 1787
October 4, 1787
November 15 (missing pp. 3,4), 29, 1787
February 7, 1788 (Printed by Hodge & Wills)
March 27, 1788
September 8, 15, 22, 29, 1788 (Edenton)
October 6, 13, 20, 27, 1788
November 3, 10, 17, 24, 1788
December 4, 11, 18, 25, 1788

January 1, 8, 15, 22, 29, 1789
February 5, 12, 19, 26, 1789
March 5, 12, 19, 26, 1789
April 2, 9, 16, 23, 30, 1789
May 7, 14, 21, 28, 1789
June 4, 11, 18, 25, 1789
July 2, 9, 16, 23, 30, 1789
August 6, 13, 20, 27, 1789
September 3, 10, 17, 24, 1789
October 1, 8, 15, 22, 29, 1789
November 5, 12, 19, 26, 1789
December 3, 10, 17, 24, 31, 1789

The Wilmington Centinel, and General Advertiser. Printed and published by Bowen and Howard.

June 18, 25, 1788
July 2, 9, 16, 23, 30, 1788
August 6, 13, 20, 27 (missing pp. 1,2), 1788
September 3, 10, 17, 24 (missing pp. 3,4), 1788
October 15, 26, 1788
November 5, 12, 19, 26, 1788
December 3, 10, 18, 25, 1788
January 8, 15, 22, 29, 1789
February 5, 12, 19, 26, 1789
March 5 (missing pp. 3,4), 1789

Fayetteville Gazette. Printed by Sibley & Howard.

August 24, 1789
September 14, 21, 1789
October 12, 1789

In indexing the extant North Carolina newspapers during the 1780s, emphasis has been placed on North Carolina and the federal Constitution. News from the remaining states has been indexed in less detail; that from overseas with the most selectivity.

In the course of indexing, the following abbreviations have been used:

Newspapers

NCG: *The North Carolina Gazette, or, Impartial Intelligencer, and Weekly General Advertiser* (New Bern); *The N. Carolina Gazette* (New Bern); *The No*ᵗʰ*-Carolina Gazette, or New-Bern Advertiser* (New Bern)

NCGH: *The North Carolina Gazette* (Hillsborough)

EI: *The North-Carolina Gazette; or the Edenton Intelligencer* (Edenton)

SG: *The State Gazette of North-Carolina* (New Bern; Edenton)

WC: *The Wilmington Centinel, and General Advertiser* (Wilmington)

FG: *Fayetteville Gazette* (Fayetteville)

Names of months

Jan: January
Feb: February
Mar: March
Apr: April
May: May
Jun: June
Jul: July
Aug: August
Sep: September
Oct: October
Nov: November
Dec: December

Identical references, principally to advertisements, addressees of letters left in post offices, and such headings as "European News" or "Marine List," in three or more consecutive issues are indicated by a hyphen after the first such reference.

A typical reference may thus be understood as follows: WC20Aug88:2 is *The Wilmington Centinel, and General Advertiser*, August 20, 1788, page 2.

INDEX

A

Abbeville County, S.C., warning from justices of court of, SG13Oct88:4

Abbot, _____, SG3Sep89:3

Abbot, Henry, WC20Aug88:2

Abbot, Stephen, WC13Aug88:3

Abbots Bromlay, England, marriage in, WC24Sep88:2

Abbott, H., SG3Dec89:3

Abraham, SG4Oct87:4

Academy, SG18Jan87:2,3, SG18Dec88:3, WC18Dec88:2, SG22Jan89:3—, SG1Oct89:3—, SG26Nov89:3

    erection of, SG31Dec89:3

Accident, SG27Oct88:2, WC15Jan89:2-3

Accounts, settlement of, SG18Jan87:2

Adam, R., SG3Dec89:2

Adam, Robert, FG24Aug89:3, SG10Sep89:3, FG14Sep89:4, FG21Sep89:4

Adams, _____, SG29Jan89:2, SG12Mar89:1,2

Adams, A. H., SG18Jan87:3, NCG15Aug87:4

Adams, Dr., review of his *Defence of the Constitutions of the United States of America*, WC8Jan89:1

Adams, John, WC18Jun88:2, SG12Mar89:1-2, SG14May89:2, SG11Jun89:3

    address to U.S. Senate by, SG21May89:1

    career of, SG22Jan89:3

    diplomacy of, WC8Jan89:2, WC22Jan89:1,2

    life of, SG4Dec88:2

    political treatise of, WC8Jan89:1

    sale of book by, SG4Oct87:4, SG29Nov87:4

    sketch of, WC29Jan89:2

    trip to New York of, SG30Apr89:2-3

Adams, Mr., WC2Jul88:2, WC27Aug88:3, SG29Sep88:3, SG12Mar89:2

    trip to N.Y. of, SG30Apr89:2

Adams, Mrs., SG10Nov88:2

Admiralty, Swedish, letter from, SG24Nov88:2

"Admirer of the Fair Sex, An," NCGH6Oct85:1

    See also Women

Advertisement, humorous, SG18Jun89:3

Affadavits, SG10Dec89:2

Africa

    convention between British and Dutch companies in, WC25Dec88:2

    exploration of, SG15Jan89:1

    slave forts in, NCG29Jul84:1

Agnew, John, SG12Jan86:4

Agricultural societies, promotion of in England and Scotland, SG19Nov89:2

Agriculture

    damage to, FG12Oct89:3

    encouragement of, SG19Nov89:2

    importance of, SG11Jun89:1, 4

    improvements in, SG11Dec88:2

    in U.S., WC6Aug88:2, SG10Sep89:2

Ague and fever, cure for, WC3Sep88:2

Albany, N.Y.

    circular letter to, SG9Apr89:1,2

    glass manufacturing in, SG10Sep89:1, FG21Sep89:2

    letter from, SG19Feb89:2

    news from, SG10Nov88:2, WC26Nov88:2, WC5Feb89:2, SG16Jul89:2

Albemarle Sound, navigation of, SG18Dec88:3, WC18Dec88:3, SG29Jan89:1-2

Albright, William, NCGH19Jan86:4, NCGH2Feb86:3

Alden, Roger, SG27Aug89:3

Alderson, _____, SG3Dec89:3

Alderson, J., SG3Dec89:3

Alderson, John, NCG2Sep84:1, NCG1Aug87:3, SG3Sep87:3

Alderson, Thomas, WC20Aug88:2

Aleck (slave), runaway, WC26Feb89:3, WC5Mar89:1

Alexander, John, NCG29Mar86:2

Alexander, R., WC20Aug88:2, SG24Sep89:3, SG3Dec89:3

Alexandria, Va., WC24Sep88:2

    damage by storm in, WC20Aug88:3

    news from, NCG2Sep84:2, NCGH23Feb86:2, WC20Aug88:3, SG10Nov88:3, SG11Dec88:2, SG26Feb89:3, SG15Oct89:3

Alford, _____, SG3Dec89:3

Alford, Jacob, SG17Sep89:3

Algiers, NCG9Dec84:3, NCGH2Feb86:2

    declaration of war against U.S., NCG3Nov85:3

    Dey of, SG19Mar89:3

    French relations with, SG6Oct88:3

    plague in, SG10Nov88:2

    prisoner in, SG20Oct88:2

    Russian relations with, SG6Oct88:3

    threat of, WC2Jul88:2

    U.S. relations with, SG12Jan86:3, NCGH2Feb86:2

Algerines, SG6Oct88:2

    capture of French vessels, SG8Oct89:2

    Christian slaves of, SG20Oct88:2

    danger from, SG6Oct88:3

    declaration of war by, NCG3Nov85:3

    depredations of, NCG29Mar86:4

    hostility against France, SG1Oct89:2

    piratical activities of, WC10Dec88:2

    ravage U.S. commerce, SG29Nov87:2

Allan, John, WC5Feb89:3, WC19Feb89:3, WC26Feb89:1,3, WC5Mar89:1

Allen

    See Hewes, Smith and Allen

Allen, Eleazer, NCG29Jul84:3

Allen, Ethan, death of, SG2Apr89:3, SG16Apr89:2, SG23Apr89:2

Allen, H., WC20Aug88:2

Allen, J., SG3Dec89:2, 3

Allen, John, NCG29Jul84:2, SG3Sep89:3

Allen, John W., SG9Jul89:3—

Allen, Nathaniel, WC20Aug88:2, SG29Jan89:1, SG9Jul89:3—

Allen, Richard, WC20Aug88:2

Allen, S., SG3Dec89:3

Allen, Shadrach, SG3Sep89:3

Alleson, J., SG3Dec89:3

Alley

    See Quince's Alley; Toomer's Alley

Alley, Charles, SG31Dec89:3

Allison, John, NCGH6Oct85:4

Allison, Robert, WC20Aug88:2

Alliteration, SG25Dec88:2

Almanacks, sale of, NCG9Dec84:4, NCG11Jul87:4, NCG1Aug87:3, NCG15Aug87:4, NCG19Dec87:4, SG7Feb88:4, SG19Feb89:4—

    See also Books

"Alonzo," SG27Mar88:2

Alston, Francis, WC10Dec88:3—

Alston, George, NCG29Mar86:2

Alves, Gavin, SG18Jan87:2

Alves, Walter, SG18Jan87:2
America
    British government in, SG22Sep88:2
    British military in, SG22Sep88:1, WC24Sep88:2
    discovery of, SG30Jul89:2
    English view of, SG10Dec89:3
    news from, WC15Jan89:2—WC5Mar89:2
    ode to freedom of, SG17Dec89:4
    satirization of affairs in by Boston newspaper,
        NCG3Nov85:3
    See also American Intelligence, American News,
        Domestic Intelligence
American Company of Comedians, SG29Nov87:4
American Intelligence, EI9Apr88:2, EI4Jun88:2,
    FG24Aug89:2, 3, FG14Sep89:2,3, FG21Sep89:2
    See also America, news from; American News;
        Domestic Intelligence
American Magazine, extracts from, SG15Jan89:1
American Museum, SG8Jan89:3
American News, NCG29Jul84:2
American Revolution, SG6Jul86:1,2, SG1Oct89:4
    history of, WC18Jun88:2
American Revolutionary, character of, SG29Jan89:2
Americans, character of, SG6Jul86:2,3,4
"Americanus," WC3Dec88:1, WC10Dec88:1,
    WC18Dec88:1, WC25Dec88:1
"Amicus Justitie," EI4Jun88:3
Amis, Thomas, EI9Apr88:3
Amsterdam
    letter from, SG24Nov88:2,3
    news from, NCGH19Dec87:2
    support of militia for, WC15Oct88:1
Anarchiad, extract from, FG12Oct89:2,3
Anchovies, found along N.Y. coast, SG8Oct89:3
Anderson, ____, SG3Dec89:3
Anderson, Ann, SG24Dec89:3, SG31Dec89:3
Anderson, James, WC20Aug88:2, SG3Nov88:2,
    SG17Sep89:2
Anderson, John, SG18Jan87:3, WC20Aug88:2
Anderson, Major, SG22Sep88:3
Anecdotes, NCG3Nov85:4, SG12Jan86:3,
    NCGH2Feb86:1,2, NCGH16Feb86:1,2,
    NCGH23Feb86:1,2, SG4Oct87:4, WC18Jun88:4;
    WC2Jul88:4, WC9Jul88:4, WC30Jul88:4,
    WC20Aug88:4, WC3Sep88:4, WC17Sep88:4,
    SG6Oct88:4, SG13Oct88:3, WC15Oct88:2,
    WC26Oct88:4, WC5Nov88:4--, SG24Nov88:3,4,
    SG4Dec88:3, SG1Jan89:4, SG8Jan89:4,
    WC15Jan89:4, SG29Jan89:4; SG5Feb89:3,4,
    WC12Feb89:4—, SG19Feb89:3—, SG16Apr89:3,
    SG14May89:4, SG18Jun89:2, SG25Jun89:4,
    SG10Sep89:4, SG17Sep89:4, FG12Oct89:4,
    SG22Oct89:3, SG26Nov89:3, SG10Dec89:2,3
Animals
    description of, FG24Aug89:4
    destruction of, SG18Jan87:3, WC18Dec88:2
    stray, SG25Dec88:3
Annapolis, Md., letter from, NCG2Sep84:3
"Another of the People," NCG9Dec84:2
"Another Subscriber," SG12Feb89:1
"Another True Federalist," FG21Sep89:2
Anson County, NCGH19Jan86:4, NCGH2Feb86:4,
    NCG29Mar86:2, NCG15Aug87:4, WC23Jul88:3—
    WC20Aug88:4, SG25Dec88:2, SG24Sep89:3,
    SG31Dec89:3
    commissioners of public buildings in, SG18Jan87:3

Anson County courthouse, SG18Jan87:3
    tobacco inspection at, SG18Jan87:3
Anson Courthouse, SG18Jan87:3
*Answers to Mr. Mason's Objections to the New
    Constitution*, sale of, SG27Mar88:2
Anthony, James, SG9Jul89:3—
Antifederalism, SG11Dec88:2, SG15Jan89:2
"ANTIFED, Senior," SG3Nov88:2
Antigua, WC17Sep88:2
    drought in, SG8Oct89:2
    earthquake in, SG3Dec89:1
    sugar in, NCGH19Jan86:2, WC13Aug88:2
Antwerp, letter from, SG25Dec88:1,2
Apprentice, wanted, EI19Dec87:1, WC23Jul88:4—,
    SG15Jan89:3, SG22Jan89:4, SG5Feb89:4—
Apthorp, Charles W., WC5Feb89:2
Apthorp, Maria, SG22Jan89:3, WC5Feb89:2
"Aratus," SG7May89:1, SG14May89:1, SG28May89:3,
    SG2Jul89:2, SG23Jul89:2, SG30Jul89:3,
    SG13Aug89:3
"Argus," SG30Jul89:4
Arithmetic, SG4Oct87:4
Armstead, John
    See Armstead, William and John
Armstead, William, Jr., SG20Oct88:3, SG27Oct88:3
Armstead, William and John, SG9Apr89:3—
Armstrong, ____, NCGH16Feb86:4, SG3Sep89:3,
    SG3Dec89:3
Armstrong, A., NCG29Jul84:3
Armstrong, Andrew, NCG15Aug87:4, FG14Sep89:3
Armstrong, Col., NCGH23Feb86:4
Armstrong, General, SG18Dec88:2—
Armstrong, J., SG29Sep88:3, SG3Dec89:3
Armstrong, James, WC19Nov88:3, WC26Nov88:3
Armstrong, John, SG12Jan86:2, WC13Aug88:3,
    SG8Jan89:3, SG15Jan89:4, SG31Dec89:3
Armstrong, Joseph, SG4Dec88:3
Armstrong, Mr., ____WC19Nov88:3, SG17Dec89:3
Armstrong, Thomas, WC20Aug88:2
Arnett, Mr., SG3Dec89:2
Arnett, S. W., WC26Nov88:3, SG4Dec88:3
Arnett, Silas W., SG4Oct87:3, SG29Nov87:4,
    SG7Feb88:4, SG29Sep88:4, SG6Oct88:4—,
    SG17Nov88:4, SG3Sep89:3
Arnett, Silas White, SG17Dec89:3
Arnold, Benedict, WC24Sep88:2, WC26Oct88:2
Arnold, John, SG25Dec88:3—, SG5Feb89:3
Arnold, William, SG25Dec88:3—, SG5Feb89:3,
    FG14Sep89:3
Arthur (slave), SG7Feb88:4
Articles of Confederation, SG6Jul86:1,2
Artillery, WC5Feb89:2
Ash, General, WC22Jan89:3
Ash, Harriet, WC22Jan89:3
Ashburn, William, SG12Jan86:4
Ashburn & Hooten, SG12Jan86:4
Ashe, John, WC25Jun88:3
Ashe, J. B., SG3Dec89:3
Ashe, John B., SG7Feb88:3
Ashe, John Baptiste, SG24Sep89:3
Ashe, Judge, EI19Dec87:2
Ashe, Mr., SG3Dec89:2
Ashe, Samuel, WC25Jun88:3, WC13Aug88:3
Ashe, Samuel, Jr., WC13Aug88:3
Ashley, Joseph
    See Will

Ashley, S., letter from, SG11Dec88:3
Asia, U.S. trade with, SG19Mar89:2
Assaults, WC12Feb89:3
Assembly of Notables, WC29Jan89:1, SG26Mar89:1
    See also France, revolution in
Assize of bread, WC5Feb89:3
Atkinson, Darley, SG22Oct89:3, SG29Oct89:3,
    SG12Nov89:4
Atkinson, Darley & Co., SG20Oct88:3, SG27Oct88:3
Atkinson, Darly, SG27Mar88:3
Attmore
    See Kaign and Attmore
Attmore, William, SG27Mar88:4
Auction, SG23Feb86:3
    mishap in, SG19Nov89:1
Augusta, Ga., SG18Dec88:3
    letter from, SG18Dec88:3, SG12Feb89:2,
        SG12Nov89:3
    news from, WC8Jan89:3, SG12Nov89:3
Austria
    losses in war with Turks, WC8Jan89:1
    performance of army of, WC25Dec88:2
    war of, WC25Dec88:2, WC22Jan89:2, FG14Sep89:2
Aux-Cayes
    letter from, WC30Jul88:2
    trade in, WC30Jul88:2

B

Bachelor
    lamentation, SG24Nov88:4
    soliloquy of, SG5Feb89:4
Backcountry, SG29Sep88:3, SG13Oct88:4
    See also Western territory
Bacot, Peter, character of, WC6Aug88:3
Bagley, Joshua, SG5Nov89:3
Bagnel, John, SG9Jul89:3—
Bagnel, Mr., NCG6Jan85:1
Bahamas
    agriculture of, NCGH6Oct85:3
    banditti from in Georgia, SG5Mar89:3
    General Assembly in, WC29Jan89:2
    General Court in, SG7May89:3
    Grand jury presentment of, SG7May89:3
    indigo in, NCGH6Oct85:3
    judiciary of, SG7May89:3
    letter from, NCG6Oct85:3
    loyalists in, NCGH16Feb86:2,3
    prejudice against, NCGH6Oct85:3
    reputation of, NCGH6Oct85:3
    supplies Indians, WC12Feb89:1
Bahama Gazette, extract from, WC29Jan89:2,
    WC5Feb89:2, SG26Feb89:3
Bailey, Thomas, Jr., NCGH19Jan86:4, NCGH2Feb86:4
Bailey, W., SG3Dec89:3
Bain, Donald, WC25Jun88:3
Baker, ____, SG3Dec89:3
Baker, Amadon, SG21May89:3, SG28May89:4,
    SG18Jun89:4
Baker, H., SG3Dec89:3
Baker, J., SG3Dec89:3
Baker, Lawrence, SG29Jan89:1, SG9Jul89:3—
Baker, Norris, SG8Jan89:3, SG15Jan89:4
Baker, Thomas, SG12Jan86:4
Baker, William, WC20Aug88:2

Baking, NCG3Nov85:3
Balcour, Peggy, WC13Aug88:3
Ball (dance), WC18Dec88:3
Ballenger, Jonathan, name of changed, SG18Jan87:2
Balloon, ascension of, SG3Sep89:2,3
Ballooning, NCG3Nov85:3
Baltic, trade in, SG5Nov89:2
Baltimore, Md., WC25Dec88:4
    meeting of tradesmen and manufacturers in,
        SG12Mar89:3
    news from, NCG2Sep84:2, NCG9Dec84:2,
        NCG3Nov85:3, NCG15Aug87:2,3,
        SG29Nov87:2, SG27Mar88:3, WC25Jun88:2,
        WC16Jul88:3, WC13Aug88:2, WC27Aug88:3,
        WC3Sep88:2, WC24Sep88:2, SG29Sep88:2,3,
        SG6Oct88:3, SG13Oct88:2, SG20Oct88:2,
        SG27Oct88:2, SG10Nov88:2,3, SG17Nov88:3,
        WC19Nov88:3, SG24Nov88:2,3, SG1Jan89:2,3,
        SG29Jan89:2, WC29Jan89:2, WC5Feb89:2,
        SG19Feb89:2, WC19Feb89:2, SG26Feb89:2,
        WC5Mar89:2, SG12Mar89:2,3, SG9Apr89:3,
        SG23Apr89:1,2, SG14May89:2,3,
        SG16Jul89:2,3, SG6Aug89:3, SG13Aug89:2,3,
        FG24Aug89:3, SG1Oct89:3,SG8Oct89:3,
        SG15Oct89:2,3, SG22Oct89:2, SG5Nov89:3,
        SG12Nov89:3, SG19Nov89:3, SG26Nov89:3,
        SG10Dec89:2, SG24Dec89:3
    newspaper extract from, NCG9Dec84:3
    protest by Capt. Stephen Waterous, SG26Nov89:2
    return of exiles to, SG12Mar89:3
    seeks capital of U.S., SG12Mar89:2
    shipping of, SG12Mar89:3
    storm in, WC13Aug88:2, WC20Aug88:3
Bank of England, WC26Nov88:1, SG5Nov89:1
Bank of Philadelphia, SG15Oct89:3
Banking, U.S., SG15Oct89:3
Bankruptcies, WC15Jan89:2
    English, SG12Nov89:2
Banks, T., SG3Dec89:3
Banks, Thomas, SG27Aug89:3, FG14Sep89:3
Baptism, SG12Jan86:2
Barbados, armed vessels at, SG12Mar89:3
Barbary pirates, NCG2Sep84:2, NCGH2Feb86:2,
    WC16Jul88:3
Barbary ports, English trade with, SG13Oct88:2
Barbary states, WC30Jul88:2, SG11Dec88:1
    finance Turkish war, SG10Nov88:2
    ports open to British ships, WC10Sep88:2
Barber, WC26Nov88:4
Barcelona, American ships in, NCG9Dec84:2
Barclay, Thomas, diplomacy of for U.S., WC25Dec88:2
Barge, Lewis, WC26Oct88:3
Barge, Mr., WC26Nov88:3, SG4Dec88:3,
    WC18Dec88:3
Barlow, Joel, voyage to France, WC25Jun88:2
Barnes, ____, SG17Sept89:3, SG3Dec89:3
Barnes, Capt., WC26Nov88:3
Barnes, E., SG3Dec89:3
Barnes, Elias, WC20Aug88:2, SG22Sep88:3
Barnes, Mr., WC18Jun88:3, WC25Jun88:3
Barney, Jacob, SG9Jul89:3—
Barnstable, Mass., letter from, SG19Mar89:3
Barret, William, SG24Sep89:3
Barringer, G. H., SG3Dec89:3
Barringer, George H., WC20Aug88:2
Barron, David, NCG9Dec84:4

Barrow, Jacob, SG22Oct89:3, SG29Oct89:3, SG12Nov89:4
Barry, Thomas, SG22Jan89:3—, SG9Jul89:3—
Barton, John, NCGH2Feb86:3, NCGH23Feb86:3, SG23Feb86:3
Barton, Thomas, NCGH2Feb86:3, NCGH16Feb86:3
Bass, Andrew, SG18Jan87:2, WC20Aug88:2
Bass, Gillam, WC22Jan89:3—
Basseterre, St. Kitts, NCG2Sep84:1,2
Bastard, Stephen, SG18Jan87:3
Bastille, SG22Oct89:2, SG5Nov89:4, SG12Nov89:2
    description of, SG19Nov89:3
    fall of, SG29Oct89:1
    narrative of prisoner of, SG19Nov89:3
    prisoners in, SG5Nov89:3
    storming of, SG1Oct89:1, SG15Oct89:1,2, SG29Oct89:3
    See also France, politics in; France, revolution in; Paris
Batavia, letter from, SG5Mar89:3
Batey, William, SG31Dec89:3
Bath (Town), N.C., NCG29Jul84:4, NCG2Sep84:3, NCG3Nov85:1, SG29Nov87:2
Bath, cold, NCG3Nov85:2
Battle, Elisha, SG12Jan86:2, WC20Aug88:2
Baum, Abraham, SG26Mar89:3
Baum, Maurice, SG23Jul89:4
Baum, Morris, SG29Jan89:1
Baum, Nathaniel, SG9Jul89:3
Baxter, Samuel, SG27Mar88:3
Bay of Honduras
    lack of food in, SG3Dec89:2
    sickness in, SG7Feb88:2
Bayne, Samuel, SG18Dec87:3
Beaufort, N.C., NCG9Dec84:3, SG1Jan89:3, SG15Jan89:4
Beaufort County, N. C., NCG2Sep84:3, NCG3Nov85:1, NCG29Mar86:2, SG25Dec88:2, SG3Sep89:3
Beale, Joseph, WC13Aug88:3
Beamon, Uzzias, SG12Jan86:4
Beauty
    description of, SG17Dec89:2
    observations on, NCG2Sep84:4
Beck, Rev. Mr., SG18Jan87:3
Beck, William, SG17Sep89:3
Becking, Mr., SG27Mar88:3
Becking, William, SG27Aug89:3
Becking, William & Co., SG4Oct87:3,4, SG29Nov87:3,4, SG7Feb88:4, SG27Mar88:4
Bedom, Elizabeth, NCG6Jan85:1
Bedom, William, NCG6Jan85:1
Beek, ____, SG3Dec89:3
Beeking, William, SG12Nov89:3
Beel, Frederick, SG9Apr89:3
Beeswax, wanted, NCGH6Oct85:4, NCGH19Jan86:3, NCGH2Feb86:4, NCGH16Feb86:4, NCGH23Feb86:4, NCG1Aug87:4, SG4Oct87:3, SG29Nov87:3, SG13Oct88:—
Beeswax and tallow, SG13Oct88:3—, SG10Nov88:4
Beet, wager over, NCG19Dec87:2
Belfast, Ireland
    letter from, NCG2Sep84:2, WC24Sep88:2, SG20Aug89:2
    manufacturing in, SW24Sep88:2
    unemployment in, WC24Sep88:2
    unrest in, WC24Sep88:2

Belgium
    emperor reported vanquished, WC25Dec88:2
    French invasion reported, WC25Dec88:2
    state of affairs in, SG6Jul86:2
Bell, ____, SG3Sep89:3, SG3Dec89:3
Bell, B., SG3Dec89:3
Bell, Bithell, WC20Aug88:2
Bell, Francis, SG30Apr89:3—
Bell, John, WC13Aug88:3
Bell, M., SG3Dec89:3
Bell, Robert, NCG29Mar86:2, SG18Jan87:3
Bell, W., SG29Sep88:3
Bellengsley, James, SG31Dec89:3
Belloc, Jude, WC26Feb89:3
Belly (slave), WC18Jun88:4, WC25Jun88:4
Beloat, Caesar, WC13Aug88:3
Ben (slave), SG2Jul89:3, SG9Jul89:4
Benbury, Dr. Bryan, SG8Jan89:3, SG15Jan89:4
Benbury, Thomas, SG29Nov87:1,2
Benford, J., SG3Dec89:3
Benford, John, WC20Aug88:2
Bengal, revenues of, SG8Jan89:2
Bennehan, Richard, NCG2Sep84:3
Bennet, P., SG17Sep89:3
Bennet, William, SG20Nov87:1
Bennett, P., SG3Dec89:3
Bennett, Sarah, SG19Nov89:3, SG26Nov89:4
Bennett, William, SG25Jun89:3, SG9Jul89:4, SG23Jul89:4
Bennington, Vt., news from, SG16Apr89:2
Bentford, ____, SG24Sep89:3
Benton, Robert, SG18Jan87:2
Benton, S., SG17Sep89:3, SG3Dec89:3
Berlin
    news from, WC3Dec88:2, SG30Apr89:2
    preparations for war in, WC5Mar89:2
Bermuda, NCG2Sep84:4
    change of governors in, WC8Jan89:2
    letter from, SG1Jan89:2, WC8Jan89:2,3
    politics in, SG1Jan89:2
    shipping of, SG9Apr89:2,3
Bernard, I., WC19Feb89:4
Bernard, Isaac, WC25Jun88:3, WC16Jul88:3—, WC5Feb89:3, WC12Feb89:3
Bernard, John, death of, WC25Dec88:3
Bernard, Lewis, SG20Oct88:3, SG27Oct88:3
Bertie County, N.C., SG18Jan87:2, EI9Apr88:1, SG25Dec88:2, SG9Apr89:3, SG16Apr89:3, SG6Aug89:3—, FG14Sep89:3, SG17Dec89:3, SG31Dec89:4
    courthouse in, SG12Jan86:4
Berwick, N.J., lawsuit in, SG10Nov88:2
Betchell, William, WC20Aug88:2
Bethel, William, SG24Sep89:3
Bethell, ____, SG3Dec89:3
Bethell, Mr., SG29Sep88:3
Beverly, Mass.
    accidental death in, SG16Apr89:2
    cotton manufacturing in, SG19Mar89:3, FG21Sep89:2
Biddle, Charles, SG15Nov87:2
Bigamy and polygamy, NCGH19Jan86:2, WC19Nov88:3
    prevention of, SG25Dec88:3
    See also Marriage
Bigar, Mr., SG20Oct88:3, SG27Oct88:3

Bigelow, N., WC19Nov88:3
Bigelow, R., WC19Nov88:3
Biggam, John, NCG6Jan85:1
Bignall, Robert, SG10Nov88:3
Billiard tables
    perniciousness of, SG2Jul89:2
    virtues of, SG8Sep88:4
Bills, Richard, NCG6Jan85:1
Bills, destroyed, SG10Dec89:3
Birds, commentary on, WC15Jan89:1
Birin, Duke de, death of, SG5Mar89:2
Birmingham, England, runaway husbands in,
    SG5Feb89:3
Bishop of London, NCG9Dec84:4
    prayer prescribed by, WC12Feb89:2
Bishoprics, English, revenue from, SG17Dec89:1
Black, Alex., EI9Apr88:3
Black, Alexander, SG8Sep88:3, SG15Sep88:4,
    SG22Jan89:3
Black, Frances, SG13Oct88:3—
Black, Samuel, SG13Oct88:3—
Black and Amis, copartnership, EI9Apr88:3
Blackeyed peas, WC25Dec88:3
Blackledge, Richard, NCG2Sep84:4, NCG3Nov85:1,
    SG4Mar88:4, SG27Mar88:4, SG8Sep88:4—
Blackledge Singleton & Co., NCG29Mar86:1
Blacks, freedom restored to, SG23Apr89:3
Blacksmiths, NCG1Aug87:3, SG2Jul89:3, FG21Sep89:2
Blackstock, John, SG6Aug89:3—
Blackstock, Mary, SG6Aug89:3—
Blackstock, Mrs., SG20Oct88:3, SG27Oct88:3
Bladen County, N.C., NCGH6Oct85:4, NCG3Nov85:2,
    SG23Feb86:2, SG6Jul86:3, SG18Jan87:2,3,
    SG7Feb88:3, WC18Jun88:4, WC23Jul88:1—,
    SG29Sep88:3, WC26Oct88:3—, WC3Dec88:1,3,
    SG18Dec88:3, WC18Dec88:3, SG25Dec88:2,
    SG10Sep89:3, FG12Oct89:4, SG31Dec89:3
    division of, SG18Jan87:2
    promotion of learning in, SG18Jan87:2
    taxes in, SG31Dec89:3
Blair, ____, SG3Dec89:3
Blair, George, SG26Mar89:3
Blair, J., SG15Jan89:3—
Blair, John, SG23Feb86:4, SG18Jan87:3, WC20Aug88:2
Blair, Mrs., SG22Sep88:3
    death of, SG26Mar89:3
Blair, Samuel, SG22Sep88:3
Blair, William, SG12Feb89:3, SG19Feb89:4,
    SG12Mar89:4, SG5Mar89:4, SG19Mar89:4
Black, Eyre, SG13Aug89:3—
Blanchard, Andrew, SG4Oct87:3, SG29Nov87:4,
    SG7Feb88:4
Blanchard
    See Hodge and Blanchard
Blanchard, Isaac, SG4Oct87:3, SG29Nov87:4,
    SG7Feb88:4
Bleakly, John, WC19Nov88:3
Bledsal, Anthony, SG12Jan86:2
Bledsoe, Anthony, SG22Oct89:3, SG29Oct89:3,
    SG12Nov89:4
Bloodworth, ____, SG3Dec89:3
Bloodworth, James, WC2Jul88:3, WC20Aug88:2
Bloodworth, Mr., SG3Dec89:3
Bloodworth, Timothy, WC20Aug88:2, SG22Sep88:2,
    WC10Dec88:3, WC10Dec88:3, SG10Sep89:3,
    SG17Dec89:3

Blount, ____, SG27Mar88:2, SG3Dec89:3
Blount, Benjamin, SG6Jul86:3
Blount, E., SG3Dec89:2
Blount, Edmund, WC20Aug88:2, SG9Jul89:3—,
    SG27Aug89:3, FG14Sep89:3
Blount, Jacob, SG26Feb89:3
    death of, SG3Sep89:3
Blount, J. G., SG3Dec89:3
Blount, John G., WC20Aug88:2, SG8Sep88:4—,
    SG17Nov88:4, SG3Sep89:3, SG17Dec89:3
Blount, Joseph, SG1Jan89:3—
Blount, Mr., SG3Dec89:2,4
Blount, Stephens, SG20Oct88:3, SG27Oct88:3
Blount, T., SG3Dec89:3
Blount, Thomas, SG3Sep89:3, SG3Dec89:4,
    SG17Dec89:3
Blount, W., SG3Dec89:3
Blount, William, NCG2Sep84:3, NCG6Jan85:1,
    NCG19Dec87:4, SG4Mar88:4, SG3Sep89:3,
    SG17Dec89:3, SG31Dec89:3
Blount, Wilson, NCG29Jul84:4, SG27Mar88:3
Blow, Richard & Co. SG15Jan89:3—, SG26Mar89:4
Boak, R., SG8Jan89:3, SG15Jan89:4
Boak, Robert, SG9Apr89:3—, SG22Oct89:3,
    SG29Oct89:3, SG12Nov89:4
Boardman, Jonathan, WC13Aug88:3
Boards, sale of, SG23Feb86:4
Bog, Thos., SG9Apr89:3—
Bogle
    See Carmichael and Bogle
Bogle, Robert, WC5Feb89:3, WC19Feb89:4
Boinod and Gaillard, NCG29Jul84:2, SG2Sep84:4
Bon mot, SG18Jun89:2
Bond, Michael, SG12Jan86:4
Bond, SG5Nov89:3
Bond, personal, NCGH19Jan86:3,4, NCGH2Feb86:3,
    NCGH23Feb86:3, SG11Dec88:3, SG25Dec88:3,4,
    SG8Jan89:4, SG15Jan89:4
Bondfield, Charles, SG9Jul89:3—
Bondfield, John, SG20Oct88:3, SG27Oct88:3
Bonds, ____, SG3Dec89:3
Bonds, John, WC20Aug88:2
Bonds, Mr., SG3Dec89:3
Bonner, James, WC20Aug88:2
Bonner, John, SG20Oct88:3, SG27Oct88:3
Bonner, Mary, SG9Jul89:3—
Books
    proposal for printing of, NCG1Aug87:4,
        EI19Dec87:1, SG8Jan89:3—, SG5Feb89:3,
        SG2Apr89:3, SG9Apr89:4, SG16Apr89:3,4,
        SG23Apr89:3,4, SG30Apr89:4—, SG4Jun89:4,
        SG18Jun89:4, SG25Jun89:4, SG9Jul89:4,
        SG16Jul89:3
    sale of, NCG9Dec84:4, SG12Jan86:4,
        NCGH2Feb86:3, NCGH16Feb86:1,
        NCGH23Feb86:1, SG23Feb86:3,
        NCG15Aug87:4, SG4Oct87:4, SG29Nov87:4,
        WC18Jun88:4, SG8Sep88:3—, SG29Sep88:3,4,
        SG6Oct88:3, WC26Oct88:3—, WC8Jan89:4—,
        SG19Feb89:3, SG12Mar89:3—
    subscriptions for, NCG11Jul87:4, SG15Oct89:3—
Boon, Joseph, WC20Aug88:2
Boot and shoemaking, SG30Apr89:3—
Bordeaux
    letter from, SG15Oct89:2,3, SG29Oct89:3
    proposed street construction in, NCG29Mar86:4

violence in, SG15Oct89:2,3
Borden, William, SG24Sep89:3
Boritz, William, NCG6Jan85:1
Borough representation, WC26Nov88:3
Boroughas, William, SG9Jul89:3—
Bosman, John, SG20Oct88:3, SG27Oct88:3
Bostick, ____, SG3Dec89:3
Bostick, Abraham, SG24Sep89:3
Bostwick, Absalom, WC20Aug88:2
Bostwick, John, SG31Dec89:3
Boswell, WC20Aug88:2
Boston, Mass.
 artillery in, WC25Jun88:2
 attitude toward federal Constitution in,
  SG11Dec88:2
 bridge in, SG19Mar89:2, SG30Jul89:2, SG10Sep89:2
 Catholic bishop expected in, SG20Oct88:2
 celebration of anniversary of independence,
  SG16Apr89:2
 custom collector accepts only American paper
  currency, FG14Sep89:3
 exports from, WC3Sep88:2
 fees of physicians in, WC9Jul88:2
 French army in, WC24Sep88:2
 French fleet departs from, WC5Nov88:2
 French packet boats to, WC3Sep88:2
 glass manufacturing in, SG10Sep89:2, FG21Sep89:2
 greets President Washington, SG3Dec89:4
 illegal shipping in port of, SG12Jan86:2
 incorporation of, SG12Jan86:2
 intended visit of president to, SG19Nov89:2
 letter from, WC24Sep88:2, SG5Feb89:2,
  SG19Nov89:2, SG10Dec89:2, SG17Dec89:2
 manufacturing in, WC5Nov88:2, SG2Jul89:2,
  SG10Sep89:1, SG3Dec89:4
 marriage in, SG26Nov89:3
 news from, NCG3Nov85:3, SG12Jan86:2,
  SG29Nov87:3, NCG19Dec87:2,3, EI9Apr88:3,
  WC25Jun88:2, WC9Jul88:2, WC6Aug88:2,
  WC27Aug88:3, WC17Sep88:2, SG22Sep88:1,
  SG3Nov88:2, WC5Nov88:2, SG10Nov88:2,
  WC19Nov88:2, SG11Dec88:2—,
  SG15Jan89:2—, WC15Jan89:2,3, SG12Feb89:2,
  WC12Feb89:1, SG19Feb89:2,4, SG5Mar89:2,4,
  SG12Mar89:2, SG19Mar89:2, SG16Apr89:2—,
  SG28May89:3—, SG30Jul89:2, SG6Aug89:2,
  SG20Aug89:1,2, SG27Aug89:2, SG10Sep89:2,
  SG15Oct89:2, SG22Oct89:2, SG19Nov89:2,
  SG26Nov89:1,2,4, SG3Dec89:3
 newspaper extract from, SG27Oct88:3,
  SG17Sep89:3, SG3Dec89:4
 preparation to receive president in, SG26Nov89:1
 proposed French newspaper in, WC12Feb89:1
 punishment of criminals in, SG10Sep89:2
 shipping of, SG22Jan89:3, SG2Jul89:2,
  SG26Nov89:3
Boston Gazette, extract from, SG20Oct88:2,
 SG23Apr89:2
Bounties, military, SG2Apr89:4, SG23Apr89:4
Boutwell, Adam, SG4Dec88:3—
Bowen & Howard, WC2Jul88:3—, WC6Aug88:2,
 WC10Sep88:3, WC26Oct88:3—, WC8Jan89:4—,
 WC26Feb89:3
Bowers, Hannah, emancipation of, SG18Jan87:2
Bowers, Jesse, alleged counterfeiting of, NCG15Aug87:4
Bowland, Robert, WC13Aug88:3

Bowman, ____, SG17Sep89:3, SG3Dec89:3
Boxing, SG20Aug89:1
Boyce, Benjamin, SG29Nov87:4
Boyd, Mrs., WC5Feb89:3
Boyd, Roger, SG29Nov87:1,4
Bracksdale, Susannah Frances, marriage of,
 WC15Jan89:3
Bradley, Ann, WC24Sep88:2
Bradley, Capt., WC19Nov88:3
Bradley, James, SG15Jan89:3—, WC15Jan89:4,
 WC22Jan89:4, SG26Mar89:4
Bradley, John, WC18Jun88:4, WC25Jun88:4,
 WC16Jul88:3, WC13Aug88:3, WC8Jan89:3,
 SG31Dec89:3
 pardon for, SG17Dec89:3
Bramhall, Mathew, WC3Sep88:3
Branan, ____, SG30Jul89:3, SG6Aug89:4
Branan, James, WC5Nov88:3, WC12Nov88:4
Branch, John, WC20Aug88:2
Brandon, WC20Aug88:2
Bransby, John, WC10Sep88:3
Brayan, William, NCG2Sep84:3
Bredgen
 See Waller and Bredgen
Brehan, James Gloster, SG27Mar88:3
Brehen, Dr. James Glister, NCG11Jul87:4
Bremen, letter from, SG26Feb89:2
Brenan, Patrick, WC17Sep88:3, WC24Sep88:1,
 WC5Nov88:3, WC12Nov88:4
Brerton, R., SG8Jan89:3, SG15Jan89:4
Brest, plot against, SG15Oct89:1
Bretigney, Marquis de, SG27Mar88:3
Brevard, ____, SG3Dec89:3
Brevard, A., SG3Dec89:3
Brevard, Adam, SG17Sep89:3
Brewster, SG9Apr89:3—
Brian, Lewis, SG20Oct88:3, SG27Oct88:3
Brice, F., WC5Feb89:3, WC12Feb89:4
Brice, Francis, SG6Jul86:3, WC29Jan89:2
Brickle, Thomas N., SG9Apr89:3—
Bricks, WC18Jun88:4—
Bridge
 See Toomer's Bridge
Bridges, William, WC20Aug88:2
Bridges, construction of, SG2Jul89:2, SG30Jul89:2
Bridgewater, Mass., accident in, WC15Jan89:2,3
Bright, S., SG3Dec89:3
Bright, Simon, SG3Sep89:3
Brimage, William, NCG3Nov85:1
Britain, Thomas, SG25Jun89:3—, SG29Oct89:3—
Britinham, Lazarus, SG19Mar89:3—
Briton, L., death of, SG29Jan89:3
Britons, quarrels of, SG16Apr89:1
Britton, Thomas, SG4Dec88:3—
Broadwater, Coventon, SG26Mar89:3—
Brocket, SG29Nov87:1
Brodut, Monsieur, SG9Apr89:3—
Brooks, Mathew, WC20Aug88:2
Brothers, James, SG19Mar89:3
Brouard, J. B., WC19Nov88:3—
Brouk, Lewis, SG20Oct88:3, SG27Oct88:3
Brown, Col., WC18Jun88:3, WC25Jun88:3,
 WC9Jul88:4
Brown, H., SG17Sep89:3
Brown, Howel, SG18Jan87:2
Brown, J., SG29Sep88:3, SG3Dec89:3

Brown, Jacob, NCG6Jan85:1
Brown, John, SG6Jul86:3, WC20Aug88:2,
    SG20Oct88:3, SG27Oct88:3, SG26Feb89:2,
    SG9Jul89:3—, FG14Sep89:3
Brown, Josiah, SG27Mar88:3
Brown, Mather, success in London as portrait painter,
    SG4Jun89:1,2
Brown, Mr., SG3Dec89:3
Brown, N., SG3Dec89:3
Brown, Neal, SG22Sep88:3
Brown, Neil, WC20Aug88:2
Brown, T., SG3Dec89:3
Brown, Thomas, NCG3Nov85:1, SG7Feb88:3,
    WC20Aug88:2, SG29Sep88:3, SG18Dec88:3,
    SG10Sep89:3
Brown, Timothy, SG27Mar88:3
Brown, William, SG3Sep89:3
Bruce, C., SG31Dec89:3
Bruce, Charles, NCGH19Jan86:4, NCGH2Feb86:4
Brun, news from, WC19Feb89:2
Brunswick County, N.C., NCG29Jul84:4, SG6Jul86:3,
    WC18Jun88:3, WC27Aug88:3, WC10Sep88:4,
    WC12Nov88:4, SG18Dec88:3, WC18Dec88:2,
    SG25Dec88:2, WC12Feb89:3—, SG10Sep89:3,
    SG31Dec89:3
Brunswick County, Va., SG18Dec88:3
Brunswick Town, N.C., SG6Jul86:3
Brussels
    letter from, SG6Jul86:2, SG8Sep88:2
    news from, SG17Dec89:1
Bryan, ____, SG30Jul89:3—
Bryan, Edward, SG6Jul86:3, SG22Oct89:3—
Bryan, H., SG29Sep88:3, SG3Dec89:3
Bryan, J., SG3Dec89:3
Bryan, J. H., WC20Aug88:2, SG3Dec89:3
Bryan, John, NCG29Jul84:4, WC20Aug88:2
Bryan, John C., SG18Jan87:3, SG7Feb88:4,
    SG27Mar88:3
Bryan, John Council, NCG29Jul84:4, SG12Jan86:3,
    SG23Feb86:4
Bryan, John H., SG3Sep89:3
Bryan, Joseph, FG24Aug89:3, SG3Sep89:3,
    FG14Sep89:3, FG21Sep89:4
Bryan, Mr., SG29Sep88:3
Bryan, N., WC20Aug88:2
Bryan, Samuel, NCG29Mar86:2
Bryan, Thomas, SG20Oct88:3, SG27Oct88:3
Bryan, William, SG23Feb86:4
Bryer, Benjamin, SG30Jul89:3
Buchanan, Hastie and company, NCG29Mar86:2
Buck (slave), WC15Jan89:4, WC22Jan89:4
Buildings
    construction of, SG31Dec89:3
    public, WC18Dec88:2
Buin, Mrs., NCG1Aug87:3
Bulgaria, alarm in at Russia, SG5Nov89:2
Bullock, Richard, SG10Nov88:3
Bultock, Captain, SG9Jul89:3—
Bunch, James, SG22Oct89:3, SG29Oct89:3,
    SG12Nov89:4
Buncombe, Thomas, SG22Oct89:3, SG29Oct89:3,
    SG12Nov89:4
Bunker, Reuben, NCG29Jul84:3
Bunn, Red., WC20Aug88:2
Burden, William, WC20Aug88:2
Burel, Jas., SG18Jan87:3

Burgess, H. J., SG4Oct87:4
Burgess, Lovet, SG9Apr89:3—
Burgess, Robert, SG9Jul89:3—
"Burgher," SG13Aug89:3
Burgwin, J., WC10Dec88:3, WC25Dec88:4
Burgwin, John, WC18Jun88:1, WC23Jul88:3,
    WC30Jul88:1, WC26Oct88:3—
Burgwin, Mr., house of burned, WC3Dec88:3
Burke, Mr.
    illness of, SG30Jul89:1
    speech of in Parliament, SG17Nov88:1,2
Burke (Burk) County, N.C., SG18Jan87:2,3,
    SG18Dec88:3, WC18Dec88:2, SG25Dec88:2,
    SG31Dec89:3
Burkit, L., WC20Aug88:2
Burks, Charles, SG2Jul89:3
Burns, John, SG12Jan86:4
Burns, Robert, reported death of, WC19Feb89:2
Burnside, James, WC29Jan89:2
Burnside, Mrs. James, WC29Jan89:2
Business, dissolution of, WC18Jun88:4, WC25Jun88:4
Burton, Benjamin, NCGH19Jan86:3
Burton, Hon. Mr., SG27Mar88:3
Burton, John W., SG19Nov88:3
Bushnel, Eusebeus, SG9Jul89:3—
Butcher, Thomas, SG11Dec88:3—
Bute County, N.C., SG18Jan87:2, NCG15Aug87:4,
    NCG29Mar86:2
Butler, Capt., SG10Dec89:3
Butler, Mr., SG10Dec89:3
Butler, Samuel, SG11Dec88:4—, SG15Jan89:3,
    SG22Jan89:4
Butler, Thomas, WC20Aug88:2
Butler, Willis, SG8Jan89:3
Byrd, Martin R., SG8Jan89:3, SG15Jan89:4
Byrne, John SG22Oct89:3, SG29Oct89:3,
    SG12Nov89:4

C

"C," NCG2Sep84:1
Cabarrus, ____, SG3Dec89:3
Cabarrus, Mr., EI4Jun88:3
Cabarrus, S., SG18Dec88:2, SG25Dec88:4, SG1Jan89:4,
    SG31Dec89:3
Cabarrus, Stephen, WC20Aug88:2, WC26Nov88:3,
    SG4Dec88:3, SG27Aug89:3, FG14Sep89:3,
    SG3Dec89:3, SG17Dec89:3
Cabinet making, WC23Jul88:4
Cade, Col., SG17Sep89:3
Cade, J., SG3Dec89:3
Cade, John, WC20Aug88:2
Cadiz, letter from, SG13Oct88:2, SG10Nov88:1,
    WC19Nov88:2, SG15Jan89:1
Cady
    See Post and Cady
Caesar, emancipation of, SG18Jan87:3
Cain, ____, SG29Sep88:3
Cain, John, SW20Aug88:2
Cain, Samuel, WC20Aug88:2
Caine, John, WC18Jun88:3
Cains, Christopher, SG6Jul86:3
Calcutta
    British government in, SG7Feb88:1
    letter from, SG7Feb88:1

news from, FG12Oct89:3
Caldwell, ___, SG29Sep88:3
Caldwell, Col., SG17Sep89:3
Caldwell, D., SG3Dec89:3
Caldwell, David, WC20Aug88:2, SG17Sep89:3,
   SG31Dec89:2
Caldwell, Mr., WC17Sep88:3, SG29Sep88:3
Calendar of Maniacs, SG22Sep88:3
Callender, Capt., WC18Jun88:3, WC25Jun88:3
Callender, Capt. T., WC17Sep88:3
Callender, T., WC24Sep88:1
Callender, Thomas, WC26Oct88:3, WC5Nov88:3,
   WC8Jan89:3—, WC19Feb89:3, WC26Feb89:1,
   SG31Dec89:3
Camas, Madam de, letters to, SG5Mar89:1,2
Camden, Lord, stoppage of a thoroughfare by,
   SG10Dec89:1
Camden County, N. C., WC26Nov88:3, SG25Dec88:3,
   SG3Sep89:3
   wardens of the poor in, SG18Dec88:3,
      WC18Dec88:3
Camden, S.C., SG14May89:1
   duel in, SG30Jul89:2
   letter from, SG30Jul89:2
Cameron, Alexander, SG9Apr89:3—
Camp, Willy, SG30Apr89:3—
Campbell, Alexander, NCG29Mar86:2
Campbell, Arth., SG27Mar88:3
Campbell, Duncan, NCG29Mar86:2
Campbell, James, SG7Feb88:4, EI9Apr88:1,
   SG8Jan89:3, SG15Jan89:4, SG22Oct89:3,
   SG29Oct89:3, SG12Nov89:4
Campbell, John, WC2Jul88:3, WC26Oct88:3,
   SG10Nov88:3, WC8Jan89:3, WCFeb89:3,
   WC19Feb89:3, WC26Feb89:1,4, WC5Mar89:1
Campbell, John A., WC20Aug88:2, SG10Sep89:3
Campbell, John Ablen, WC2Jul88:3—,
   WC12Feb89:3—
Campbell, W., WC10Sep88:1, WC17Sep88:4
Campbell, William, NCG29Mar86:2, SG6Jul86:3,
   WC18Jun88:3, WC25Jun88:3, WC9Jul88:4,
   WC8Jan89:3
Campbell's Station, SG18Dec88:3—
Campbellsborough, proposed town of, EI9Apr88:1
Campbellton, proposal for, EI9Apr88:1
Canada, SG19Feb89:1
   anecdote from, SG20Aug89:4
   British expenses in, SG22Sep88:1
   British supply Indians from, WC12Feb89:1
   expedition of explorers in, FG21Sep88:2
   trade of, SG18Jan87:3
   tranquillity of, NCGH23Feb86:3
   U.S. investigation of, FG21Sep89:2
Canal, SG18Jan87:3, SG25Dec88:3, SG23Apr89:3,
   SG7May89:4, SG13Aug89:3
   cutting of, SG31Dec89:3
   See also Raleigh Canal
Caner, ___, NCG6Jan85:1
Cannon, David, WC13Aug88:3
Cannon, James, SG27Mar88:3
Cannon, inscription on, SG25Jun89:2
Canoe, stolen, SG19Mar89:3—
Canton
   account of voyage to, WC15Oct88:1
   imports from, WC19Nov88:2
   U.S. trade with, NCGH23Feb86:2, WC10Sep88:2,

SG6Oct88:3, WC15Oct88:1, SG10Nov88:2,
   SG17Nov88:2,3, SG16Apr89:3, SG2Jul89:3
   See also China
Cape Coast Castle, Africa, school in, SG1Oct89:3
Cape Fear River, WC18Jun88:3, WC25Jun88:3,
   WC9Jul88:4
   navigation of, SG31Dec89:3
   pilotage of, SG18Jan87:3
Capehart, George, SG12Jan86:4
Capital
   See U.S., capital of
   See N.C., capital of
Capitol
   See U.S., capitol of
Card playing, NHGH2Feb86:3, SG20Aug89:4
Carding machine, FG21Sep89:2
Carlisle, Pa.
   cotton manufacturing in, SG2Apr89:3
   letter from, SG12Jan86:2,3
Carmalt, John, SG27Mar88:3
Carman, Dr., WC19Nov88:3
Carmen, James, SG9Jul89:3—
Carmichael, Maurice, WC5Feb89:3—
Carmichael and Bogle, WC5Feb89:3—
Carney, James, SG29Nov87:4, NCG19Dec87:4,
   SG7Feb88:4
Carolina, price of British goods in, SG11Dec88:1
Carpelen, Baronde, SG4Dec88:1
Carpenter, George, SG23Feb86:4
Carpenter, P., WC19Feb89:3, WC26Feb89:1
Carpenters, house, WC3Dec88:3—
Carr, Joseph, WC13Aug88:3, SG8Jan89:3, SG15Jan89:4
Carragan, Hugh, WC13Aug88:3
Carrel, John, WC20Aug88:2
Carruth, ___, SG3Dec89:3
Carruth, Major, SG24Sep89:3
Carson, J., SG3Dec89:2
Carson, Mr., SG29Sep88:3
Carson, Thomas, WC20Aug88:2
Carter, L., SG3Dec89:3
Carter, Mr., SG6Jul86:3
Carter, Sandon, SG29Nov87:3
Carteret County, N.C., NCG2Sep84:3, SG29Nov87:4,
   SG22Sep88:3, WC26Nov88:3, SG18Dec88:3,
   WC18Dec88:3, SG25Dec88:2, SG24Sep89:3
Cartagena, American immigrants to, SG23Jul89:3
"Castigator," EI9Apr88:4
Castle Inn, rent of, SG5Mar89:3
Castlew, James, SG9Jul89:3—
Castor oil, manufacture of, FG21Sep89:2
Caswell, ___, NCG19Dec87:4
Caswell, Richard, SG23Feb86:4, SG6Jul86:4,
   NCG19Dec87:4, SG7Feb88:4, WC26Nov88:3,
   SG4Dec88:3, SG3Sep89:3, SG3Dec89:4
   death of, SG3Dec89:4
   funeral of, SG17Dec89:2
Caswell, Richard, Sr., NCG6Jan85:1
Caswell, William, NCG6Jan85:1
Caswell, Winston, SG23Feb86:4, SG6Jul86:4,
   SG3Sep89:3
Caswell County, N.C., NCG9Dec84:4,
   NCGH16Feb86:1, NCGH23Feb86:1, SG22Sep88:3,
   SG18Dec88:3, WC18Dec88:2, SG25Dec88:2,
   SG17Sep89:3
Catawba River, SG18Dec88:3
Catherine, Empress of Russia, letter from,

WC18Dec88:2
Celestial phenomenon, SG6Oct88:2
Celibacy, WC9Jul88:1
Cemetery, WC29Jan89:2
Centre Benevolent Society, establishment of,
    SG31Dec89:3
Certificates
    Auditor's, sale of, SG4Jun89:1, SG9Jul89:3,
        SG23Jul89:3
    counterfeited, NCG15Aug87:4
    Loan-Office, WC18Jun88:3, WC2Jul88:1,
        WC9Jul88:1, SG29Sep88:3, SG6Oct88:3,
        SG10Nov88:4
    lost, NCG1Aug87:4
    N.C., redemption of, NCG9Dec84:2
Certificates and Claims, N.C. commissioners of,
    SG10Dec89:3
Chaise, sale of, WC5Feb89:3—
Chambers, ____, SG3Dec89:3
Chambers, Mr., SG3Dec89:3
Chambers, Maxwell, SG17Sep89:3
Chambers, Thomas, SG9Apr89:3—
Champlain, Adam, SG20Oct88:3, SG27Oct88:3
Chandler, Samuel, NCG3Nov85:4
Chapman, Benjamin, NCGH19Jan86:3
Chapman, Samuel, NCG29Jul84:4, SG27Mar88:3
Chaponel, J., NCG3Nov85:4
Chaponel, Mons., NCG6Jan85:1
Charity, NCGH23Feb86:2
Charles III, death of, SG23Apr89:2
Charles, Michael, NCGH2Feb86:3, NCGH16Feb86:3
Charles River, Mass., bridge over, SG19Mar89:2
Charleston, S.C.
    assault on members of S.C. legislature in,
        WC22Jan89:3
    citizens of, SG4Dec88:4
    executions in, WC18Jun88:2, WC2Jul88:2
    fire in, SG6Jul86:2
    Glasgow immigrants to, SG10Nov88:3
    letter from, NCG9Dec84:2, WC19Feb89:3,
    lighthouse in harbor of, WC22Jan89:3
    magazine extract from, SG4Jun89:3
    news from, NCGH2Feb86:2, SG23Feb86:2,
        SG6Jul86:2, WC18Jun88:2, WC25Jun88:2,
        WC2Jul88:2, WC9Jul88:2, SG7Feb88:2,
        WC10Sep88:3, WC17Sep88:1,2,3,
        SG22Sep88:3, WC24Sep88:2, SG3Nov88:2,
        SG10Nov88:3, WC12Nov88:3, SG24Nov88:3,
        WC26Nov88:2, SG4Dec88:4, WC8Jan89:1,
        WC22Jan89:2,3, WC12Feb89:2,
        WC19Feb89:1,3, SG12Mar89:3, SG28May89:3,
        SG30Jul89:2,3, SG27Aug89:3, FG21Sep89:2,
        SG5Nov89:3, SG12Nov89:3
    newspaper extract from, SG29Nov87:2,3
    poor in, SG3Nov88:2
    Scottish immigration to, SG10Nov88:2
    shipping of, WC26Nov88:3
Charleston City Gazette, extract from, WC10Dec88:3
Charlestown, Mass.
    growth of, SG12Jan86:2
    news from, SG12Jan86:2
Charlestown, N.H., births in, SG26Feb89:4
Charlton, Thomas, SG23Apr89:3—
Charrier, Mons., SG27Mar89:3
Chastelleaux, Marque de, death of, SG19Feb89:2
Chateloux, Marquis, reported death of, WC19Feb89:2

Chatham, Earl of, SG5Feb89:4
    character of, SG6Jul86:2
    named governor-general of Bengal, WC5Nov88:2
Chatham County, N.C., SG18Jan87:2,3, SG22Sep88:3,
    WC12Nov88:3—, SG25Dec88:2, SG17Sep89:3,
    SG17Dec89:3
    court of, NCGH19Jan86:3, SG18Jan87:2
Cheek, Thomas L., SG27Mar88:3
Cheeke, Thomas L., NCG29Jul84:4
Cherokee lands, letter from, SG9Apr89:3
Chesson, ____, SG3Dec89:3
Chesson, Samuel, SG27Aug89:3, FG14Sep89:3
Cheney, Benjamin, SG18Jan87:3
Chezon, ____, SG3Dec89:3
Child, Francis, SG23Feb86:4, SG6Jul86:4, SG18Jan87:3,
    WC6Aug88:4
    See also Comptroller of Accounts
Child, Sylvester, WC13Aug88:3
Child, deformed, SG8Oct89:2
Childrearing, WC10Sep88:4
Chimney sweeps, SG2Jul89:3
China, SG11Jun89:3
    civil war in, SG5Mar89:3
    European conflict in, SG5Mar89:3
    laws of, SG12Feb89:3
    trade in, SG23Feb86:2
    U.S. diplomatic relations with, SG23Feb86:3
    U.S. trade with, NCGH23Feb86:2, WC18Jun88:2,
        WC6Aug88:2, WC10Sep88:2, SG6Oct88:1,
        WC15Oct88:1, WC19Nov88:2, WC26Nov88:2,
        SG2Jul89:3
    See also Canton
Chockzim, articles of capitulation of, WC5Feb89:1,2
Chowan County, N.C., NCG2Sep84:4, SG12Jan86:4,
    NCG29Mar86:2, SG29Nov87:1, WC26Nov88:3,
    SG25Dec88:2, SG22Jan89:4—, SG23Apr89:3—,
    FG14Sep89:3
    court of, SG1Jan89:3—
    militia observance of Washington's birthday,
        SG19Feb89:2
    See also Edenton, N.C.; Edenton and Chowan
        County
Christ Church (New Bern, N.C.), SG17Dec89:2
Christ Church Parish (Craven County, N.C.),
    SG18Jan87:3
Christie, James, SG8Jan89:3, SG15Jan89:4
Christie, Thomas, NCG29Mar86:2
Christmas, ____, SG24Sep89:3
Christmas, J., SG17Sep89:3, SG3Dec89:3
Christmas, T., SG3Dec89:3
Christmas, Thomas, WC20Aug88:2, SG24Sep89:3
Christmas, W., SG3Dec89:3
Church of England, WC12Feb89:2
Cicaty, Augustine, FG14Sep89:3
Cincinnati, Society of
    See Society of Cincinnati
Cities, European, population of, SG19Feb89:1
"Citizen, A," WC18Jun88:3
"Citizen and Soldier, A," SG22Sep88:3, SG11Jun89:2
    response to, SG20Oct88:3
"Citizen of North-Carolina, A," SG15Sep88:3
    response to, SG3Nov88:1,2
Citizenship, British definition of, WC10Dec88:2
Claimants, U.S. military, NCGH19Jan86:4
Clark, Christopher, SG12Jan86:4, SG29Nov87:1,
    SG29Jan89:1, SG9Jul89:3—

Clark, Col., NCG2Sep84:2, SG24Sep89:3
Clark, Hans, SG20Oct88:3, SG27Oct88:3
Clark, J., SG3Dec89:3
Clark, Joseph, WC19Feb89:3
Clark, Mrs., SG12Jan86:4, WC13Aug88:3
Clark & Weir, SG12Jan86:4
Clarke, Ichabod, SG9Apr89:3—
Clarke, Jas., SG20Oct88:3, SG27Oct88:3
Clarke, Thomas, SG20Oct88:3, SG27Oct88:3,
    SG9Apr89:3—
Clarksville, N.C., SG31Dec89:3
Clapp, George, NCGH19Jan86:4, NCGH2Feb86:3
Claret, sale of, SG29Nov87:4, NCG19Dec87:4,
    SG7Feb88:4
Clause, G., SG23Feb86:4
Clayton, Francis, WC26Feb89:3, WC5Mar89:1
Clay, ___, SG17Sep89:3
Clear, Timothy, SG7Feb88:3
Cleary, Simon, SG18Dec88:3
Clendenin, John, SG20Oct88:3, SG27Oct88:3,
    SG8Jan89:3, SG15Jan89:4
Clendenning, Matthew, WC13Aug88:3
Clergy, French, petition and remonstrance of,
    SG15Sep88:1
Clerks, N.C. county courts, NCG2Sep84:3
Clinch Mountain, SG18Dec88:3—
    settlement in, SG29Nov87:2
Clinton, ___, SG29Jan89:2, SG3Dec89:3
Clinton, Geo., WC20Aug88:3
Clinton, George, WC23Jul88:3
    address of, WC22Jan89:1
    address to, SG6Aug89:3
    letter of, WC20Aug88:3
    proclamation of, SG10Nov88:2
    response of, SG6Aug89:3
    speech of to N.Y. legislature, WC22Jan89:1
Clinton, General, SG18Dec88:2—, SG17Sep89:3
Clinton, Robert, WC20Aug88:2
Clocks and watches, SG18Jan87:4, SG25Dec88:3
Clodfelter, Reuben, NCGH19Jan86:4, NCGH2Feb86:4
Cloe (slave), NCG15Aug87:4
Cloth, SG11Dec88:2
Clothes, stolen, SG30Apr89:3—
Coal, Thomas, NCG6Jan85:1
Coates, James W., SG20Oct88:3, SG27Oct88:3
Cob, Thomas, NCG29Jul84:3
Cobb, Benjamin, SG20Oct88:3, SG27Oct88:3
Cobbler, merits of, SG22Sep88:4
Cobham, Dr. Thomas, SG6Jul86:3
Cobham, Miss, WC18Jun88:4, WC25Jun88:4
Coble, Anthony, NCGH2Feb86:3, NCGH16Feb86:3,
    NCGH23Feb86:3
Cochran, Robert, SG8Jan89:3, SG15Jan89:4
Cocke, William, SG18Dec88:2—
Cockton, John, SG9Jul89:3—
Coffee House, SG29Nov87:3, WC12Feb89:2,3
Coffield, John, SG30Apr89:3—
Coffield, John, Sr., SG9Apr89:3—
Coffield, Michael, SG9Jul89:3—
Coffield, Thomas, SG12Jan86:4
Cogdale, ___, SG3Sep89:3
Cogdell, R., NCG6Jan85:1
Cogdell, Richard, NCG29Jul84:2
Coinage
    copper, SG10Sep89:2
    English, SG12Nov89:2

U.S., NCG15Aug87:2
    See also Money
Cole and Stevenson, NCG19Dec87:4
Coleman, John, WC9Jul88:3
Collier, John, NCG2Feb86:3, NCGH16Feb86:3,
    NCGH23Feb86:3, SG23Feb86:3
Collier, Mary, SG27Mar88:3
Collins, John, WC13Aug88:3
Collins, Josiah, WC20Aug88:2, WC19Nov88:3,
    WC26Nov88:3, SG4Dec88:3, SG29Jan89:1,
    SG9Jul89:3—
Collins, Mary, SG26Feb89:3
Colson, John, SG18Jan87:2,3, WC18Dec88:3
Colson, William, SG18Jan87:3
Comedies, sale of, SG15Oct89:3—, SG12Nov89:3—
Comet, SG24Nov88:2
    study of, SG29Sep88:2,3
Commerce
    See France; N.C.; U.S.
Commission store, NCG15Aug87:4
"Commissioner, A," SG13Aug89:3
Commissioners for Improving the Navigation of
    Albemarle Sound, SG9Jul89:3—
Commissioners of Navigation (Cape Fear River),
    WC18Jun88:4—
Commissioners of Pilotage, Charleston, S.C.,
    WC22Jan89:3
Commissioners of the Town of Edenton, SG5Feb89:3
Commissioners of the Town of Wilmington,
    WC5Feb89:2,3—
    election of, WC8Jan89:3
Commodities, unmerchantable, exportation of,
    SG31Dec89:3
"Common Sense," WC16Jul88:2, WC23Jul88:2
Compositor, wanted, SG11Dec88:3—
Comptroller of Accounts, WC23Jul88:4—
Concord, N.H.
    accident in, SG24Nov88:2
    letter from, WC16Jul88:3
Confiscated property, SG23Feb86:1, SG6Jul86:3
    commissioners of, SG18Jan87:3
Confiscation Acts, NCGH16Feb86:3,
    NCG29Mar86:1,2,3,4
Congregational Church, SG19Nov89:4
Congregational ministers, New Haven, address to
    President Washington, SG19Nov89:4
Congress, U.S., NCGH23Feb86:3, SG16Apr89:2,
    SG30Apr89:2,3, SG18Jun89:2, SG10Sep89:3
    accidental injuries to members of, SG16Jul89:2
    acts of, WC12Feb89:1, SG18Jun89:2, SG30Jul89:4,
        SG20Aug89:3, FG24Aug89:2,4, SG27Aug89:4,
        SG10Sep89:4, SG17Sep89:4, FG21Sep89:4,
        SG24Sep89:4, SG1Oct89:3, SG22Oct89:3,
        SG29Oct89:4, SG12Nov89:4
    address to, SG16Apr89:1
    adjournment of, SG22Oct89:3,4
    approves federal Constitution, WC13Aug88:2
    attitudes of members of, SG7May89:3
    bills of, SG11Jun89:2, SG3Sep89:4
    calls for presidential election, WC15Oct88:1
    compensation of members of, SG3Sep89:1,
        SG24Sep89:2,3
    considers amendments to federal Constitution,
        FG14Sep89:4
    considers impost collection bill, SG25Jun89:3
    considers judicial system, SG18Jun89:2

considers location of capital of U.S., SG10Sep89:1,2,3, SG1Oct89:2, SG22Oct89:2

considers tonnage duties, SG6Aug89:1

considers western lands, SG6Aug89:2,3

debate over titles, SG11Jun89:3

election of members of, WC12Feb89:1

evaluation of, SG12Jan86:3

extract from journals of, WC23Jul88:2

financial report of, SG15Nov87:1,2, WC17Sep88:1

first meeting of under new government, SG23Apr89:3

Indian relations of, SG3Sep89:1,4

ineptitude of, SG12Jan86:3

legislation prescribing oath of office, SG18Jun89:2

letter from member of, SG17Sep89:2,3, SG1Oct89:3, SG22Oct89:2

meeting of, SG2Apr89:2

members of, WC8Jan89:3, SG16Jul89:3

N.C. delegates to, SG7Feb88:3

organizes new government, WC23Jul88:2

payment of members of, SG17Sep89:2,3

petitions for establishment of permanent capital, FG21Sep89:3

place of meeting of, WC27Aug88:3

proceedings of, SG23Feb86:3, SG27Mar88:2, WC25Jun88:1, WC3Sep88:2, SG8Sep88:2, WC17Sep88:1,2, SG22Sep88:2, SG29Sep88:2, SG23Apr89:3, SG30Apr89:2,3, SG7May89:1,2, SG14May89:3, SG21May89:3, SG28May89:1,2, SG4Jun89:2,3, SG25Jun89:1,3, SG2Jul89:1,2, SG9Jul89:1,2, SG16Jul89:1, SG23Jul89:3, SG30Jul89:3, SG6Aug89:1,2, SG13Aug89:4, SG20Aug89:3, FG24Aug89:2, SG3Sep89:1,4, SG10Sep89:2, FG14Sep89:4, SG17Sep89:1,2,3, FG21Sep89:3,4, SG24Sep89:1,4, FG12Oct89:3, SG15Oct89:3, SG22Oct89:4, SG29Oct89:1,3

proclamation of, SG29Sep88:1

provides protection for western territories, WC17Sep88:2

qualifications for members of, WC12Nov88:2

receipt of federal Constitution, SG4Oct87:3

receipt of New Hampshire's ratification, WC23Jul88:2

rejection of Kentucky statehood, WC13Aug88:1

requisitions by, SG15Nov87:1,2 WC17Sep88:1,2, SG29Sep88:2

resolution of, NCGH19Jan86:4, NCGH2Feb86:4, NCG29Mar86:1, NCG15Aug87:2, SG4Oct87:3,4, SG29Nov87:4, WC25Jun88:1, WC13Aug88:1, WC3Sep88:1, SG29Sep88:1, SG6Oct88:3, WC15Oct88:1, SG11Dec88:3, SG29Jan89:3, SG17Sep89:4, SG24Sep89:3

sale of acts of, SG10Sep89:4—, SG29Oct89:3, SG19Nov89:3, SG26Nov89:3, SG17Dec89:3

seeks status of Rhode Island, SG2Jul89:1

survey directed by, SG24Sep89:3

travel allowance to members of, SG10Sep89:3

Congressman, U.S., accident to, SG16Jul89:2

Congressmen, N.C., appointment of, SG31Dec89:3

election of, SG17Dec89:3, SG31Dec89:2,3

Conkling, Joseph, SG27Mar88:3

Connecticut

anecdote about thief in, SG10Dec89:3

congressmen of, SG17Nov88:3, SG19Feb89:3

consideration of constitutional amendments, SG26Nov89:2,3

description of, SG28May89:4

elections in, WC18Jun88:3, WC26Nov88:2, WC15Jan89:3, SG29Jan89:2, WC26Feb89:2, SG18Jun89:2

electors of, WC12Feb89:1, SG19Feb89:3

legislation of, WC26Nov88:2

legislative address of, SG19Nov89:4

legislature of, WC26Nov88:2

manufacturing in, WC5Nov88:2, WC12Feb89:1, SG23Apr89:3, SG21May89:3, SG10Sep89:1,2

newspaper extract from, SG16Apr89:3

politics in, WC18Jun88:3, SG17Nov88:3, SG24Nov88:2, WC15Jan89:3, SG29Jan89:2, SG19Feb89:3, SG18Jun89:2, SG26Nov89:2,3

presentation of suits of clothes to congressmen by, SG21May89:3

Quakers in, SG24Nov88:2

troops in, WC19Feb89:2

Connely, Nuton, WC13Aug88:3

Conner, Dempsey, WC26Nov88:3, SG4Dec88:3, SG29Jan89:1, SG9Jul89:3, SG23Jul89:4

Connor, Dempsey, WC19Nov88:3, SG16Jul89:4

Conolly, Col., NCG9Dec84:3

Constable, WC5Feb89:3

Constable, Rucker and Co., SG8Sep88:4—

Constantin

See Henrion & Constantin

Constantinople, news from, WC19Feb89:2

Constitution, N.C., interpretation of, NCG11Jul87:2

Constitutional Convention, Mass., SG25Dec88:3

Constitutional Convention, N.C., SG4Dec88:2,3, WC10Dec88:3

convening of, WC10Dec88:3

members of, WC20Aug88:2

proposed meeting of, WC5Nov88:2, WC26Nov88:3

Constitutional Convention, Philadelphia, NCG11Jul87:3, NCG15Aug87:3, WC29Aug88:4, WC10Dec88:1

N.C. representatives to, SG18Jan87:3, WC26Nov88:3

resolution of, SG4Oct87:3

sale of publications relating to proceedings of, WC18Jun88:4

See also Fayetteville Convention; Hillsborough Convention

Constitutions, nature of, SG12Feb89:1

Contentment, commentary on, SG22Sep88:4

Continental Commissioner of Accounts, memorial of, SG3Sep89:1

Continental Intelligence, SG4Jun89:1

See also European Intelligence; Foreign Intelligence

Convicts, English, SG26Feb89:3, SG12Mar89:1

importation of, SG6Oct88:3, WC19Nov88:3

Cook, Benjamin, SG29Nov87:1

Cook, Capt., NCGH19Jan86:2, WC19Feb89:3

Cook, John, NCG3Nov85:1

Cook, Harvey, NCGH16Feb86:3

Cooke, Captain, SG20Oct88:3, SG27Oct88:3

Cooke, Henry, NCGH2Feb86:3, SG23Feb86:3

Cooke, Silas, NCG2Sep84:3, SG6Jul86:3

Cooley, Mrs., SG9Jul89:3—

Cool Spring Tavern, FG21Sep89:4

Cooper, Charles, NCGH23Feb86:3

Cooper, Henry Batts, NCG2Sep84:4

Cooper, John, NCG2Sep84:4

Cooper, Capt. John, SG12Jan86:3

Cooper, Samuel, NCG29Jul84:3
Cooper's Town, N.Y., letter from, SG2Jul89:3
Coor, James, NCG2Sep84:3, NCG6Jan85:1,
    SG27Mar88:3, WC16Jul88:2, WC23Jul88:1
Copeland, James, SG12Jan86:4
Copenhagen
    letter from, SG18Jun89:2
    news from, WC18Dec88:2
Copyright, U.S., bill for, SG16Jul89:1
Cork, newspaper extract from, SG3Nov88:2
Cornell, Samuel, NCG3Nov85:1, NCG29Mar86:2
Cornwall Chronicle (Montego Bay), extract from,
    WC22Jan89:1
Cornwallis, Lord, SG20Oct88:1
"Correspondent, A," WC9Jul88:2
Cosby, Philips, SG13Oct88:2
Cotter, Capt. NCG29Jul84:3
Cotterell, John, WC13Aug88:3
Cotton, manufacturing of, FG21Sep89:2
Council, James, WC26Oct88:3
Council (Jamaica), address to Prince William Henry,
    WC22Jan89:1
Council of State, France, order of, SG6Aug89:4
Council of State, N.C., members of, SG4Dec88:3,
    SG31Dec89:3
Counterfeiting, NCG15Aug87:2, SG1Jan89:2,
    WC8Jan89:2, SG18Jun89:2, SG20Aug89:2,
    SG19Nov89:2
    See Money, counterfeit
Counties, N.C., empowered to levy taxes, SG18Jan87:3
Country produce, NCG29Jul84:4, WC25Dec88:3
    sale of, WC3Sep88:3, WC10Sep88:4
County courts, SG18Jan87:3, SG18Dec88:3,
    SG25Dec88:3
    clerks of, SG6Jul84:4, SG12Feb89:3
    diminution of revenue in, WC18Dec88:2
    jurisdiction of, SG18Jan87:2, WC19Nov88:3,
        SG25Dec88:3
    meeting times of, SG18Jan87:3
    neglect by, WC18Dec88:2
    powers of, SG18Jan87:2
Court of equity, SG3Dec89:3
    Hillsborough District, WC18Jun88:4, WC25Jun88:3
Court of the King's Bench, England, proceedings of,
    SG16Jul89:2
Court Law, N.C., 1777, SG31Dec89:3
Court cases pending, SG29Nov87:4, WC18Jun88:4—,
    WC18Dec88:3, SG25Dec88:3, WC25Dec88:1,
    SG1Jan89:3—, WC8Jan89:4—, SG9Apr89:4—,
    SG20Aug89:4—
Courtney, William, NCG6Jan85:1, SG20Oct88:3,
    SG27Oct88:3
Courtney and Watts, NCGH19Jan86:3,
    NCGH2Feb86:4, NCGH16Feb86:3,
    NCGH23Feb86:3
Courts, N.C.
    act to erect, SG12Jan86:1
    business of, SG17Dec89:3
    delays in, WC12Nov88:3
    establishment of, SG3Dec89:3
    Justice in, WC12Nov88:1
Courtship, SG12Oct89:4
Courthouse
    Fayetteville, FG24Aug89:3, FG14Sep89:4,
        FG21Sep89:4
    Pitt County, SG31Dec89:3

Covent Garden Theater, London, play in,
    SG19Feb89:1
Covington, Benjamin, WC20Aug88:2
Cowan, ____, SG3Dec89:3
Cowan, John, SG10Sep89:3
Coward, Capt., WC22Jan89:4
Cowen, J., SG3Dec89:2
Cowhides, wanted, NCGH6Oct85:4
Cox, J., WC20Aug88:2
Cox, John, SG8Jan89:3, SG15Jan89:4, SG9Apr89:3—,
    SG22Oct89:3, SG29Oct89:3, SG12Nov89:4
Cox, Thomas, SG11Dec88:4—, SG15Jan89:3,
    SG22Jan89:4
Craike, Mr., WC29Jan89:4—
Craven County, N.C., NCG29Jul84:2,3, NCG9Dec84:4,
    NCG3Nov85:1,2, NCG29Mar86:2, SG18Jan87:2,
    SG7Feb88:3, SG25Dec88:2, SG3Sep89:3
    clerk of court of, SG18Jan87:3
    poorhouse in, SG18Jan87:2
Crawford, Gideon, SG27Mar88:3
Crawford, Mr., consul at Rotterdam, SG7Feb88:1
Crawford, Nancy, SG27Mar88:3
Creecy, ____, SG3Dec89:2,3
Creecy, Lemuel, SG27Aug89:3, FG14Sep89:3
    letter from, EI4Jun88:2,3
Creecys, ____, SG8Jan89:3
Cricket, NCGH19Jan86:2
Crime, English, SG20Aug89:1
Criminal offenders, N.C., fines and imprisonments of,
    SG17Dec89:3
Criminals, punishment of, WC26Nov88:2,3,
    SG10Sep89:2
Crockery, sale of, WC25Dec88:3
Croisic, France
    description of, SG15Jan89:2
    letter from, SG15Jan89:2
Cromwell, Rowlin, NCG6Jan85:1
Cronstadt-Mole, Russia, letter from, SG10Nov88:3
Cropton, Charles, WC23Jul89:3
Croswell, Charity, NCGH19Jan86:4, NCGH2Feb86:4
Crump, ____, SG3Dec89:3
Crump, John, FG14Sep89:3
Cuba, trade of, FG21Sep89:2
Cuffee (slave), ran away, WC12Feb89:3—
Cumberland County, N.C., SG23Feb86:2,
    WC23Jul88:3—, SG22Sep88:3, SG20Oct88:2,
    WC26Oct88:3—, SG18Dec88:3, WC18Dec88:3,
    SG25Dec88:2, WC5Feb89:3, SG10Sep89:3,
    SG31Dec89:3
    elections in, FG24Aug89:3
    inspectors in, WC18Dec88:3
Cumberland Gazette (Portland), extract from,
    SG27Aug89:2
Cumming, Henry, WC16Jul88:3
Cummins, Robert, SG18Jan87:2
Cunningham, James, SG20Oct88:3, SG27Oct88:3
Cunningham, William, NCG29Mar86:2
Currency
    emission of, SG12Jan86:2
    paper, WC5Nov88:2, WC18Dec88:3
    redemption of, SG23Feb86:1, SG18Jan87:3,
        WC18Dec88:2
    scale of depreciation of, SG25Dec88:4
    See also Money
Currie, John, WC13Aug88:3
Currier and tanner, NCGH16Feb86:1, NCG23Feb86:1

Currituck County, N.C., NCG3Nov85:1, NCG29Mar86:2, WC26Nov88:3, SG25Dec88:2, SG31Dec89:3
Curtis, Ivy, NCG6Jan85:1
Curtis, Tho., NCG29Mar86:1
Customs laws, violation of, SG27Aug89:2
Customs officers, U.S., appointment of, SG27Aug89:2,3
Cutting, Rev. Dr., SG18Jan87:4, SG18Jun89:3
Cutting, Rev. Leonard, SG20Oct88:3, SG27Oct88:3
Cuyler, John, SG27Mar88:4

D

D____, Capt., SG18Jan87:3
Dabney, J., SG3Dec89:3
Dabney, John, SG24Sep89:3
Dalkey, obituary of King of, SG18Jun89:1
Dalling, Mary, SG20Oct88:3, SG27Oct88:3
Dalrymple, Sir John, memoirs of, SG24Nov88:2
Daly, Elizabeth, SG25Dec88:3
Dalzell, John, SG12Jan86:4
Dameron, John, SG25Dec88:3—
Dance, public, NCG23Feb86:3, SG23Feb86:3
Dancing
    instructor for, NCG29Jul84:4
    school of, SG23Feb86:4
Daniel, Mark, SG22Oct89:3, SG29Oct89:3, SG12Nov89:4
Daniel, S., WC27Aug88:3—
Dantzic
    commerce of, WC25Jun88:2
    future of, WC25Jun88:2
Danvers, Mass., death of woman in tavern in, WC3Sep88:2, WC24Sep88:2
Danville, Ky.
    convention in, SG16Apr89:1
    letter from, WC30Jul88:3
Dartmouth University, SG16Apr89:3
Dauge, ____, SG3Dec89:2,3
Dauge, Peter, WC20Aug88:2, SG3Sep89:3
Davidson, Brig.-Gen., SG20Oct88:1, SG18Dec88:3—
Davidson County, N.C., SG18Jan87:2, SG27Mar88:4, WC23Jul88:2, WC26Nov88:3, WC18Dec88:2,3, SG25Dec88:2,4, SG1Jan89:4, WC5Mar89:1, SG31Dec89:2
    court of, SG31Dec89:3
    description of, SG20Oct88:1, SG19Feb89:1, WC5Mar89:1
    division of, SG22Jan89:3
    essay concerning legislation for raising troops to protect, WC6Aug88:1,2
    raising troops in, SG18Jan87:2
    superior court in, WC18Dec88:2
Daves, John, SG27Mar88:3
Davie, ____, WC6Aug88:2, SG3Dec89:3
Davie, Col., SG20Oct88:3, SG24Sep89:3
Davie, Mr., WC20Aug88:2, SG3Dec89:2,4, SG17Dec89:3
Davie, W. R., NCG15Aug87:3
Davie, William R., SG2Sep84:4, SG18Jan87:3, WC20Aug88:2, SG31Dec89:3
Davie, William Richardson, NCG19Dec87:4
Davis, D., SG3Dec89:3
Davis, Devotion, WC20Aug88:2, SG27Aug89:3, FG14Sep89:3

Davis, Dolphin, FG14Sep89:3, FG21Sep89:4
Davis, Jehu, WC15Oct88:1
Davis, John, WC22Jan89:3
Davis, Jonathan, NCG15Aug87:4
Davis, Joseph, SG27Mar88:3
Davis, Josoph, NCG6Jan85:1
Davis, Thomas, WC2Jul88:3—, WC18Dec88:3, SG25Dec88:3—, WC25Dec88:1, WC8Jan89:4—, SG20Aug89:4—, SG24Sep89:4—
Davis, William, SG27Mar88:3
Dawley, Dennis, SG29Jan89:3—
Dawson, John, SG15Jan89:3—, SG26Mar89:4, SG9Apr89:4, SG16Apr89:4, SG30Apr89:4
Dawson, Levi, SG18Jan87:3
Dawson, Mrs., SG12Jan86:4
Dawson, W. J., WC26Nov88:3, SG3Dec89:2
Dawson, William J., WC20Aug88:2, FG24Aug89:1, SG27Aug89:3, FG14Sep89:3
Dawson, W. Johnston, SG17Dec89:3
Dawson, William Johnston, SG8Sep88:3, SG15Sep88:4—, SG4Dec88:3, SG9Jul89:3
Day, Luke, NCG15Aug87:1
Dayton, Henry, WC29Jan89:3—
Dean, Joseph, SG6Jul86:4
Dean, Thomas, WC12Feb89:3, WC19Feb89:4
Deane, Silas, death of, SG24Dec89:1
Death, accidental, SG24Nov88:2, SG18Dec89:3
DeBretigny, ____, SG18Jun89:4
Debretigny, Marquis, NCG6Jan85:1
Debt, N.C., payment of, SG17Dec89:3, SG31Dec89:3
Debt, U.S., WC17Sep88:1,2, WC5Nov88:1
    specie payment of, SG13Oct88:2
Debtors
    deceased, proceedings against, SG31Dec89:3
    relief of, SG29Jan89:3—, SG23Apr89:3, SG14May89:3, SG21May89:4
Debts, recovery of, WC19Nov88:3, SG25Dec88:3
Declaration of Rights
    France, SG19Nov89:2
    North Carolina, WC20Aug88:1, SG19Nov89:2
Deeds, registration of, SG18Dec88:3
Deekings, ____, SG17Sep89:3
Deerskins, wanted, NCGH19Jan86:3, NCGH2Feb86:4, NCGH16Feb86:4, NCGH23Feb86:4
Defence of the Constitutions of Government of the United States of America, A, sale of, SG4Oct87:4, SG29Nov87:4
DeGlaubeck, Baron, petition to Congress, SG1Oct89:4
Dekeyser, Col., WC19Nov88:3
Delahunty, Daniel, NCG6Jan85:1
De la Luzerne, Chevalier, NCG29Jul84:2
Delaware
    description of, SG28May89:4
    election of U.S. senators, WC3Dec88:3
    incorporation of physicians in, SG19Mar89:3
    legislation of, SG19Mar89:3
    politics in, SG17Nov88:3, WC3Dec88:3, SG19Feb89:2
Delaware River, navigation of, SG29Jan89:2
Delinquent accounts, WC23Jul88:4—
Denmark, SG18Dec88:1
    alliance with Russia, WC26Feb89:2
    attack on Scottish brig, WC25Dec88:2
    attitude toward Russo-Swedish war, WC15Jan89:1
    Russia rejects mediation offer of, FG14Sep89:2
    support of for Russia, WC18Dec88:2

truce of with Sweden, WC12Feb89:2
   war of, WC22Jan89:2, WC26Feb89:2
D'eous, Dr. John Y. Samuel Lees Gud, SG22Oct89:3,
   SG29Oct89:3, SG12Nov89:4
Department of State, U.S., congressional deliberation
   over creation of, SG16Jul89:1
Department of War, U.S., act to establish, SG10Sep89:4
Depreciation, scale of, SG18Dec88:2
Devane, Thomas, WC20Aug88:2,3
Devane, William, SG22Sep88:3
Devereaux, John, SG29Nov87:4, SG7Feb88:3
Dickens, ____, SG3Dec89:3
Dickins, Robert, NCG9Dec84:4, WC20Aug88:2
Dickinson, Benjamin and son, SG20Oct88:3,
   SG27Oct88:3
Dickson, ____, SG3Dec89:3
Dickson, Col., WC17Sep88:3, SG29Sep88:3
Dickson, J., SG3Dec89:3
Dickson, Joseph, SG18Jan87:3, SG24Sep89:3
Dickson, R., SG3Dec89:3
Digs, R., WC20Aug88:2
Dinwiddie, Crawford and company, NCG29Mar86:2
"Diogenes," SG30Jul89:3, SG13Aug89:3
Disinterments, N.Y., SG12Mar89:2
Distillery, WC18Jun88:4, WC25Jun88:4
Divorce, SG12Feb89:2
Dixon, Jonathan, WC13Aug88:3
Dixon, Joseph, SG31Dec89:3
Dixon, Robert, SG22Sep88:3, SG17Sep89:3,
   SG31Dec89:3
Dixon, William, WC20Aug88:2
Dobbins, W., SG3Dec89:3
Dobbs, Edward Brice, NCG29Mar86:2
Dobbs, Governor, NCG29Mar86:3
Dobbs County, N.C., NCG2Sep84:3, SG23Feb86:2,4,
   NCG29Mar86:2, SG6Jul86:4, SG4Oct87:4,
   WC6Aug88:2, WC26Nov88:3, SG18Dec88:3,
   WC18Dec88:2, SG25Dec88:2, SG2Jul89:3,
   SG9Jul89:4, SG23Jul89:3, SG3Sep89:3
Dobins, William, WC20Aug88:2
Dodd, David, WC20Aug88:2
Dog
   rabid, NCGH23Feb86:1, WC17Sep88:2
   sagacity of, SG17Nov88:3
Doherty, George, NCGH2Feb86:3, NCGH16Feb86:4,
   NCGH23Feb86:4
Dollars
   counterfeiting of Spanish milled, SG1Jan89:2
   silver, WC19Feb89:3, WC26Feb89:3
   wanted, WC5Oct88:2, WC26Oct88:4—
Domestic Intelligence, WC18Jun88:2—,
   WC5Nov88:2—, WC25Dec88:3, WC8Jan89:1,2,
   WC29Jan89:2
   See also American Intelligence
Dominica
   letter from, SG29Oct89:2
   ships in port of, SG29Oct89:3
   slave violence in, NCG29Mar86:1
   storm in, SG8Oct89:2
Dominico Gazette, selection from, WC10Sep88:1
Donald, Captain, WC15Jan89:3
Donaldson
   See Stott and Donaldson
Donan, David, SG15Jan89:3—, SG26Mar89:4,
   SG9Apr89:4, SG16Apr89:4, SG30Apr89:4
Donelson, Stokely, WC20Aug88:2

Donelson, William, WC20Aug88:2
Dongan, Thomas, WC20Aug88:2
Donggan, Thomas, WC18Dec88:2
Donnell, Robert, SC25Dec88:3, SG27Aug89:3
Donnell, Robert & Co., SG29Nov87:3
Dorance, Daniel, SG27Mar88:3
Dorr, E., SG20Oct88:3, SG27Oct88:3
Dorsey, L., WC3Dec88:3
Dorsey, La., WC10Dec88:3
Dorsey, L. A., WC18Dec88:1, WC25Dec88:3,4,
   WC8Jan89:3
Dorsey, Lawrence, WC13Aug88:3, WC26Feb89:3,
   WC5Mar89:1
Dorsey, Lawrence A., WC8Jan89:3—
Dorsey, Mr., WC3Dec88:3
Dorsey's Tavern, WC3Dec88:3
Dotten, James, NCG29Mar86:2
Doud, Corn., WC20Aug88:2
Dougherty, Patrick, SG30Apr89:3
Douglas, ____, WC17Sep88:3, SG29Sep88:3,
   SG3Dec89:3
Douglas, John, SG27Mar88:3
Douglas, Joseph, WC20Aug88:2, SG17Sep89:3,
   SG3Dec89:3
Douglas, Robert, WC3Sep88:1
Douglass, Benjamin, SG22Sep88:3
Douglass, David, SG22Oct88:2
Douglass, E., SG3Dec89:3
Dowd, C., SG3Dec89:3
Dowd, Conner, SG31Dec89:3
Dowd, Cornelius, SG24Sep89:3
Dowd, Mary, SG31Dec89:3
Drama, WC17Sep88:3
Dramatic performances, WC19Feb89:1
   tax on, WC19Nov88:3, SG25Dec88:3
Drawing school, SG4Oct87:4
Dray, Nicholas A., SG6Jul86:3
Dress
   female mode of, SG29Jan89:3
   manner of, SG12Jan86:4
Drew, ____, SG3Dec89:3
Dromgoole, Alexander, WC22Jan89:3
Drought, SG23Feb86:4, SG6Jul86:4
Drowning, WC26Oct88:3
Drugs and medicines, sale of, NCG29Jul84:3,
   NCG2Sep84:3, SG12Jan86:3, SG18Jan87:4,
   SG27Mar88:4
Drumgole, ____, SG26Feb89:3, WC5Mar89:2
Drummond, Va., SG26Mar89:3—
Dry, William, NCG29Jul84:3
Dry goods, sale of, NCG29Jul84:4, NCG2Sep84:4,
   NCG3Nov85:3, NCGH19Jan86:3, NCGH3Feb86:4,
   NCGH16Feb86:4, NCGH23Feb86:2,3,4,
   SG4Oct87:3, SG29Nov87:3,4, SG7Feb88:4,
   SG27Mar88:4, WC18Jun88:4, WC25Jun88:4,
   WC26Oct88:3, SG27Oct88:3, WC5Nov88:3,
   WC25Dec88:3, SG29Jan89:3—, FG24Aug89:3,
   FG14Sep89:4, FG21Sep89:4
Dry and wet goods, sale of, SG18Jan87:4
Dublin
   convicts from sent to Nova Scotia, WC12Feb89:1
   insurrection in, NCG29Jul84:2
   letter from, WC9Jul88:2, WC5Feb89:1,
      SG27Aug89:2
   news from, NCG2Sep84:3, SG6Jul86:2,
      WC3Sep88:1, SG11Dec88:2, WC25Dec88:2,

WC15Jan89:2, WC29Jan89:1
newspaper extracts from, SG17Nov88:3,
SG11Dec88:4, SG18Dec88:4
opposition in to Police Bill, SG6Jul86:2
Dubrutz, ____, WC19Nov88:3—
Dubrutz, Gabriel, WC2Jul88:3—
Duchess of Devonshire, poetry of, NCGH6Oct85:4
Duckenfield, Sir Nathaniel, SG12Jan86:4
Ducket, Christopher, SG20Oct88:3, SG27Oct88:3
Duckett, Christopher, SG9Apr89:3—
Duckinfield, Nathaniel, SG29Mar86:2
Dudley, Agatha, WC6Aug88:3
Dudley, G., WC24Sep88:2, WC15Oct88:2—
Dudley, Guilford, SG20Oct88:3, SG27Oct88:3,
FG24Aug89:3, FG14Sep89:4, FG21Sep89:2
Dudley, William, NCG19Dec87:4
Duelling, WC10Sep88:3, SG22Sep88:3, WC22Jan89:3,
SG23Jul89:2, SG30Jul89:2, SG27Aug89:1
Duff, James, Consul, letter to, SG13Oct88:2
Dugan, Mr., SG29Sep88:3
Dugan, Thomas, FG14Sep89:3
Duguid, Alexander, SG20Oct88:3
Duke, ____, SG3Dec89:2,3
Duke de Choiseul, anecdote about, NCG3Nov85:3
Duke of Dorset, letter from, SG15Oct89:1,2
Duke of Orleans, arrival of in London, WC3Sep88:1
Duke of York, proposed marriage of, NCG19Dec87:2
Duke's Place, London, anecdote about, SG10Sep89:4
Dumbarton
letter from, SG5Mar89:2,3
storm in, SG5Mar89:2
Duncan, Alexander, WC18Jun88:4, WC25Jun88:4
Duncan, Ancrum, and Schaw, WC18Jun88:4,
WC25Jun88:4
Dunkins, John, WC20Aug88:2
Dunlap, John, NCG29Mar86:2
Dunn, Capt., WC26Nov88:3
Duplin County, N.C., NCG29Jul84:3, SG23Feb86:2,
SG6Jul86:3, SG7Feb88:3, SG22Sep88:3,
SG25Dec88:2, SG17Sep89:3
Dupre, Cornelius, WC15Oct88:2—
Dupre, Lewis, WC20Aug88:2, WC15Oct88:2—,
SG10Sep89:3
Dupre, Sterling, WC20Aug88:2
Dye, Martin, WC2Jul88:3

E

Eaborn, John, SG3Sep89:3
Eachran, Duncan, WC13Aug88:3
Eagles, Joseph, NCG29Jul84:4
Earl of Chatham, character of, SG6Jul86:2
Earth, Mrs., SG22Oct89:3, SG29Oct89:3,
SG12Nov89:4
Earthquake, NCGH16Feb86:3, SG3Dec89:1
Easley, Daniel W., WC15Jan89:3—
East Florida, SG7May89:3
U.S. shipping to, SG26Mar89:2
East India Company, NCGH19Jan86:2, SG22Sep88:1,
WC25Dec88:2, SG19Mar89:2, SG26Mar89:2,
SG23Jul89:1, FG24Aug89:2, SG29Oct89:1
commerce of, SG8Oct89:2
British squadron sent to, WC30Jul88:2
execution of Almas Ali Cawn, FG24Aug89:2
news from, SG11Jun89:3, FG12Oct89:3

pleas to from wife of Almas Ali Cawn, FG24Aug89:2
seeks recovery of treasure from sunken ship,
WC25Dec88:2
shipping in, FG12Oct89:3
wealth of, SG23Jul89:1
East Indies
news from, SG11Jun89:3
proposed Spanish company for trade with,
SG27Oct88:2
shipping in, FG12Oct89:3
Easton, Conn., letter from, SG26Nov89:2
proceeding of court of oyer and terminer in,
SG26Nov89:2
Easton, J., SG3Dec89:2
Easton, John, NCG29Jul84:3, SG24Sep89:3
Eaton, Gen., WC19Nov88:3, SG18Dec88:2—
Ebersdorf, Germany, scarcity of provisions in,
SG29Jan89:2
Eborne, John, WC20Aug88:2
Eccles, John, WC23Jul88:3, WC30Jul88:3
Eccles, William, SG20Oct88:3, SG27Oct88:3
Edenton, NCG29Jul84:3, SG12Jan86:4, SG6Jul86:4,
SG18Jan87:3, SG29Nov87:1, SG7Feb88:3,
EI4Jun88:4, SG8Sep88:3,4, SG15Sep88:4—,
SG13Oct88:3,4, SG20Oct88:3,4—, SG4Dec88:3,
SG11Dec88:3,4, SG18Dec88:3,4, SG25Dec88:3,4,
SG8Jan89:3, SG15Jan89:3,4, SG22Jan89:4,
SG29Jan89:3,4, SG5Feb89:4—, SG12Mar89:3,
SG2Apr89:3—, SG23Apr89:3,4, SG30Apr89:3,4,
SG7May89:3,4, SG14May89:4—, SG18Jun89:3,4,
SG25Jun89:3,4, SG2Jul89:4, SG9Jul89:3,4,
SG16Jul89:4, SG23Jul89:3,
SG30Jul89:3,SG6Aug89:3,4,SG13Aug89:3,
SG20Aug89:3,4, SG3Sep89:3, SG10Sep89:3,4,
FG14Sep89:3, SG22Oct89:3—, SG17Dec89:3—
address to freeholders and others in, SG10Dec89:3
celebration of ratification of federal Constitution,
SG3Dec89:2
dance to honor Washington's birthday,
SG19Feb89:2
exports from, SG26Mar89:3
fire in, SG10Dec89:3
fire prevention for, SG10Dec89:3
government of, SG5Feb89:3—, SG13Aug89:3
illegal trade by slaves in, SG13Aug89:3
jailbreak in, SG26Feb89:3
letter from, SG4Jun89:3, SG1Oct89:2
meeting in, SG29Nov87:1
need for better protection in, SG10Dec89:3
news from, SG29Nov87:1, EI9Apr88:2, EI4Jun88:2,
SG8Sep88:2, SG22Sep88:3—, WC15Jan89:3,
SG3Sep89:3, FG14Sep89:3, SG17Sep89:3,
SG1Oct89:3—
politics in, SG2Apr89:3, SG15Oct89:3
slaves in, SG30Jul89:3, SG13Aug89:3
taxes in, SG18Jan87:3
Edenton and Chowan County, report of meeting in,
SG29Nov87:1
Edenton District, SG25Dec88:4
"Edentoniensis," SG10Dec89:3
Edgecomb(e) County, NCG29Mar86:2, WC26Nov88:3,
SG25Dec88:2, SG9Apr89:3, SG3Sep89:3
Edinburgh
death of the Rev. Adam Gib in, SG13Oct88:2
letter from, EI4Jun88:2, SG24Nov89:2
news from, WC9Jul88:2

Edinburgh Amusement, extract from, SG2Apr89:1
Edison, A., SG3Dec89:3
Education, NCG9Dec84:4, NCG3Nov85:4,
  WC30Jul88:3, SG8Sep88:3—, WC15Oct88:2—,
  WC18Dec88:1,2, SG22Oct89:3, SG26Feb89:2,
  SG1Oct89:3, SG31Dec89:4
  essay on, SG24Dec89:4
  nature of, FG12Oct89:3
  in Philadelphia, FG21Sep89:2
  See Academy; New-Bern Academy, School
Edwards, ____, SG17Sep89:3, SG3Dec89:3
Edwards, David, SG27Mar88:3
Edwards, G., SG24Sep89:3, SG3Dec89:3
Edwards, Mary, NCG15Aug87:4
Edwards, Quan, SG22Oct89:3, SG27Oct89:3,
  SG12Nov89:4
Edwards, R., SG3Dec89:3
Egan, ____, SG25Jun89:2
Egan, Mr., SG11Dec88:3, SG25Dec88:4,
  SG23Apr89:3—, SG3Dec89:3, SG31Dec89:3
Egan, Robert, SG25Dec88:3, SG8Jan89:3,
  SG15Jan89:3,4, SG22Jan89:4, SG5Feb89:4,
  SG12Feb89:4
Egan's Tavern, SG3Dec89:2, SG24Dec89:3
Egremont, Lord, anecdote about, NCGH16Feb86:1,2
Ehorn, I., SG3Dec89:3
Elections, N.C., NCG2Sep84:3, SG18Jan87:3,
  SG27Aug89:3
Electricity, experiment with, SG29Jan89:2
Elizabeth Town, N.J., letter from, SG5Nov89:3
Elizabeth Town, N.C., NCGH19Jan86:4,
  NCGH2Feb86:3, WC15Jan89:4, SG31Dec89:2
Ellery, Christopher, WC26Oct88:3, WC5Nov88:3
Elletson, Goodin, WC18Jun88:4, WC25Jun88:4
Elliot, George, WC20Aug88:2
Ellis, James, WC18Dec88:3, SG25Dec88:3—,
  WC25Dec88:1, WC8Jan89:4—, SG20Aug89:4—
Ellis, Joseph, NCG6Jan85:1
Ellis, Richard, NCG29Jul84:2, NCG6Jan85:1,
  SG12Jan86:2, NCG19Dec87:4
Ellison, ____, SG3Dec89:3
Ellison, Alderson, NCG29Jul84:4, SG3Sep89:3
Ellison, Goodin, WC20Aug88:2
Elopement, SG22Jan89:2
Elsinier (Elsineur), letter from, WC15Oct88:1,
  SG29Oct89:2
Emigration, western, WC5Mar89:2
Emmet, Col., NCGH16Feb86:3
Empress of Russia, letter of, SG1Jan89:2
England, NCG9Dec84:4
  attitude toward U.S., SG18Jun89:2
  bankruptcies in, WC3Sep88:1,2
  characterization of politicians in, SG10Sep89:1
  China trade of, SG22Jan89:2,3
  comment on politics in, NCGH16Feb86:2
  commerce of, NCGH19Jan86:2, SG22Jan89:2,3,
    SG3Dec89:1
  customs of, WC22Jan89:2
  customs duties of, WC3Sep88:1
  customs receipts of, WC12Feb89:2
  debt of, WC22Jan89:2
  deportation of convicts of, SG12Mar89:1
  enmity of with France, SG24Nov88:3
  export of corn from, SG29Oct89:1
  government officials in, NCGH19Jan86:2
  history of, WC16Jul88:4, SG19Feb89:1, SG2Apr89:2

humorous handbill in, WC25Jun88:2
incitement of Indians by, SG12Feb89:3
intention to sign commercial treaty with U.S.,
  WC13Aug88:2
land in, SG29Nov87:3
life in, SG11Dec88:3, SG22Jan89:1,2
manufacturing in, SG26Feb89:2
monarchy of, SG26Feb89:1
Moroccan relations with, SG22Jan89:2
navy of, NCGH19Jan86:2, WC15Jan89:2,
  WC22Jan89:2, WC5Feb89:2
opposition to U.S. by, SG12Feb89:3
politics in, NCGH16Feb86:2, WC18Jun88:2,
  SG12Feb89:3, WC19Feb89:3, SG5Mar89:3,
  SG19Mar89:1,2, SG2Apr89:3, SG9Apr89:3,
  SG16Apr89:1, SG23Apr89:3, SG30Apr89:1,3,
  SG28May89:2,3, SG23Jul89:1, SG3Sep89:2,3,
  SG26Nov89:2
refuses French request for food, FG12Oct89:3
regency proposed for, SG19Mar89:1, SG2Apr89:3,
  SG16Apr89:3, SG23Apr89:3, SG30Apr89:2,
  SG14May89:1
regulation of tobacco trade of, WC9Jul88:2,
  SG10Dec89:1
regulation of trade of, NCGH6Oct85:1,2,3,
  WC25Jun88:2
relations with Russia, WC10Sep88:2
restrictions on grain imports from U.S.,
  WC26Oct88:2,3
robbery in, SG5Mar89:2, SG20Aug89:1
royal family of, SG25Jun89:2, SG30Jul89:2
satirization of public figures of, NCGH2Feb86:1
shipping of, NCG29Jul84:2
Spanish relations of, WC25Jun88:2
squadron of sent to East Indies, WC30Jul88:2
tax revenues of, SG4Dec88:1
taxes on imports of, WC25Jun88:2
trade to South Sea and Orient, NCGH19Jan86:2
treaty with Prussia, WC10Sep88:2
U.S. attitude toward, SG20Oct88:2
U.S. relations with, SG18Jun89:2
English lady, SG22Jan89:2
English Monthly Review, extract from, WC8Jan89:1
English Review, extract from, SG19Mar89:1
English, Thomas, NCGH2Feb86:4
Entails, SG31Dec89:3
Entertainment, public, SG29Nov87:4, SG27Mar88:3,
  WC18Jun88:3, WC24Sep88:2, WC26Oct88:3,
  SG3Nov88:3, WC5Nov88:3, WC19Nov88:3,
  WC10Dec88:3, SG25Dec88:3,
  WC25Dec88:3, WC26Feb89:3
  See also Performances, dramatic; Kenna Company
Ephraim (slave), SG26Mar89:3, SG9Apr89:4,
  SG16Apr89:4
Episcopal Church, SG12Nov89:2
Episcopal Society of Newbern, SG31Dec89:3
Epitaph, SG11Dec88:4, SG4Jun89:4
Erichson, Severin, WC18Jun88:3—, WC10Sep88:3
Err, Joseph, SG22Oct89:3, SG29Oct89:3, SG12Nov89:4
Erwin, John, WC25Jun88:3
Essays, reflection of English life in, SG22Jan89:1,2
Estates, SG2Sep84:4, SG18Jan87:2, FG14Sep89:3
  administration of, NCG29Jul84:3, SG4Oct87:3,
    SG29Nov87:4, SG7Feb88:4, SG27Mar88:3,4,
    WC18Jun88:4, WC25Jun88:4, WC23Jul88:3—,
    SG13Oct88:3—, SG6Aug89:3—

descent of, SG3Dec89:3
execution of, NCG29Jul84:2, NCG9Dec84:4,
    NCGH6Oct85:4, SG7Feb88:2, EI9Apr88:1,
    WC8Jan89:3, WC15Jan89:3, WC19Feb89:3,
    SG30Jul89:3, SG1Oct89:3
forfeited, NCGH19Jan86:3, SG23Feb86:1
intestate, management of, SG3Dec89:3
management of, SG31Dec89:3
suits about, WC25Jun88:4
Estis, J., NCGH19Jan86:3, NCGH2Feb86:4,
    NCGH16Feb86:4
Europe
    confederacy in, WC8Jan89:2
    deaths in, SG25Dec88:3
    letter from traveller in, SG5Feb89:3
    news from, WC15Jan89:2, WC29Jan89:1,
        WC5Feb89:1,2, WC26Feb89:2, FG12Oct89:3
    See Foreign Intelligence
    politics in, NCG29Jul84:1, NCG2Sep84:2,
        SG12Jan86:1,2, NCGH2Feb86:2,
        NCGH16Feb86:2, NCGH23Feb86:2,
        NCG11Jul87:2, NCG15Aug87:2,3,
        SG29Nov87:2, NCG19Dec87:2,3,
        SG7Feb88:1,2, SG27Mar88:3, WC18Jun88:2,
        WC25Jun88:2, WC2Jul88:2, WC9Jul88:2,
        WC30Jul88:2,3, WC3Sep88:1,2,
        SG8Sep88:1,2,3, WC10Sep88:2, SG22Sep88:1,
        WC24Sep88:1,2, SG6Oct88:1,2, SG13Oct88:2,
        WC15Oct88:1, SG20Oct88:2, WC26Oct88:2,
        SG27Oct88:2, SG3Nov88:2, WC5Nov88:2,
        SG10Nov88:1,2,3, WC12Nov88:2,
        SG17Nov88:1,2, WC19Nov88:1,2,3,
        SG24Nov88:1,2,3, WC26Nov88:1,2,
        WC3Dec88:2,3, SG4Dec88:1,2,3,4,
        WC10Dec88:2, SG11Dec88:1,2,
        SG18Dec88:1,3, WC18Dec88:2, SG2588:1,2,3,
        WC25Dec88:2,3, SG1Jan89:1,2,3,
        SG8Jan89:2,3, WC8Jan89:2, SG15Jan89:1,2,3,
        WC15Jan89:1, WC22Jan89:2, SG29Jan89:2,
        WC29Jan89:2, SG5Feb89:2, WC5Feb89:1,2,
        SG12Feb89:2, WC12Feb89:2, SG19Feb89:1,2,
        WC19Feb89:2, SG26Feb89:1,2, WC26Feb89:2,
        SG5Mar89:3, WC5Mar89:2, SG12Mar89:1,2,
        SG19Mar89:2, SG26Mar89:2, SG2Apr89:2,
        SG30Apr89:2, SG14May89:1, SG28May8:3,
        SG4Jun89:1,2, SG11Jun89:3, SG18Jun89:1,2,3,
        SG25Jun89:1,2, SG2Jul89:4, SG16Jul89:1,2,3,
        SG23Jul89:1, SG30Jul89:1,2, SG20Aug89:1,2,
        FG24Aug89:2, SG3Sep89:2, SG10Sep89:1,
        FG14Sep89:2, SG17Sep89:1, SG1Oct89:2,3,
        SG8Oct89:1,2,3, SG15Oct89:2, SG29Oct89:2,
        SG5Nov89:1,2,3, SG12Nov89:2,
        SG19Nov89:1,3, SG26Nov89:1,3,4,
        SG10Dec89:2, SG17Dec89:1,2, SG24Dec89:3,
        SG31Dec89:1
    population of cities in, SG19Feb89:1
    storm in, SG26Feb89:2
    war in, WC18Jun88:2, WC30Jul88:2, WC10Sep88:2
        WC24Sep88:1,2, SG6Oct88:2, WC15Oct88:1,
        WC26Oct88:2, WC27Oct88:2, SG3Nov88:2,
        WC5Nov88:2, SG10Nov88:2,3, WC12Nov88:2,
        SG17Nov88:1,2, WC19Nov88:1,2,3,
        SG24Nov88:1,2,3, WC26Nov88:1,
        WC3Dec88:2,3, SG4Dec88:1,2, WC10Dec88:2,
        SG11Dec88:1, SG18Dec88:1, SG25Dec88:2,
        SG1Jan89:1,2,3, SG8Jan89:2,3,

SG15Jan89:1,2,3, WC22Jan89:2, SG29Jan89:2,
    SG5Feb89:2, WC5Feb89:1, WC26Feb89:2,
    WC5Mar89:2, SG30Apr89:2, SG30Jul89:1,
    SG14May89:1, SG18Jun89:2, SG25Jun89:1,2,
    FG14Sep89:2, SG1Oct89:3, SG8Oct89:2,
    SG15Oct89:2, SG5Nov89:2, SG10Dec89:2,
    SG31Dec89:1
Euster, Nathaniel, SG20Oct88:3, SG27Oct88:3
Evans, Major, NCG11Jul87:4
Evans, Thomas, WC20Aug88:2
Everagin, Edward, SG27Aug89:3, FG14Sep89:3
Everegain, Edward, WC20Aug88:2
Evergain, ____, SG3Dec89:3
Everitt, Joseph, NCG29Jul84:3
Everitt, Richard, SG8Jan89:3, SG15Jan89:4
Everton, John, SG23Apr89:3
Ewans, William, WC19Feb89:3, WC26Feb89:1
Ewans and McCauslan, WC19Feb89:3, WC26Feb89:1
Ewing, ____, SG3Dec89:3
Ewing, R., SG3Dec89:3
Execution, WC19Feb89:2, SG12Mar89:2, SG30Apr89:3
Exeter, N.H.
    news from, WC26Nov88:2
    newspaper extract from, WC16Jul88:1
Exuma, Bahamas, price of salt in, WC27Aug88:3

F

Fable, SG29Nov87:4, SG11Dec88:4
Falkner, William, SG20Oct88:3, SG27Oct88:3
Falmouth, England, WC3Sep88:1
    enrollment of seamen in, WC3Sep88:1
Falmouth, New England, SG12Jan86:2
Falvey, Michael, NCG9Dec84:4
Fan (slave), runaway, NCG29Jul84:4
Fanning, Edmund, NCGH2Feb86:3, NCGH16Feb86:3,
    NCGH23Feb86:3, NCG29Mar86:2
Farange, Mr., SG9Jul89:3—
Farm, wanted to rent, SG23Jul89:3—, SG20Aug89:3
"Farmer," SG30Jul89:3
"Farmer, A," SG11Jun89:2
Farmer, William, WC20Aug88:2
Farmer, eulogy of, SG8Oct89:4
Farmers
    education of, SG26Feb89:2
    need to manufacture cloth, WC5Nov88:2
Farr, John, SG20Oct88:3, SG27Oct88:3, SG8Jan89:3,
    SG15Jan89:4
Farret, Elizabeth, NCG6Jan85:1
Fayette, Ky., letter from, SG29Sep88:3
Fayetteville, N.C., NCGH6Oct85:4,
    NCGH19Jan86:3,4, NCGH2Feb86:3,
    NCGH16Feb86:1,3, NCGH23Feb86:4,
    SG23Feb86:2, SG18Jan87:2, NCG11Jul87:4,
    NCG15Aug87:4, WC18Jun88:3, WC2Jul88:2,3,
    WC23Jul88:2,3, WC30Jul88:3, WC6Aug88:3,
    WC3Sep88:2, SG8Sep88:4—, WC17Sep88:3,
    WC24Sep88:2, WC26Oct88:3,4, WC5Nov88:2,3,
    WC12Nov88:3, WC19Nov88:3, WC26Nov88:4,
    WC3Dec88:3, SG4Dec88:3, WC10Dec88:1,3,
    SG18Dec88:3, WC18Dec88:1,3, SG25Dec88:4,
    SG1Jan89:4, WC15Jan89:3, WC29Jan89:2,3,
    WC5Feb89:1,2,3, WC12Feb89:1,3,4,
    WC26Feb89:1,3,4, WC5Mar89:1, SG30Jul89:3,
    SG6Aug89:4, FG24Aug89:3, SG10Sep89:3,

FG14Sep89:3, FG21Sep89:2,4, FG12Oct89:4,
SG3Dec89:3, SG17Dec89:3, SG31Dec89:3
celebration of Fourth of July in, WC23Jul88:3
courthouse in, FG21Sep89:4
elections in for members of legislature and
    Fayetteville Convention, FG24Aug89:3
improvements in, WC23Jul88:3
letter from, WC6Aug88:3, SG26Feb89:2,3,
    WC5Mar89:2, SG5Nov89:3, WC19Nov88:3
news from, FG24Aug89:3, FG14Sep89:3,
    FG21Sep89:2, SG24Sep89:3, FG12Oct89:3,
    SG3Dec89:4
public buildings in, SG18Dec88:3
regulation of, SG18Dec88:2,3, WC18Dec88:2
representation of, SG3Dec89:3
state house in, WC19Nov88:3
Fayetteville Convention, SG1Oct89:2, SG5Nov89:3
members of, SG27Aug89:3
legislative call for elections to, WC10Dec88:3
proceedings of, SG3Dec89:2,3, SG17Dec89:3
Fayetteville District, SG25Dec88:4
prisons and stocks for, WC18Dec88:2
Fayetteville Gazette, FG21Sep89:2
Federal Constitution, WC18Jun88:4, WC25Jun88:4,
    WC9Jul88:1, SG13Aug89:3, WC3Sep88:4
amendment of, WC25Jun88:2, WC16Jul88:2,
    WC13Aug88:3, WC20Aug88:1,2, SG15Sep88:3,
    SG13Oct88:1,2, SG17Nov88:3, WC22Jan89:1,
    SG29Jan89:2, WC5Feb89:2, SG12Feb89:1,2,
    SG5Mar89:2, SG19Mar89:2, SG9Apr89:2,
    SG16Apr89:2, SG23Apr89:2, SG7May89:3,
    SG25Jun89:3, SG9Jul89:1, SG16Jul89:4,
    SG20Aug89:2,3, FG24Aug89:1,2, SG10Sep89:2,
    FG14Sep89:1,2,3,4, SG17Sep89:4,
    FG21Sep89:2,3, SG24Sep89:3, FG12Oct89:1,2,
    SG22Oct89:4, SG29Oct89:1, SG26Nov89:2,3,
    SG17Dec89:2
amendments submitted to states, SG29Oct89:1
approval of, SG28May89:3, WC25Jun88:2,
    FG24Aug89:2,3
British view of, SG6Aug89:3,
celebration of ratification of, WC6Aug88:2
commentary on proposed amendments for,
    SG16Jul89:4
Congressional approval of, WC13Aug88:2
Congressional consideration of amendments to,
    SG9Jul89:1
copy of, SG4Oct87:1,2,3
criticism of, SG4Jun89:3
Del. consideration of, SG29Nov87:2
effects of ratification of, WC17Sep88:2
essay on, WC29Jan89:1
European praise for, WC9Jul88:2
examination of nature of, NCG19Dec89:1,2,3,
    SG7Feb88:2, SG27Mar88:1,2, SG3Nov88:1,2,
    WC18Dec88:1, WC29Jan89:1, SG23Apr89:1,2,
    SG4Jun89:3, FG21Sep89:1,2,
Ga. ratification of, SG7Feb88:2
Mass. attitude toward, SG29Nov87:2, SG27Mar88:3,
    SG5Mar89:2
N.H. attitude toward, SG27Mar88:3
N.J. attitude toward, SG7Feb88:2
N.Y. attitude toward, NCG19Dec87:3,
    WC6Aug88:2, WC20Aug88:2, WC27Aug88:3,
    SG27Oct88:2, SG12Feb89:3
N.Y. celebration of ratification of, SG27Mar88:3

N.C. attitude toward, SG29Nov87:1,
    SG27Mar88:1,2, SG6Oct88:1, SG15Sep88:1,2,3,
    SG22Sep88:3, WC5Nov88:1,2, WC12Nov88:3,
    SG28May89:3, SG20Aug89:2, SG26Nov89:3
N.C. reconsiders decision about, WC12Nov88:3
observations on, SG29Jan89:2
ode to, SG14May89:4
opposition to, NCG19Dec87:2,3, SG27Mar88:3,
    EI9Apr88:4, WC13Aug88:2, SG11Dec88:2,3,
    SG26Mar89:2, SG30Apr89:3
praise for, SG16Jul89:2
proposed celebration of ratification of, WC9Jul88:2
Pa. attitude toward, SG29Nov87:2, WC10Sep88:1
proposed commercial regulations of, WC16Jul88:2
publications about, SG27Mar88:3
ratification of, EI19Dec87:2, SG27Mar88:3,
    EI9Apr88:2,4, EI4Jun88:1,2, WC18Jun88:2,
    WC25Jun88:2, WC2Jul88:2, WC9Jul88:2,3,
    WC16Jul88:2,3, WC23Jul88:2, WC30Jul88:2,3,
    WC6Aug88:2,3, WC13Aug88:1,3,
    WC20Aug88:2,3, WC27Aug88:3, WC3Sep88:2,
    SG8Sep88:2,3, SG15Sep88:1, WC17Sep88:2,3,
    SG22Sep88:3, SG6Oct88:3, WC5Nov88:1,2,
    WC3Dec88:1,2, WC10Dec88:1, WC18Dec88:1,
    WC25Dec88:4, WC15Jan89:3, SG29Jan89:3,
    SG12Feb89:2, SG19Feb89:2, SG5Mar89:2,3,
    FG14Sep89:3, SG1Oct89:2, SG3Dec89:2,
    SG10Dec89:2, SG17Dec89:2,3
reflections upon in St. George's, Grenada,
    WC13Aug88:2
R.I. attitude toward, WC12Feb89:3, SG23Apr89:3,
    SG23Jul89:3, SG15Oct89:2
signatories of, SG4Oct87:3
support for, WC9Jul88:1
Vt. attitude toward, WC24Sep88:2
Va. attitude toward, EI4Jun88:1,2, WC16Jul88:2,
    SG9Apr89:2
Wilmington ratification celebration of,
    WC16Jul88:2
Federal district
    See U.S., capital of
Federal Gazette, extract from, SG16Jul89:4
Federalism, SG29Sep88:3
Federalist (ship)
    presented to George Washington, WC16Jul88:3
    sails to Mt. Vernon, WC25Jun88:2
Fellon, Andrew, SG18Jan87:3
Fell's Point, N.Y., births in, SG26Feb89:2
Felons, in Edenton, N.C., SG26Feb89:3
Fencing, instruction in, NCG29Jul84:4
Fennell, Michael, SG20Oct88:3, SG27Oct88:3,
    SG9Jul89:3—
Fenner, Robert, NCGH19Jan86:2,3, SG27Mar88:3,
    SG20Oct88:3, SG27Oct88:3, SG15Jan89:3,
    SG22Jan89:1,4, SG29Jan89:4, SG5Feb89:3,4,
    SG12Feb89:4, SG26Feb89:4—, SG26Mar89:4,
    SG9Apr89:4—
    See also Fenner, W. R., and Robert
Fenner, W. R., and Robert, SG27Mar88:3
Ferebee, Joseph, WC20Aug88:2
Ferebee, S., SG3Dec89:2
Ferebee, W., SG3Dec89:2
Ferebee, William, WC20Aug88:2
Ferguson, Alexander, SG9Apr89:3—, SG22Oct89:3,
    SG29Oct89:3, SG12Nov89:4
Ferguson, Dr. Walter, SG3Dec89:3

Ferrand, Mr., SG27Mar88:3
Ferries, WC2Jul88:3, WC9Jul88:3, WC23Jul88:4,
	WC3Sep88:3, WC15Oct88:2, WC5Nov88:4,
	WC3Dec88:4
	Kemp's, NCG29Mar86:1
	Neuse River, NCG2Sep84:4
Festival of St. John the Baptist, WC8Jan89:1
Field, John, Jr., NCG29Mar86:2
Field, Joseph, NCG29Mar86:2
Field, William, NCG29Mar86:2
Fields, Jeremiah, SG31Dec89:3
Fields, Robert, SG31Dec89:3
Fields, William, NCGH2Feb86:4, NCGH19Mar86:4
Figs, preserving of, SG18Jun89:4
Figures, Matthew, SG18Jan87:2, SG18Dec88:3,
	WC18Dec88:3
Finney, Thomas, EI4Jun88:4
Fire, WC10Sep88:3
Fire engine, WC5Feb89:3—
Fire house, WC5Feb89:3—
Firebuckets, SG30Apr89:3—
Fishing, SG27Aug89:2, SG8Oct89:3
Fishkill, N.Y., letter from, SG9Apr89:2
Fitt, Thomas, SG20Oct88:3, SG27Oct88:3,
	SG8Jan89:3, SG15Jan89:4
Fitz Gerald, John, WC19Feb89:3
Fitzgerald, Jasper, SG27Mar88:3
Fitzgerald & Maxwell, SG9Jul89:3—
Fitzwilliam, General, estate of, SG12Nov89:2
"Flagellator Scurrarum," SG28May89:3, SG30Jul89:3
Flanders, discontent in, SG3Dec89:1
Flax, machine to break and dress, SG7May89:3
Flaxseed, wanted, NCGH19Jan86:3, NCGH2Feb86:4,
	NCGH16Feb86:4, NCGH23Feb86:4,
	NCG1Aug87:4
Fleeming, WC30Jul88:3, WC12Nov88:3,
	WC19Nov88:3
Fletcher, James, WC20Aug88:2
Florida, WC9Jul88:2
	Spanish troops in, NCGH2Feb86:2
Flowers, David, WC13Aug88:3
Flowers, Mr., WC12Nov88:3, WC19Nov88:3
Foldick, Samuel, WC13Aug88:3
Fontaine & Morin, WC26Oct88:3, WC5Nov88:3
Fool Warrior, WC24Sep88:2
Forbes, Arthur, WC20Aug88:2
Ford
	See Greer and Ford
Foreign Affairs, SG2Apr89:1, FG24Aug89:2,
	SG14Sep89:2, SG12Oct89:3
	Department of, SG27Aug89:4
	See also Europe, news from; Foreign Intelligence
Foreign Intelligence, NCG29Jul84:1, NCG2Sep84:2,
	EI19Dec87:2, EI4Jun88:2, WC18Jun88:2—,
	WC30Jul88:2, WC13Aug88:1, WC3Sep88:1,
	WC10Sep88:2, WC24Sep88:1, WC15Oct88:1—,
	WC8Jan89:2, WC29Jan89:1
	See also Europe, news from; Foreign Affairs
Foreman, Caleb, WC20Aug88:2
Fort, W., SG3Dec89:3
Fort, William, WC20Aug88:2, SG3Sep89:3
Fort, erection of, WC18Dec88:3
Fort Chisel, letter from, WC24Sep88:2
Fort Harmar, letter from, SG1Jan89:2, WC15Jan89:1
Foster, A. M., WC20Aug88:2
Foster, Robert, NCGH2Feb86:3, NCGH16Feb86:3,

	NCGH23Feb86:3
Foullon, J. B., SG22Oct89:3, SG29Oct89:3,
	SG12Nov89:4
Foulon, Mr., SG20Oct88:3, SG27Oct88:3
Fourth of July, celebration of, WC23Jul88:3,
	SG29Sep88:1,3, SG23Jul89:2,3
Fox, Mr., SG4Jun89:4
Foy, James, WC16Jul88:3
France, NCGH23Feb86:3, SG18Dec88:1, WC26Feb89:3
	army desertions in, SG12Nov89:1
	attitude of Louis XVI toward unrest in, FG12Oct89:3
	bankruptcies in, SG3Sep89:2
	clergy in, SG4Dec88:1
	constitution of, SG8Oct89:2, SG15Oct89:4,
		SG22Oct89:1,2, SG5Nov89:2
	critical commentary on, SG30Jul89:1
	death of Dauphin of, FG14Sep89:2
	departure of squadron of from Boston, SG8Oct89:3
	desertion of Swiss soldiers in, SG26Nov89:2
	diplomat of, SG29Oct89:3
	disturbances in, WC3Sep88:2, WC10Sep88:2
	encouragement given to importation of U.S. grain,
		WC26Feb89:2
	enmity with England, SG24Nov88:3
	failure of courts to operate in, WC3Dec88:3
	fleet of leaves Boston, WC5Nov88:2
	food needed in, SG4Jun89:3
	free press in, SG16Jul89:2, SG10Dec89:4
	hatred for queen in, WC5Feb89:1
	importation of grain to, SG19Mar89:3
	involvement in wars by, SG8Jan89:2
	launch of ship "America," WC24Sep88:1
	letter from, SG5Nov89:3
	liberation of slaves in islands considered,
		FG12Oct89:3
	mail from to U.S., SG30Jul89:4
	meeting of Assembly of Notables in, WC29Jan89:1,2
	meeting of States General in, SG3Sep89:2
	meeting of Third Estate in, SG17Sep89:1
	military preparations in, NCGH19Jan86:1,
		WC25Jun88:2
	minister of to U.S., SG5Nov89:2
	money in, NCG2Sep84:2
	navy of, SG15Sep88:1, WC24Sep88:2,
		WC5Nov88:2, SG8Oct89:3, SG15Oct89:3
	news from, NCG29Mar86:4, SG25Jun89:2
	packet boats to U.S., SG30Jul89:4
	politics in, SG23Feb86:2, WC10Sep88:2,
		SG15Sep88:1, WC24Sep88:1, SG6Oct88:1,2,3,
		SG13Oct88:2, SG3Nov88:2,3,4, WC12Nov88:2,
		SG17Nov88:2, WC19Nov88:2, SG24Nov88:3,
		WC3Dec88:3, SG25Dec88:1, WC29Jan89:1,2,
		WC5Feb89:1, SG19Mar89:3, SG26Mar89:1,
		SG16Apr89:1,2, SG7May89:3, SG16Jul89:2,
		SG6Aug89:4, SG3Sep89:2, FG14Sep89:2,
		SG17Sep89:1, SG24Sep89:2, SG1Oct89:2,
		FG12Oct89:3, SG15Oct89:2,4, SG5Nov89:3,4,
		SG12Nov89:1,2, SG19Nov89:1,2, SG3Dec89:1,
		SG10Dec89:1, SG17Dec89:1
	presumed U.S. sympathy for, SG1Oct89:3
	price of corn in, SG23Jul89:1
	prohibition of foreign trade by, SG29Jan89:2
	proposed new constitution of, SG8Oct89:2
	refugees from, SG8Oct89:2
	regulation of trade by, WC12Feb89:1, SG20Aug89:1
	remonstrance of the clergy in, SG13Oct88:2

reports of revolution in, WC3Sep88:2
revolution in, WC13Aug88:1,2, WC3Sep88:2,
    SG8Sep88:1,2, SG25Dec88:3, SG18Jun89:2,
    SG25Jun89:2, SG24Sep89:2, SG1Oct89:1,2,
    SG8Oct89:1,2, SG15Oct89:2,3, SG22Oct89:1,
    SG29Oct89:1,2,3, SG5Nov89:1,2,3,
    SG19Nov89:2, SG24Dec89:1,2,3,
    SG31Dec89:1,2
  role of queen in revolution in, SG3Dec89:2
  role of women in revolution in, SG19Nov89:1,2
  royal family in saves money, SG16Apr89:1
  slave trade of, SG27Aug89:4
  States General of, SG4Dec88:1
  trade of, WC3Sep88:2, WC12Feb89:1, SG4Jun89:4
  U.S. ministers to, SG16Jul89:3
  U.S. relations with, SG27Mar88:2,3, SG22Oct89:4,
    SG5Nov89:2
  U.S. trade with, NCG29Jul84:2, WC18Jun88:2,
    SG6Aug89:4
  unrest in, SG6Oct88:3, SG13Oct88:2,
    SG17Nov88:3
  vessel of seized by Russian privateers, WC25Dec88:2
  vintage in, WC29Jan89:2
  visit of naval squadron to Boston, SG15Sep88:1
  War Office of, WC15Oct88:1
  women's address to the National Assembly,
    SG10Dec89:1
Frankford, news from, WC18Jun88:2
Frankland
  See Franklin, State of
Franklin, ____, SG27Mar88:2, SG29Jan89:2,3
Franklin, Benjamin, NCG3Nov85:3, SG29Jan89:2,3
  health of, NCG29Mar86:4, SG5Nov89:3
  observations of on parties, SG12Mar89:3
Franklin, Dr., NCG29Mar86:4, SG29Sep88:3
  arrival of in Philadelphia, NCG3Nov85:3
  debility of, SG5Nov89:3
  his observations on parties, SG12Mar89:3
Franklin, Jesse, SG31Dec89:3
Franklin, William, SG20Oct88:3, SG27Oct88:3
Franklin County, N.C., SG18Jan87:2,3,
    NCG15Aug87:4, SG10Nov88:3, SG25Dec88:2,
    SG24Sep89:3, SG31Dec89:3
Franklin, State of, SG29Nov87:3, WC6Aug88:3,
    WC8Jan89:3, SG29Jan89:2, SG30Jul89:2
  conference in, SG29Nov87:3
  government in, SG29Nov87:2
Frazel, John, SG2Jul89:3, SG23Jul89:4
Frazier, J., SG3Dec89:3
Frazier, Jeremiah, SG27Aug89:3, FG14Sep89:3
Fredericksburg, Va., SG5Mar89:3
  letter from, SG6Oct88:3
  news from, SG9Apr89:3, SG10Sep89:3
Frederick-Town, Md., news from, SG20Oct88:2
Free blacks, SG7Feb88:2
Free Masons, WC8Jan89:3, SG29Jan89:3,
    WC19Feb89:1, SG3Dec89:4, SG17Dec89:3
  Charleston, S.C., WC8Jan89:1
  Edenton, N.C., SG29Jan89:3, SG25Jun89:2,3
  N.C., NCG19Dec87:4, SG7Feb88:3, SG17Dec89:2
  revival of, WC25Dec88:3
  S.C., WC8Jan89:1, WC19Feb89:1
  Wilmington, N.C., WC8Jan89:2
  See also Grand Lodge
Freedom of the press, NCGH19Jan86:2
Freeholders, SG13Aug89:3

Freeman, Robert, SG18Jan87:3
Freemasonry, SG25Jun89:2
French
  assessment of, SG19Nov89:3
  character of, SG24Nov88:3, SG16Jul89:2,
    SG30Jul89:1, SG19Nov89:3
French Broad, letter from, WC5Mar89:2, SG30Apr89:3
Freneau, Capt., poetry of, WC26Oct88:4
Friend, Jonathan, SG29Nov87:1
"Friend to Common Sense, A," SG6Jul86:3
Fulford, J., SG3Dec89:2
Fulford, John, SG22Sep88:3, SG24Sep89:3
Fulgiron, SG21May89:3, SG28May89:4, SG18Jun89:4
Fullerton, Andrew, SG27Mar88:3
Fullmer, Mrs., SG18Jan87:3
Fulsher, Shadrack, SG18Jan87:3
Fungus, John, SG22Oct89:3, SG29Oct89:3,
    SG12Nov89:4
Fur trade, SG26Feb89:1
Furniture, WC26Oct88:3, WC5Nov88:3

                        G

G. M. D. and Co., SG27Oct88:3
Gaillard
  See Boinod and Gaillard
Gains, James, WC20Aug88:2
Gainsborough, SG24Nov88:1
Gaither, B., SG29Sep88:3
Galagher, Peter, SG13Aug89:3—
Gallispie, D., SG17Sep89:3
Galloway, ____, WC6Aug88:2, SG3Dec89:3
Galloway, Charles, WC20Aug88:2
Galloway, James, SG9Jul89:3—, SG17Dec89:3
Galloway, Joseph, WC20Aug88:2, SG24Sep89:3
Galloway, Mr., SG29Sep88:3, SG3Dec89:2,
    SG17Dec89:3
Galphin, ____, SG15Oct89:3
Galphin, John, SG30Jul89:2,3
Gamble, Edward, SG20Oct88:3, SG27Oct88:3
Gamble, James, and Company, NCG29Mar86:2
Gaming, SG13Oct88:2, SG18Dec88:3, WC18Dec88:2
  discouragement of, WC19Nov88:3, SG25Dec88:3,
    SG22Jan89:1
  regulation of, SG23Feb86:1
Gaol (jail), construction of, SG31Dec89:3
Gardner, Alexander, SG27Mar88:3, SG7Feb88:2
Gardner, Capt., SG12Jan86:3
Gardner, Matthew, SG27Mar88:3
Gardoqui, Don Diego de, SG24Sep89:3, SG5Nov89:2
Garrison, Relph, SG18Jan87:3
Garvey, P., SG13Aug89:3—
Garvey, Patrick, SG20Oct88:3, SG27Oct88:3,
    SG8Jan89:3, SG15Jan89:4, SG27Mar88:3
Gaskins, Adams, SG12Nov89:3
Gass, John, SG22Oct89:3, SG29Oct89:3, SG12Nov89:4
Gaston, Alexander, SG18Jan87:2
Gates County, N.C., SG25Dec88:2, SG28May89:3
Gator, ____, SG29Sep88:3
Gator, Capt., SG17Sep89:3
Gator, Mr., WC17Sep88:3
Gause, William, SG10Sep89:3
Gauss, William, SG6Jul86:3
Gautier, J., SG3Dec89:3
Gautier, Joseph, WC20Aug88:2, SG10Sep89:3

Gauze, SG3Dec89:2

Gaw, William, NCG6Jan85:1

Gazette d' Agriculture, extracts from, WC18Jun88:2

Gazetteer of the United States, proposal for, EI19Dec87:1

Gearman, Joseph, SG23Feb86:4

Geddes, Alexander, WC13Aug88:3

Geekie, James, WC18Jun88:3, WC25Jun88:3

Geer, Gilbert, WC13Aug88:3

Gefford, Robert, WC13Aug88:3

Gellespie, James, WC13Aug88:3

General Assembly, N.C., NCG2Sep84:4,
    NCGH16Feb86:3, WC23Jul88:4, WC30Jul88:4,
    WC6Aug88:4, SG26Feb89:2,3
  acts of, NCG9Dec84:1,2, NCG6Jan85:1,2,
      SG12Jan86:1,2,4, NCGH19Jan86:3,
      SG23Feb86:1,2, NCG29Mar86:1, SG6Jul86:3,
      SG18Jan87:2,3, NCG11Jul87:4, SG29Nov87:4,
      SG7Feb88:2, SG27Mar88:3, WC16Jul88:2,
      WC23Jul88:2, SG18Dec88:3, WC18Dec88:2,3,
      SG25Dec88:3, SG22Jan89:1, SG12Feb89:3,
      SG19Feb89:4, SG5Mar89:4, SG12Mar89:4,
      SG19Mar89:4, SG2Apr89:4, SG16Apr89:4,
      SG23Apr89:4, SG7May89:4, SG18Jun89:4,
      SG25Jun89:4, SG16Jul89:4, SG3Dec89:3,
      SG31Dec89:3,4
  ball given for members of, WC18Dec88:3
  bills considered by, WC19Nov88:3
  commentary on legislation of, WC23Jul88:1,
      WC30Jul88:1,2, WC6Aug88:1,2
  consideration of location of capital of N.C.,
      WC26Nov88:3
  destroys paper money, WC18Dec88:3
  election of members of, NCG11Jul87:1,
      WC17Sep88:3, SG31Dec89:3
  journals of, WC16Jul88:3, WC24Sep88:1,
      SG8Jan89:3
  laws and journals of, SG6Jul86:3
  meeting of, WC5Nov88:2
  meeting places of, WC26Nov88:3, SG4Dec88:3
  members of, SG22Sep88:3, SG29Sep88:3,
      WC18Dec88:3, SG27Aug89:3
  memorial to, WC12Nov88:1
  proceedings of, SG12Jan86:2, NCGH19Jan86:3,
      EI9Apr88:2,3, WC12Nov88:3, WC26Nov88:3,
      SG8Jan89:3, SG22Jan89:3, SG3Dec89:3,
      SG17Dec89:3, SG31Dec89:3
  recommendation to convene constitutional
      convention, WC26Nov88:3
  resolutions of, SG4Dec88:2,3, WC10Dec88:3
  and Thomas Vail, EI9Apr88:2,3, SG27Oct88:1
  usurpations of, NCG15Aug87:3

General Assembly, Pa., SG9Apr89:3
  act of, SG1Oct89:3
  proceedings of, SG27Oct88:2
  resolution of, SG2Apr89:3

General Assembly, R.I., WC12Feb89:3, SG23Jul89:2

Geneva, revolution in, SG14May89:1

Genius, editorial on, FG12Oct89:3

Gentleman
  extract from journal of, SG12Mar89:2
  poem on death of, SG15Oct89:3

Gentlemen, conduct of, SG5Feb89:1,2

Geographer General of the U.S., SG11Jun89:3

George III, WC8Jan89:2, SG12Mar89:1, SG2Apr89:1,2,
    SG7May89:3, SG14May89:3, SG20Aug89:1,
    SG17Sep89:1
  birthday celebration of, WC9Jul88:2
  character of, SG5Mar89:3
  health of, WC8Jan89:2, WC15Jan89:3,
      WC5Feb89:1,2,3, WC12Feb89:1,2,3,
      WC19Feb89:1,3, SG12Mar89:3,
      SG19Mar89:1,2, SG30Apr89:3, SG20Aug89:1,
      SG17Sep89:1
  popular support for, SG4Jun89:1
  recovery of, SG14May89:3
  reported death of, WC15Jan89:3, SG29Jan89:2,
      WC12Feb89:1, SG5Mar89:2
  treatment of John Adams by, SG1Jan89:1,2,
      WC8Jan89:2
  tribute to, SG19Feb89:1

George, Marcus, SG22Oct89:3

Georgetown (George-Town) Md.
  commerce of, SG28May89:3
  escort for George Washington in, SG14May89:3
  letter from, SG14May89:2
  news from, SG26Mar89:2, SG28May89:3,
      SG3Dec89:2

Georgia, WC18Jun88:1, SG18Dec88:3, SG12Feb89:3,
    SG7May89:3
  address of chief justice of, SG28May89:3
  agriculture of, SG5Mar89:3
  attacks on, SG5Mar89:3
  British supply Indians in, WC12Feb89:1
  climate of, SG25Dec88:2
  consideration of amendments to federal
      Constitution, SG16Apr89:3
  constitutional convention of, SG18Jun89:3
  crops in, SG5Mar89:3
  description of, SG28May89:4
  governor calls meeting of General Assembly of,
      WC17Sep88:2
  Indians in, SG12Feb89:3
  Indian disturbances in, SG24Nov88:3,
      SG12Feb89:3, SG24Sep89:3, SG12Nov89:3
  Indians relations of, WC17Sep88:2
  letter from, SG25Dec88:2, SG5Mar89:3
  politics in, WC17Sep88:2, SG12Feb89:2
  ratification of federal Constitution by, SG7Feb88:2
  refusal of General Assembly to convene,
      SG12Feb89:2,3
  relations with North Carolina, WC22Jan89:2
  runaway slaves in, WC9Jul88:2
  superior court trial in, SG27Aug89:3
  wages in, SG25Dec88:2

Gerard, C., SG3Dec89:3

German, Joseph, NCG19Dec87:4

Germany, WC18Dec88:2
  declining health of emperor of, WC19Feb89:3

Gerock, Samuel, SG27Aug89:3

Gerrard, Charles, NCG6Jan85:1, SG31Dec89:3

Gerry, E., NCG19Dec87:3

Gerry, Elbridge
  address to voters of Middlesex County, Mass.,
      SG5Mar89:2
  letter of, SG9Apr89:3
  support for federal Constitution, SG27Mar88:3

Gib, Adam, SG13Oct88:2

Gibble, Dederick, NCG29Jul84:3

Gibbs, William, NCG6Jan85:1

Gibraltar, WC15Oct88:1
  attitude of governor of toward Algeriens,
      WC2Jul88:2

difficulty securing provisions for, WC3Sep88:1
English provisioning of, WC25Jun88:2
famine in, WC15Oct88:1
letter from, WC30Jul88:2, WC3Sep88:1,
    WC24Sep88:2, SG6Oct88:2, SG4Jun89:2
threatened by Morocco, WC30Jul88:2
Gibson, Mr., WC19Nov88:3
Gibson, William, NCG6Jan85:1
Giffard, Alexander, WC13Aug88:3
Gilbert, Mr., SG3Dec89:2
Gilbert, Mrs., SG8Oct89:4
Gilchrist, Mrs., SG15Oct89:4
Gilchrist, Thomas, NCG2Sep84:3, SG1Oct89:3,
    SG15Oct89:4
Gillaspie, ____, SG3Dec89:3
Gillespie, A., NCG29Jul84:3
Gillespie, D., SG3Dec89:3
Gillespie, Daniel, WC20Aug88:2
Gillespie, J., SG3Dec89:3
Gillespie, James, NCG29Jul84:3, SG9Apr89:3—,
    WC20Aug88:2
Gillies, Malcom, NCG29Jul84:4
Gillies, Malcor, SG27Mar88:3
Gilliken, George A., SG22Oct89:3, SG29Oct89:3,
    SG12Nov89:4
Gillispie, James, SG31Dec89:3
Gillispie's Fort on Holstein, SG11Dec88:2
Gilmoor, William, NCG6Jan85:1
Gilmour, William, SG20Oct88:3, SG27Oct88:3
Gladin, John, SG6Jul86:3
Glasgow, James, SG23Feb86:4, SG6Jul86:4,
    NCG19Dec87:4, SG27Mar88:3, WC19Nov88:3,
    WC26Nov88:3, SG4Dec88:3, SG17Dec89:3
Glasgow
    exports to N.C., NCG29Mar86:1, SG27Oct88:3—,
        SG3Nov88:4
    passengers from, SG10Nov88:3
Glasgow Advertiser, extract from, WC2Jul88:1
Glass, manufacture of, WC5Nov88:2, FG21Sep89:2
Glass works, SG10Sep89:2
Glaubeck, Baron de, SG22Oct89:4
    military exploits of, SG1Oct89:4
Gloster, Thomas, SG20Oct88:3, SG27Oct88:3,
    SG9Apr89:3—
Goa, ship from, SG16Apr89:1
Goagh, Caleb C., NCG29Jul84:3
Godden, David, SG6Jul86:3
Godwin, James V., SG9Apr89:3—
Godwin, Mr., SG3Nov88:3
Gold, imported into R.I., SG2Jul89:2
Gold Coast, unrest among Negroes, NCG29Jul84:1
Goldsmith and jeweler, journeyman wanted by,
    NCGH6Oct85:4
Good, Mary, SG20Oct88:3
Good, William, SG4Oct87:4, SG20Oct88:3
Goodrich, Solomon, SG18Jan87:3
Gordon, Dr.
    proposed history of Revolution by, SG6Jul86:2,3
    publication of history by, WC18Jun88:2
Gordon, (Lord) George, SG4Oct87:4, SG5Mar89:2
    marriage of, SG22Sep88:2
    petition of, SG5Nov89:1,2
Gorrell, Robert, SG22Oct89:3, SG29Oct89:3,
    SG12Nov89:4
Gorsia, John, SG9Jul89:3—
Gottenburg, letter from, WC5Feb89:1

Goudy, William, WC20Aug88:2
Gould, Daniel, WC20Aug88:2
Government
    nature of, SG6Jul86:1,2, NCG11Jul87:3,4,
        NCG1Aug87:1,2,3, SG3Nov88:1,2,
        WC3Dec88:1, WC10Dec88:2,4, WC18Dec88:1,
        WC25Dec88:1, SG7May89:1,3, SG14May89:1,
        SG28May89:3, SG2Jul89:3, SG23Jul89:2,
        FG24Aug89:3, SG5Nov89:2
    nature of judiciary of, SG4Jun89:1
Governors, titles of, SG27Aug89:3
Gowdy, ____, SG17Sep89:3, SG3Dec89:3
Gowdy, Mr., SG29Sep88:3
Gracey, Ebenezer, SG20Oct88:3, SG27Oct88:3
Graham, Dr., NCG19Dec87:2
Graham, Dr. James, arrest in London of, SG5Feb89:2
Graham, J., SG3Dec89:3
Graham, Joseph, WC20Aug88:2
Graham, Major, SG17Sep89:3
Graham, William, SG27Mar88:3
Grain, scarcity of in N.Y., SG16Jul89:2
Grainger, William, NCG6Jan85:1
Grand Jury, Edenton District, report of, SG29Nov87:1
Grand Lodge, N.C., WC26Nov88:3
    meeting of, SG7Feb88:3, SG4Dec88:3
    officers of, SG17Dec89:3
    See also Free Masons
Grand Seignor, deposing of, NCG3Nov85:3
Granday, ____, SG3Dec89:3
Grandy, Charles, WC20Aug88:2, SG3Sep89:3
Grange, John, WC30Jul88:4, WC29Jan89:3,
    WC5Feb89:4
Grange, John, Sr., WC23Jul88:3—
Grange, William, SG27Mar88:3
Grant, John, WC2Jul88:3—, WC12Feb89:3—
Grant, Reuben, SG22Sep88:3
Granville County, N.C., NCGH6Oct85:4,
    NCG29Mar86:2, SG18Jan87:2,3, SG29Sep88:3,
    SG10Nov88:3, SG25Dec88:2, SG17Sep89:3,
    SG24Dec89:3, SG31Dec89:2,4
    glebe land to be sold, SG18Jan87:3
    wardens of the poor in, SG18Jan87:3
Grasse, Comte de, duels of, SG29Jan89:2
Graves, ____, SG17Sep89:3, SG3Dec89:3
Graves, John, WC20Aug88:2, SG22Sep88:3
Gray, Eleanor, SG23Jul89:3
Gray, Etheld., WC20Aug88:2
Gray, Ethelred, SG3Sep89:3
Gray, George, SG4Dec88:3, SG9Jul89:3—
Gray, Robert, SG29Nov87:1
Gray, Stevens, SG20Oct88:3, SG27Oct88:3
Gray, William, SG9Jul89:3—
Gray, John and Co., NCG6Jan85:1
Greane, Lear, SG20Oct88:3, SG27Oct88:3
Great Britain, SG18Dec88:1
    accessions to peerage of, WC19Feb89:3
    Algerine emissary to, WC25Dec88:2
    attempt to stop counterfeiting in, WC8Jan89:2
    bankruptcies in, SG12Nov89:2
    budget of, SG27Aug89:2
    coinage in, SG12Nov89:2
    commerce of, SG7Feb88:2,3, WC10Sep88:2,
        SG13Oct88:2, SG19Nov89:2, SG24Dec89:3
    corn in, FG12Oct89:3
    dispute among officers of naval vessel of,
        WC5Feb89:2

enlisting sailors for government service in, WC22Jan89:2

evaluation of Russian trade of, SG3Dec89:1

frigate of captures Moorish vessel, WC25Dec88:2

growth of, SG19Feb89:1

introduction of manufactures to America, SG10Sep89:2

involvement in European politics, SG26Feb89:1

liberty of the press in, WC9Jul88:2

military presence in North America, WC24Sep88:2

naval blockade of Moroccan ship, WC25Dec88:2

naval command of in Halifax, Nova Scotia, WC5Feb89:2

navy of, SG27Mar88:3, WC15Oct88:1, WC25Dec88:2, WC22Jan89:2

neutrality of in war between Russia and Sweden, WC19Nov88:3

outfitting a naval expedition of, WC25Dec88:2

overtures of alliance made to, WC25Dec88:2

politics in, SG19Mar89:2, SG3Sep89:2

Prince of Wales, SG19Mar89:1

prohibits wheat imports from U.S., WC24Sep88:2

regency for, SG19Mar89:1

revenues of, WC22Jan89:2

seeks apology from Denmark, WC25Dec88:2

settlement of African Company of with that of Holland, WC25Dec88:2

settlement with Morocco, WC24Sep88:2

shipping insurance of, SG27Oct88:2

supplies Indians in U.S., WC12Feb89:1

tax on pens in, WC22Jan89:2

tobacco bill of, SG29Oct89:3

trade of with Barbary ports, SG13Oct88:2

trade regulations of, NCGH6Oct85:1,2,3, WC24Sep88:2, WC26Oct88:2

treaty of with Prussia, SG28May89:2, SG2Jul89:4

treaty of with Spain, NCG2Sep84:2

U.S. commerce with, SG8Sep88:3, SG22Sep88:1, SG27Oct88:2, WC10Dec88:2, SG19Nov89:2

U.S. relations with, SG12Jan86:3, WC2Jul88:2, WC26Nov88:2

See also England

Great Tassel, WC6Aug88:3

Greatree, General, NCG6Jan85:1

Greeks, drinking customs of, SG26Mar89:1

Green, George, WC24Sep88:2

Green, James, NCG29Mar86:2

Green, James, Jr., SG12Jan86:3

Green, John, NCG2Sep84:3, NCG6Jan85:1, SG12Jan86:4, SG7Feb88:3, SG4Mar88:4, SG27Mar88:3,4, WC24Sep88:2

Green, Joseph, SG18Jan87:2, WC16Jul88:3

Green, S., SG3Dec89:3

Green, Solomon, SG24Sep89:3

Green, William, WC6Aug88:3, WC24Sep88:2

Greene, Nathaniel, SG19Feb89:2

Greene (Green) County, N.C., SG18Jan87:2, SG18Dec88:3, WC18Dec88:3, SG25Dec88:2

letter from, SG11Dec88:2,3, SG29Jan89:2, SG16Apr89:3

Greenlee, James, WC20Aug88:2

Greensville, N.C., SG27Mar88:4

Greenville, N.C., establishment of, SG18Jan87:2

Greenville, Tenn., SG16Apr89:3

Greenville County, Va., NCG9Dec84:4

Greenwich, Jamaica, explosion of vessel in harbor of,

WC27Aug88:3

Greer, ____, SG3Dec89:3

Greer, Samuel, NCG6Jan85:1

Greer and Ford, SG27Mar88:3

Gregg, Frederick, NCG29Mar86:2

Gregory, General, SG18Dec88:2—

Gregory, Isaac, SG12Jan86:2, WC20Aug88:2, SG29Jan89:1, SG3Sep89:3

Gregory, J., SG3Dec89:2

Gregory, James, NCG6Jan85:1, WC20Aug88:2

Greig, Admiral, SG25Dec88:2, WC5Mar89:2

death of, SG12Mar89:3

Grenada, free port bill for, WC13Aug88:2

Grenville, W., NCG19Dec87:3

Grieves, Rhoda, SG20Oct88:3, SG27Oct88:3

Griffin, ____, SG3Dec89:3

Griffin, Cyrus, SG29Sep88:1

Grigg, Frederic, SG6Jul86:3

Grimes, Major, WC17Sep88:3, SG29Sep88:3

Grist, ____, SG3Dec89:3

Grist, Mr., SG3Dec89:2

Grist, Richard, SG3Dec89:3

Gristmill, NCG9Dec84:4

sale of, NCG6Jan85:4

See also Saw mill and gristmill

Groceries, sale of, SG23Feb86:2

Grove, ____, SG3Dec89:3

Grove, William Barry (W. B., William B.), WC18Jun88:3, WC25Jun88:3, WC9Jul88:4, WC20Aug88:2, SG22Sep88:3, FG24Aug89:3, SG10Sep89:3, FG21Sep89:2, FG12Oct89:4, SG3Dec89:3, SG17Dec89:3

Grundy, George, SG8Jan89:3, SG15Jan89:4

Guadaloupe, SG28May89:3

Guerard, John, WC13Aug88:3, WC8Jan89:3—

Guilford County, N.C., NCGH19Jan86:4, NCG29Mar86:2, SG18Jan87:2,3, SG29Sep88:3, SG25Dec88:2, SG17Sep89:3, SG31Dec89:3

Guion, ____, SG3Dec89:3

Guion, Dr., SG3Sep89:3

Guion, Frederick, NCG2Sep84:4, SG23Feb86:2

Guion, Isaac, NCG6Jan85:1, SG4Oct87:4, SG29Nov87:4, SG27Mar88:3

Guittar (guitar), WC5Nov88:3—

Gun

invention of, WC25Jun88:2

stolen, SG19Nov89:3, SG26Nov89:4

Gunsmith and locksmith, SG2Jul89:3—

H

Habrick, Robert, SG22Oct89:3, SG29Oct89:3, SG12Nov89:4

Hackett, Redmond, SG14May89:3, SG21May89:4

Hagan, John, SG22Oct89:3, SG29Oct89:3, SG12Nov89:4

Hagan, Mr., SG2Apr89:3, SG9Apr89:4, SG23Apr89:3—, SG18Jun89:4, SG25Jun89:4, SG9Jul89:4, SG23Jul89:4, SG10Sep89:3, SG17Sep89:3, SG24Sep89:4

Hagins, Robert, SG20Oct88:3, SG27Oct88:3

Hague, The

letter from, WC24Sep88:2, SG25Dec88:1

news from, SG7Feb88:1, WC18Jun88:2

Hairdressing, SG12Jan86:4

Halifax, N.C., SG2Sep84:4, NCGH16Feb86:3,
  NCG29Mar86:1,2,3,4, SG18Jan87:3,
  NCG19Dec87:4, SG8Sep88:4—, WC26Nov88:3,
  SG15Jan89:3, SG22Jan89:1,4, SG29Jan89:4,
  SG12Feb89:3, SG9Apr89:4—, SG24Sep89:3,
  SG1Oct89:3—, SG26Nov89:3, SG17Dec89:3
  regulation of, SG18Jan87:3, WC18Dec88:3
Halifax, N.S., SG19Feb89:2
  British naval command in, WC5Feb89:2
  fire in, SG19Feb89:2
  government of, NCG9Dec84:2
  influence of French Revolution in, SG19Nov89:2
Halifax Congress, SG7May89:1, SG2Jul89:3
Halifax County, N.C., SG25Dec88:2, SG24Sep89:3
Halifax District, SG18Jan87:3, SG25Dec88:4
Hall, Durham, WC20Aug88:2
Hall, J., SG3Dec89:2
Hall, Jane, SG22Oct89:3, SG29Oct89:3, SG12Nov89:4
Hall, John, WC23Jul88:3—, WC29Jan89:3,
  WC5Feb89:4, SG23Apr89:3—, SG10Sep89:3
Hall, Kitching, SG8Jan89:3, SG15Jan89:4
Hall, Parry, SG29Sep88:3
Hall, William, FG14Sep89:3
Halling, Solomon, NCG29Jul84:3, NCG2Sep84:2
Halling and Pasteur, SG12Jan86:3, SG18Jan87:4
Halsey, Henry, WC13Aug88:3
Halsey, Mallachi, SG22Oct89:3, SG29Oct89:3,
  SG12Nov89:4
Halstead, Jesse, SG9Apr89:3—
Ham, Mr., address of at Philadelphia, SG6Oct88:4
Hamburg (Hamburgh)
  letter from, SG26Feb89:2, SG25Dec88:1,
    SG5Feb89:2
  peace in, SG13Aug89:2
  religious toleration in, SG12Jan86:3
Hamilton, ____, SG17Sep89:3, SG3Dec89:3
Hamilton, Alexander, SG9Apr89:2, SG14May89:3
  circular letter of, SG9Apr89:1,2
  communication to N.Y. voters, SG14May89:3
Hamilton, Archibald, NCG29Mar86:2
Hamilton, James, SG18Jan87:3
Hamilton, John, NCG29Mar86:2, WC20Aug88:2,
  SG13Aug89:3, SG27Aug89:3, FG14Sep89:3,
  SG15Oct89:3, SG3Dec89:3, SG17Dec89:3,
  SG31Dec89:3
  address to Edenton voters, SG13Aug89:3
Hamilton, Lt. Gov., SG12Jan86:2
Hamilton, Mr., SG29Sep88:3, SG17Dec89:3
Hammer, Solomon, WC13Aug88:3, WC5Nov88:3,
  WC12Nov88:4
Hammond, A. G., SG20Oct88:3, SG27Oct88:3
"Hampden," NCG1Aug87:3
Hampton, Va., SG17Dec89:3
Hancock, Governor, EI9Apr88:4, WC27Aug88:3
  response of Mass. legislature to, WC26Feb89:2,3
Hancock, John, NG23Feb86:3
  family of, SG2Apr89:4
  extract of message from, SG19Feb89:2
  on the federal Constitution, EI9Apr88:2
  response of Mass. legislature to, SG12Mar89:3
Handley, ____, SG3Dec89:3
Hands, Capt., WC26Nov88:3
Hands, John, WC23Jul88:3, WC30Jul88:1
Handy, Mr., SG3Dec89:3
Hanging, WC5Nov88:4
Hankins, Dennis, SG10Sep89:3

Hanly, James, WC20Aug88:2, SG3Sep89:3
Hann, Joseph, SG27Mar88:3
Hanover, letter from, SG23Jul89:1
Hanover County, Va., SG1Oct89:3
Happiness, nature of, WC25Jun88:1
Haragan, ____, SG3Dec89:3
Hardiman, Thomas, WC20Aug88:2
Hardin, Judge, Sr., SG16Apr89:3
Hardware, sale of, SG23Feb86:2
Hardware and pewter, sale of, EI9Apr88:4, EI4Jun88:4
Hardy, Agness, NCG29Jul84:3
Hardy, Francis, NCG29Jul84:3
Hardy, Humphry, SG12Jan86:4
Hardy, Mr., SG12Jan86:4
Hardy, Robert, NCG29Jul84:3
Harger, Frederick, WC20Aug88:2
Harget, ____, SG3Dec89:3
Harget, Frederick, SG3Sep89:3, SG31Dec89:3
Harnett, C., WC5Feb89:4
Harnett, Cornelius, WC29Jan89:3
Harnett, Mrs., WC26Nov88:3, WC5Feb89:4
Harnett, Mrs. Cornelius, WC29Jan89:3
Haron, Dennis, SG29Nov87:4
Harper, Arthur, WC25Jun88:3
Harper, James, WC25Jun88:3
Harracks, Thomas, WC22Jan89:3
Harrel, Samuel, WC20Aug88:2
Harrington, Wm., SG27Mar88:3
Harris
  See Springs and Harris
Harris, Thomas, SG22Oct89:3, SG29Oct89:3,
  SG12Nov89:4
Harrisburg, N.C., NCG19Dec87:4
Harrisburg, Pa., meeting to support federal Constitution,
  SG13Oct88:1,2
Harrison, Christopher, SG30Apr89:3—
Harry (slave), WC5Nov88:4, WC12Feb89:3—,
  SG2Jul89:3
Hart, Anthony, SG20Oct88:3, SG27Oct88:3,
  SG8Jan89:3, SG15Jan89:4
Hartford, John, SG8Jan89:3, SG15Jan89:4
Hartford, Conn., news from, SG24Nov88:2,
  SG19Mar89:2, SG23Apr89:2
Hartley & Nicholson, SG12Jan86:4
Harvey, John, SG20Oct88:3, SG27Oct88:3,
  SG9Jul89:3—
Harvey, Joseph, SG27Aug89:3, FG14Sep89:3
Harvey, Miles, SG9Jul89:3—, SG20Aug89:4,
  SG24Sep89:4
Harvey, Thomas, WC20Aug88:2
Harvey's Neck, SG22Jan89:3—
Harvie, David, WC5Nov88:3, WC12Nov88:4
Haslen, Capt., SG17Dec89:2
Haslen, Thomas, SG6Jul86:3
Haslin, Mr., SG29Nov87:3
Haslin, Thomas, SG27Mar88:3
Hastings, Mr., NCG15Aug87:3, SG8Sep88:2,
  SG17Nov88:1, SG6Aug89:3
  illness of, WC9Jul88:2
  trial of, WC25Jun88:2, SG22Sep88:1,
    SG12Mar89:1, SG6Aug89:3, SG20Aug89:1
Hastings, Warren, WC9Jul88:2
  petition of, SG25Jun89:4
  trial of, WC16Jul88:1, SG29Sep88:3, SG10Nov88:1,
    WC19Nov88:2, SG16Jul89:3, SG20Aug89:1
Hat, lost, WC26Feb89:3

Hatch, Edward, Jr., SG7Feb88:3
Hatch, N., SG20Oct88:3
Hatcher, Priscilla, WC26Nov88:4, WC3Dec88:3
    See Johnson, Priscilla
Hathaway, James, SG22Oct89:3
Hathaway, Sarah, death of, SG22Oct89:3
Hatrick, Robert, SG27Mar88:3
Havanna, port opened to importation of slaves,
    FG21Sep89:2
Haverhill, Mass.
    drowning in, SG24Nov88:2
    Pres. Washington stays in, SG17Dec89:2
Havre-de-Grâce
    letter from, SG5Mar89:3, SG4Jun89:4
    prices for imports to, SG4Jun89:3
Hawkins, ____, SG13Aug89:3, SG3Dec89:2,3
Hawkins, B., SG3Dec89:3
Hawkins, Benjamin, NCG6Jan85:1, SG18Jan87:3,
    SG7Feb88:3, SG18Dec88:2—, SG24Sep89:3,
    SG17Dec89:3, SG31Dec89:3
Hawkins, John, SG20Oct88:3, SG27Oct88:3,
    SG9Jul89:3—
Hawkins, Mr., SG3Dec89:4
Hawkins, P., SG3Dec89:3
Hawkins, Philemon, SG24Sep89:3
Hawkins, W., SG3Dec89:3, SG31Dec89:3
Hawkins, Wyat(t), WC20Aug88:2, SG24Sep89:3
Hawkins County, N.C., SG18Jan87:2, SG18Dec88:3,
    WC18Dec88:3, SG25Dec88:2, SG31Dec89:2,3
    courthouse of, SG31Dec89:3
Hawley, William, SG27Mar88:3
Hay, J., SG3Dec89:2
Hay, John, SG23Feb86:2, SG10Sep89:3
Hay, Joseph, SG4Dec88:3
Hayn, Mr., WC19Nov88:3
Hays, Joseph, SG11Dec88:4—
Hays, W., SG3Dec89:3
Haywood, Egbert, WC20Aug88:2
Haywood, J., SG25Dec88:2
Haywood, John, SG8Sep88:4—
Haywood, John, Jr., NCG6Jan85:1
Haywood, Joseph, SG22Sep88:3
Haywood, S., SG15Sep88:4—, SG18Dec88:2—
Hazard, Capt. George, WC13Aug88:3
Healing Springs, NCG3Nov85:2
Health, NCG3Nov85:2,3, NCGH16Feb86:2,
    SG11Dec88:3
    protection of, SG5Mar89:2
    remedies of, NCG1Aug87:3
    See Ague and fever
Healton, Ralph, SG27Mar88:3
Hearring, John, SG9Apr89:3—
Hearring, Jonathan, SG20Oct88:3, SG27Oct88:3
Hellstedt, Charles, letter to in Philadelphia,
    SG24Nov88:2
Hemp
    cultivation of, SG10Sep89:2
    wanted, NCGH19Jan86:3, NCGH2Feb86:4,
        NCGH16Feb86:4, NCGH23Feb86:4
Hemphite, James, NCG6Jan85:1
Henderson, N., SG3Dec89:3
Henderson, Pleasant, NCG6Jan85:1
Henderson, Richard, SG18Dec88:3, WC18Dec88:2
Henderson, Robert, SG9Apr89:3—
Hendre, Jean, WC13Aug88:3
Hendrickson, Saluthiel, NCG29Jul84:3

Hendry, William, WC13Aug88:3
Henley, John, SG12Jan86:4
Hennon, Peter, NCG6Jan85:1
Henrion & Constantin, NCG29Mar86:1
Henry, Joel, SG27Mar88:3
Henry, Paddy (Patrick), SG29Jan89:2
Henry, William, SG27Mar88:3
Hepburn and Reynolds, SG6Jul86:3
Herald of Freedom, extract from, SG5Feb89:1,2
Herndon, Col., FG14Sep89:3
Herndon, J., SG3Dec89:3
Herndon, Joseph, WC20Aug88:2
Hero, Mr., NCG6Jan85:1, SG6Jul86:4, SG29Nov87:3
Herriman, Thomas, SG20Oct88:3
Herritage, William, NCG19Dec87:4
Hertford County, N.C., SG18Jan87:2, WC26Nov88:3,
    SG25Dec88:2, SG14May89:3, SG21May89:4,
    SG27Aug89:3, FG14Sep89:3
    courthouse of, SG12Jan86:4
Hesse, Manifesto of Prince of, WC26Feb89:2
Hewes, Smith and Allen, SG8Jan89:3, SG15Jan89:4
Hewill, Benjamin, SG20Oct88:3, SG27Oct88:3
Hibernia Chronicle, extracts from, NCG19Dec87:3
Hibernian gentlemen, NCGH16Feb86:3
Higgenson, Stewart, SG8Jan89:3, SG15Jan89:4
Higgins, Cormick, SG7Feb88:4
Hill, ____, SG27Aug89:3, FG14Sep89:3
Hill, A., SG3Dec89:3
Hill, Aaron, FG14Sep89:3
Hill, Elizabeth, WC12Nov88:3
Hill, H., SG3Dec89:3
Hill, Henry, SG29Nov87:1, WC20Aug88:2,
    SG24Sep89:3
Hill, J., SG3Dec89:3
Hill, John, WC3Dec88:3—, WC19Feb89:3—
Hill, Jordan, SG24Sep89:3
Hill, Joseph, SG22Sep88:2, SG9Jul89:3
Hill, Joshua, SG20Oct88:3, SG27Oct88:3
Hill, Margaret, WC5Nov88:3, WC3Dec88:3—,
    WC19Feb89:3—
Hill, W. H., WC3Dec88:3—, WC22Jan89:3,4,
    WC19Feb89:3—, SG3Dec89:3
Hill, Whitmill (Whitm., Whitmil), SG7Feb88:3,
    WC20Aug88:2, SG20Oct88:3, SG27Oct88:3,
    WC19Nov88:3—, SG29Jan89:1
Hill, William, WC19Feb89:3—
Hill, William H., WC12Nov88:3, SG10Sep89:3
Hill, William Henry, SG23Jul89:3—
Hilliard, ____, SG3Sep89:3
Hilliard, J., SG3Dec89:3
Hillsborough, N.C., NCG2Sep84:4, NCG9Dec84:4,
    NCG6Jan85:4, NCGH6Oct85:4,
    NCGH19Jan86:2,3, NCGH2Feb86:2,3,4,
    NCGH16Feb86:1,3,4, NCGH23Feb86:1,3,4,
    SG23Feb86:1,3, SG18Jan87:2,3, WC16Jul88:3,
    WC23Jul88:4, WC6Aug88:2,3, SG8Sep88:4,
    SG15Sep88:4, SG22Sep88:3,4, SG29Sep88:4—,
    WC26Nov88:3, SG4Dec88:3, SG17Sep89:3,
    SG3Dec89:3, SG31Dec89:3
    letter from, WC6Aug88:3, SG20Oct88:2
    news from, NCGH6Oct85:3, NCGH19Jan86:2,3,
        NCGH2Feb86:2, NCGH16Feb86:3,
        NCGH23Feb86:3, WC20Aug88:1,2
    regulation of, SG18Dec88:2,3, WC18Dec88:2
Hillsborough Convention, WC18Jun88:2,
    WC23Jul88:3, WC6Aug88:2,3, WC13Aug88:3,

WC20Aug88:1, SG8Sep88:3, WC17Sep88:3,
SG20Oct88:3, SG3Nov88:1,2, WC5Nov88:1,2,
WC19Nov88:3, WC3Dec88:1, WC10Dec88:1,
WC18Dec88:1, SG25Dec88:3, SG3Dec89:3
approves amendments to federal Constitution,
WC13Aug88:3
approves Declaration of Rights, WC13Aug88:3
criticism of, WC3Dec88:1, WC10Dec88:1,
WC18Dec88:1, WC25Dec88:1
decides location of state capital, WC13Aug88:3,
SG8Sep88:3
proceedings of, WC20Aug88:1,2
Hillsborough District, SG18Jan87:2
Hilton, Peter, NCGH2Feb86:3, NCGH16Feb86:3,
NCGH23Feb86:3
Hinduism, SG19Feb89:3
Hines, ____, SG3Dec89:3
Hines, Thomas, WC20Aug88:2, SG17Sep89:3,
SG3Dec89:3
Hingham, Mass., description of, SG17Sep89:3
Hinreon, Peter, SG6Jul86:3
Hinton, James, WC20Aug88:2
Hinton, Mr., SG29Sep88:3
Hispaniola
letter from, SG29Nov87:2
ports open for trade, SG22Oct89:2
U.S. trade with, SG29Nov87:2
History, writing of, SG24Nov88:2
History of the American Revolution, The, by David
Ramsay, proposal to publish, SG8Jan89:3—
History of Kentucky, sale of, NCG9Dec84:4
*History of the Rise, Progress and Establishment of the United
States, The*, by William Gordon
available to subscribers, SG15Oct89:3
proposed publication of, SG2Apr89:3—
Hodge & Blanchard, SG18Jan87:1, NCG1Aug87:4
Hodge & Wills, SG8Sep88:3,4, SG15Sep88:4—,
SG6Oct88:3,4, SG13Oct88:4, SG27Oct88:1,4,
SG3Nov88:3—, SG2Apr89:3—, SG20Aug89:2,
SG3Dec89:3
considered for public printers, SG3Dec89:3
Hodge, J., SG3Dec89:3
Hodge, Joseph, SG17Sep89:3
Hodgeson, WC13Aug88:3
Hogarth, Mr., anecdote of, WC3Dec88:4
Hogg, Gavin, SG18Jan87:2
Hogg, James, SG31Dec89:3
Hogg, Robert, NCG29Jul84:2
Hogg, Walter, name of changed, SG18Jan87:2
Hogiston, Archibald, SG22Oct89:3, SG29Oct89:3,
SG12Nov89:4
Holland, ____, SG3Dec89:3
Holland, James, SG31Dec89:3
Holland, NCGH23Feb86:3, SG3Dec89:3
ascendance of Prince of Orange in, WC27Aug88:3
decline of, WC10Sep88:2
emigration from, NCGH19Jan86:2
government of, SG7May89:3
meeting of Council of State, WC3Dec88:2
politics of, WC27Aug88:3
price of bread in, SG5Nov89:2
revolt on East India ship of, NCG2Sep84:2
settlement of African company of with that of Great
Britain, WC25Dec88:2
succumbs to influence of France, SG17Nov88:1
price of wheat in, SG29Oct89:1,2

support for Russia by, WC3Dec88:2
trade of, NCG19Dec87:3
U.S. relations with, SG12Mar89:2
Hollowell, James, SG3Nov88:2
Holmes, H., SG3Dec89:3
Holmes, Hardy, WC20Aug88:2, SG22Sep88:3,
SG17Sep89:3
Holmes, Lewis, SG20Aug88:2
Holmes, Thomas, SG9Apr89:3—
Holston, NCG11Jul87:4
Homer, Charles, SG20Oct88:3, SG27Oct88:3,
SG22Oct89:3, SG29Oct89:3, SG12Nov89:4
Honduras, Spanish depredations in, SG8Oct89:2
"Honest Man, An," SG27Oct88:2
"Honestus," NCG15Aug87:2, WC18Jun88:2,
WC27Aug88:3, WC3Sep88:2, WC10Sep88:3
Honey, ____, SG12Jan86:4
Hooper, ____, WC18Jun88:3
Hooper, George, WC18Jun88:3—, WC8Jan89:3,
WC19Feb89:3, WC26Feb89:1
Hooper, Thomas, SG6Jul86:3
Hooper, William, WC16Jul88:3
Hooper, William, Jr., WC23Jul88:1, WC30Jul88:1
Hooper, George & Co., WC18Dec88:3, WC15Jan89:3,
WC22Jan89:4
Hooten
See Ashburn and Hooten
Hooten, Mr., SG12Jan86:4
Hopewell, Treaty of, SG29Sep88:1
Hopkins, Patrick, SG2Apr89:3
Hopkinson, F., ode by, WC3Sep88:4
Hopkinson, John, WC16Jul88:1
Hops, SG18Dec88:3
"Horatius," NCG11Jul87:2
Horn, ____, SG27Aug89:3, FG14Sep89:3
Horne, Joseph, SG29Nov87:1
Horse
aged, SG19Nov89:2
apprehended, EI19Dec87:1
prevention of theft of, SG18Jan87:2, SG25Dec88:3
punishment of theft of, SG18Jan87:2
sale of, SG1Jan89:4, SG15Jan89:4, SG22Jan89:4,
SG19Feb89:4, SG5Mar89:4—, SG7May89:1
stolen, SG6Jul86:4, SG21May89:3, SG28May89:4,
SG18Jun89:4
strayed or stolen, NCG2Sep84:3, FG24Aug89:3,
FG14Sep89:3, FG21Sep89:4
stud, NCGH23Feb86:3, SG23Feb86:2,
NCG29Mar86:1, SG27Mar88:3,4
Horse racing, NCG2Sep84:3, SG29Nov87:3,
SG8Sep88:2—, WC24Sep88:2, WC15Oct88:2—,
WC19Nov88:3, FG14Sep89:3, FG21Sep89:2,
SG3Dec89:4
Horse thief, SG25Dec88:3, WC15Jan89:3
Horton, Nathan, SG9Apr89:3—
Hoskins, Henry, WC8Jan89:3
Hosmer, Dr. S., SG20Oct88:3, SG27Oct88:3
Hostler, Alexander, WC5Feb89:3
Hostler, Mr., WC13Aug88:3
House, rent of, SG6Jul86:3, NCG15Aug87:4,
SG4Oct87:4, SG29Nov87:4, WC25Jun88:3—,
WC24Sep88:1, WC12Nov88:3, WC19Nov88:3,
WC3Dec88:3, WC10Dec88:1,3, SG11Dec88:4,
WC18Dec88:1—, SG8Jan89:3, SG15Jan89:4,
WC15Jan89:3—, SG29Jan89:4—, SG12Mar89:3
sale of, NCG2Sep84:4, SG11Dec88:4—,

WC26Feb89:3, WC5Mar89:1

House of Assembly, Jamaica, honors Prince William
  Henry, WC15Jan89:3
House of Burgesses, Va., WC3Dec88:2
  See also Virginia, politics in
House of Commons, England, SG9Apr89:3,
  SG23Apr89:1
  proceedings of, WC3Sep88:1, SG9Apr89:3,
    SG23Apr89:3
  See also England, politics in
House of Commons, N.C., SG8Sep88:4, SG15Sep88:4
  committee of, SG28May89:3
  proceedings of, NCGH19Jan86:2,3, SG9Apr89:3,
    SG23Jul89:1, SG3Dec89:3, SG17Dec89:3
  reports to, NCGH19Jan86:2
  resolutions of, SG29Sep88:4
  See also General Assembly, N.C.; North Carolina,
    politics in
House of Delegates, Va., proceedings of, SG15Nov87:2,
  WC3Dec89:2,3
  See also Virginia, politics in
House of entertainment, SG11Dec88:3, SG26Feb89:4
  See also Tavern
House of Lords, proceedings of, SG13Oct88:1,
  SG12Feb89:2, WC19Feb89:2, SG25Jun89:4,
  SG3Sep89:1
  consideration of regency by, WC19Feb89:2
House of Representatives, Mass.
  legislation of, SG19Mar89:2
  motion to petition Congress to consider amendments
    to federal Constitution, SG16Jul89:3
House of Representatives, U.S.
  address of, SG21May89:2
  composition of, SG22Jan89:3, SG17Sep89:3
  consideration of revenue bill by, SG4Jun89:3
  consideration of tariff duty by, SG21May89:3,
    SG28May89:1,2
  discussion of citizenship by Mr. Smith of S.C.,
    SG18Jun89:3
  proceedings of, SG21May89:3, SG4Jun89:3,
    SG15Oct89:3
  response to George Washington, SG21May89:2
Household goods
  sale of, SG26Feb89:3—, SG30Jul89:3
  stolen, SG14May89:4
Houser, ____, SG29Sep88:3
Houser, G., SG24Sep89:3, SG3Dec89:3
Hovey, James, WC24Sep88:1
Hovey, Samuel, WC17Sep88:3
Hovey, Seth, WC20Aug88:2
Howard
  See Sibley & Howard
Howard, Elijah, SG27Mar88:3
Howard, James, SG18Jan87:4, WC13Aug88:3
Howard, John H., SG18Jan87:3
Howard, Martin, NCG3Nov85:1
Howard, Samuel Harvey, SG29Nov87:4
Howard, Thos., SG9Apr89:3—
Howe, Arthur, WC13Aug88:3, WC27Aug88:3—
Howe, General, SG23Feb86:3
Howe, John, SG9Apr89:3—, SG22Oct89:3,
  SG29Oct89:3, SG12Nov89:4
Howell, John, NCG6Jan85:1, WC9Jul88:3,
  WC16Jul88:3
Howell, Joseph, SG22Sep88:3
Howsser, George, SG20Oct88:3, SG27Oct88:3

Hubac, Louis, SG9Apr89:3—
Hudson, N.Y., fire in, SG5Feb89:2
Hughes, John, SG27Mar88:3
Human nature, disquisition on, SG6Jul86:1,2
Human Nature in Its Fourfold State, by Thomas Boston,
  proposal to publish, SG16Apr89:3—
Hume, David, professorial appointment of,
  SG24Nov88:2
Humour, instance of, WC26Feb89:1
Humphreys, John, EI4Jun88:4
Humphries, John, WC20Aug88:2, SG20Oct88:3,
  SG27Oct88:3, SG9Apr89:3—
Hunley, Richard, SG6Jul86:4
Hunly, Capt., SG18Jan87:3
Hunt, J., SG8Sep88:3,4, SG15Sep88:4—,
  SG10Nov88:4, SG24Nov88:4
Hunt, John, SG3Dec89:2,3, SG17Dec89:3,
  SG31Dec89:3,4
Hunt, L., SG3Nov88:3, SG17Nov88:4
Hunt, M., SG18Dec88:2, SG10Dec89:3
Hunt, Memucan, SG29Sep88:3
Hunt, Robert, NCG6Jan85:1
Hunter, Isaac, SG8Sep88:3
Hunter, Miles, death of, WC15Jan89:3
Hunter, Robert, WC13Aug88:3
Hunter, Thomas, SG18Jan87:3, WC20Aug88:2,
  SG8Jan89:3, SG15Jan89:4, SG3Sep89:3,
  SG3Dec89:3
Hunting, NCG3Nov85:4, SG29Nov87:4
  regulation of, SG18Jan87:2
Huntington, Roswell, NCGH6Oct85:4
Huntington, Samuel, address to President Washington,
  SG19Nov89:4
Hurricane, WC20Aug88:3, WC10Sep88:2,
  SG29Sep88:3, SG6Oct88:3, SG13Oct88:3,
  WC26Oct88:1,2
  See also Storm
Husband
  choice of, WC25Jun88:1
  desertion by, SG5Feb89:3
Huske, ____, SG3Dec89:3
Huske, John, NCG29Jul84:2, WC18Jun88:3—,
  WC29Jan89:3, WC5Feb89:2,4, SG10Sep89:3
Hutchings, Thomas, SG29Nov87:4
Hutchins, Thomas, Geographer General of U.S., life of,
  SG11Jun89:3
Hutchinson, John, Jr., SG8Jan89:3, SG15Jan89:4
Hyde County, N.C., NCG2Sep84:3, NCG3Nov85:1,2,
  SG18Jan87:3, WC26Nov88:3, SG25Dec88:2,
  SG3Sep89:3, SG31Dec89:3
  elections in, SG18Jan87:3
Hymns, sale of, NCG9Dec84:4

I

Illinois country, description of, SG8Jan89:1,
  SG15Jan89:3, SG29Jan89:4
Immigration, NCG2Sep84:2, SG29Oct89:2
Impeachment, SG25Dec88:3
  trial of, WC19Nov89:3
Imperial Crowns, Confederacy of, SG8Sep88:1
Impey, Sir Elijah, anecdote of, WC2Jul88:4
Independence
  American celebration of anniversary of, SG6Jul86:3,
    SG29Sep88:3

ode to, FG24Aug89:4
"Independent Citizen," NCG1Aug87:2,
    NCG15Aug87:1
"Independent Citizen, An," SG11Jun89:2
"Independent Citizen, or the Majesty of the People,
    The," publication of, NCG15Aug87:3
India, SG8Jan89:2, SG11Jun89:3, SG6Aug89:3,
    SG19Nov89:3
    anecdote about, SG22Oct89:3
    British government in, SG7Feb88:1
    Cornwallis in, WC10Dec88:2
    death of British soldiers in, NCGH19Jan86:2
    distress in, WC10Dec88:2
    government of, WC5Nov88:2
    letter from, SG12Nov89:3
    newspaper from, SG2Jul88:2
    peace in, SG8Jan89:2
    reports from, WC10Dec88:2, SG23Jul89:1
    unrest in, SG19Nov89:3
    U.S. commerce with, WC12Feb89:1, SG26Nov89:3
    war in, SG11Jun89:3
Indians, WC18Jun88:3, WC6Aug88:3, SG8Sep88:3,
    WC17Sep88:2, WC29Sep88:2, SG20Oct88:1,
    SG3Nov88:2, SG24Nov88:2,3, SG4Dec88:4,
    SG1Jan89:2, SG15Jan89:2, WC15Jan89:1,
    WC22Jan89:2,3, WC12Feb89:1, WC19Feb89:2,
    SG26Feb89:3, SG5Mar89:3, WC5Mar89:2,
    SG2Apr89:2,3, SG9Apr89:2,3, SG23Apr89:2,
    SG30Apr89:3, SG30Jul89:2, SG1Oct89:3,
    SG8Oct89:3, SG15Oct89:3, SG29Oct89:3,
    SG5Nov89:3
    attacks of, SG29Nov87:2, WC30Jul88:3,
        WC24Sep88:2, SG6Oct88:3, SG15Jan89:2,
        SG29Jan89:2, WC5Mar89:2
    attacks by whites on Cherokee, SG13Oct88:4
    captive of, SG26Feb89:3
    Cherokee, NCG2Sep84:2, WC23Jul88:2,
        SG8Sep88:3, SG29Sep88:1, SG6Oct88:3,
        SG13Oct88:4, SG27Oct88:3, SG4Dec88:3,
        WC22Jan89:2,3, SG26Feb89:3, WC5Mar89:2,
        SG2Apr89:2,3, SG13Aug89:1, SG26Nov89:3,
        SG17Dec89:3, SG31Dec89:3
    Chickamauga, SG20Oct88:2, WC22Jan89:2,3,
        SG31Dec89:3
    Creek, SG8Sep88:2, WC17Sep88:2, SG20Oct88:2,
        SG4Dec88:3, SG18Dec88:3, WC22Jan89:2,
        SG26Mar89:2, SG13Aug89:1, SG3Dec89:2
    commissioners for, SG22Jan89:3, WC22Jan89:2
    confederation of, NCGH2Feb86:2
    depredations of, SG12Jan86:2, SG11Dec86:2,3,
        SG24Sep89:3, SG12Nov89:2,3
    exchange of prisoners with, WC19Feb89:2,
        SG26Feb89:3
    hostility of, SG29Nov87:2
    message to Cherokee, SG26Nov89:3
    negotiations with, FG21Sep89:3,4, SG5Nov89:3,
        SG12Nov89:3
    Pa. relations with, SG12Mar89:2
    Seminoles, SG5Mar89:3
    Seneca, SG3Sep89:3
    Shawnee, NCG2Sep84:2
    supplied by British, SG12Feb89:2
    support from Canada, SG12Feb89:3
    treaty with, SG12Mar89:2, SG13Aug89:2,
        SG24Sep89:3
    trouble with, SG17Dec89:2

U.S. relations with, SG10Sep89:2, SG17Sep89:4,
    SG24Sep89:2
    war with, WC24Sep88:2, SG29Jan89:2,
    WC5Mar89:2
Indigo, NCGH6Oct85:3, WC15Oct88:2
Influenza, epidemic of, SG26Nov89:2
Ingles, John, SG20Aug89:2, SG27Aug89:4,
    SG10Sep89:3, SG24Sep89:3, SG1Oct89:4
Ingles, Mrs., returned as captive by Indians,
    WC5Mar89:2
Ingraham, Dr., WC2Jul88:3
Ingram, Dr., SG30Jul89:3, SG6Aug89:4
Ingram, J., SG3Dec89:2
Ingram, John, FG24Aug89:3, SG10Sep89:3,
    FG14Sep89:4, FG21Sep89:4
Ingrum, Dr., WC18Jun88:3, WC25Jun88:3, WC9Jul88:4
"Inhabitant of Wilmington, An," WC16Jul88:2
Inkpowder, SG13Oct88:4
Innes, James, SG23Feb86:4
Inquisition, Spanish, WC12Feb89:1
Insolvency, SG26Nov89:2
Insolvents, allowances for, SG18Jan87:3
Inspectors of exports, WC8Jan89:3
Insurance, NCGH2Feb86:2
Insurrection, domestic, SG18Dec88:3
Intelligence, WC18Dec88:3
"Intelligencer," SG23Apr89:2
Intemperance, fatal effects of, SG27Oct88:3
Invention, NCG2Sep84:2, WC25Jun88:2,
    SG26Feb89:1,2, SG5Mar89:3, SG7May89:3,
    SG20Aug89:2
Inverness, Scotland, aged pensioner in, SG12Nov89:2
Iredell, ____, WC6Aug88:2
Iredell, James, EI19Dec87:2, SG8Sep88:4—,
    SG27Oct88:1,4, SG3Nov88:3, SG10Nov88:3,
    SG17Nov88:4, WC19Nov88:3, WC26Nov88:3,
    SG4Dec88:4, SG15Jan89:3—, SG9Jul89:3,
    SG23Jul89:3—, FG24Aug89:1
    address of, SG2Apr89:3
    declines election as Edenton town commissioner,
        SG2Apr89:3
Iredell County, N.C., SG17Sep89:3, SG31Dec89:2
Ireland, NCG29Mar86:2
    Attorney General of, WC22Jan89:2
    bankruptcies in, WC15Jan89:2
    convicts of, WC12Feb89:1
    emigration from, NCG2Sep84:3, WC25Jun88:2,
        SG29Oct89:2
    expenses of government in, SG27Aug89:2
    freedom of the press in, NCG29Jul84:2,
        NCG2Sep84:2
    letter from, SG3Sep89:3, SG29Oct89:2
    Lord Chancellor of, WC22Jan89:2
    mail theft in, WC9Jul88:2
    mortgage payments in, SG26Feb89:2
    newspaper extract from, NCG2Sep84:2,
        SG23Jul89:4
    payments of to England, SG26Feb89:2
    peasant in, SG10Dec89:3
    politics in, WC22Jan89:2, SG23Jul89:1
    prices in, SG22Jan89:3, WC29Jan89:2,
        SG17Dec89:1
    rebels in, SG20Aug89:2
    ships in distress from, NCG9Dec84:2
    U.S. exports to, NCG2Sep84:3, SG29Oct89:2
Iron works, encouragement of, SG18Dec88:3,

WC18Dec88:2
Irvine, W., SG3Dec89:2
Irwin, Robert, WC20Aug88:2
Isham, James, SG18Jan87:2
Isle of Wight County, Va., SG2Sep84:4
Italy, SG18Dec88:1
Ives, SG23Feb86:4
Ivey, Curtis, WC20Aug88:2

J

Jack (slave), sale of, SG23Jul89:3, SG6Aug89:4,
    SG13Aug89:4
Jackass, NCG3Nov85:3
Jackson, Capt., SG27Mar88:3
Jackson, Mr., NCGH19Jan86:3
Jackson, William, SG12Jan86:4, NCGH16Feb86:1,
    NCGH23Feb86:4
Jacob (slave), WC22Jan89:3, WC29Jan89:4
Jacob, George, WC24Sep88:2, SG18Dec88:3,
    WC18Dec88:3
Jail, lack of, WC18Jun88:3
Jailbreak, SG16Apr89:2
Jamaica
    Council of, WC22Jan89:1
    favors U.S. trade, NCGH19Jan86:2
    lieutenant governor of, WC22Jan89:2
    politics in, WC15Jan89:2,3
    slave code of, WC15Jan89:2, WC22Jan89:2
    slaves in, SG10Sep89:2
    sugar exports from, WC25Dec88:2
    suspected pirate captured in, SG25Jun89:2
    trade of, SG3Dec89:1
    trade restrictions of, NCGH19Jan86:2
    See also Kingston, Jamaica
Jambo, African prince, story of, SG10Sep89:4
Jameson, John, NCG29Mar86:1
Jamieson, Dr., SG25Dec88:3—
Jamison, David, SG24Sep89:3
Jasper, ____, SG3Dec89:3
Jasper, James, WC20Aug88:2, SG3Sep89:3
Jay, John, NCG19Dec87:3, SG14May89:2
    letter to, WC26Feb89:2
Jefferson, Thomas
    address of, SG10Dec89:2
    letter from, WC26Feb89:2
Jem (slave), SG9Apr89:3, SG16Apr89:3
Jemison, Mr., SG3Dec89:2
Jenness, John, SG9Jul89:3—
Jennett, Capt. Thomas, WC13Aug88:3
Jennins, John, SG22Oct89:3, SG29Oct89:3,
    SG12Nov89:4
Jennings, Thomas, WC13Aug88:3
Jerden, Thomas, NCG19Dec87:4
Jernigan, ____, SG3Dec89:3
Jesuits, reestablishment of, SG26Mar89:1
Jewkes, Charles, WC19Feb89:3, WC26Feb89:1
Jewkes, Charles & Co., WC26Oct88:3—
Jews, collection of money in Charleston, S.C.,
    WC17Sep88:1
Jocelin, A., WC18Jun88:3, WC9Jul88:4, WC19Feb89:3
Jocelin, Amaziah, WC18Dec88:3, WC25Dec88:3,
    WC29Jan89:3, WC5Feb89:3
Joe (slave), NCG29Jul84:2
Johnson, C., SG3Dec89:2

Johnson, Charles, WC20Aug88:2, SG29Jan89:1,
    SG9Jul89:3—, SG27Aug89:3, FG14Sep89:3,
    SG3Dec89:2,4, SG31Dec89:3
Johnson, Dr., predictions of, SG5Feb89:2
Johnson, Jacob, SG3Sep89:3
Johnson, John, WC20Aug88:2
Johnson, Matthew, WC19Nov88:3, WC26Nov88:4,
    WC3Dec88:3
Johnson, Priscilla, WC3Nov88:3, WC26Nov88:4,
    WC3Dec88:3
    See also Hatcher, Priscilla
Johnson, William, NCGH16Feb86:3, NCGH23Feb86:3
Johnston, Capt., FG14Sep89:3
Johnston, Charles, SG7Feb88:3
Johnston, Dr., letter of, SG7Feb88:4
Johnston, Governor, SG7Feb88:3, WC23Jul88:3,
    WC6Aug88:2, SG22Jan89:3
    See also Johnston, Samuel
Johnston, Hezekiah, SG27Mar88:3
Johnston, J., SG3Dec89:2,3
Johnston, James, WC20Aug88:2
Johnston, John, SG27Aug89:3, FG14Sep89:3
Johnston, Matthew, WC19Feb89:3, WC26Feb89:1
Johnston, Robert, NCG6Jan85:1
Johnston, Samuel, NCG19Dec87:4, SG7Feb88:3,
    WC20Aug88:2, SG8Sep88:3, SG20Oct88:3,
    WC5Nov88:2, WC19Nov88:3, SG24Nov88:3,
    WC26Nov88:3, SG15Jan89:3, SG22Jan89:4,
    SG29Jan89:1,3, SG9Jul89:3—, SG27Aug89:3,
    FG14Sep89:3, SG15Oct89:3, SG3Dec89:2,3,
    SG17Dec89:3
    address of, WC26Oct88:3
    address to, SG8Sep88:3, WC17Sep88:3
    to George Washington, FG24Aug89:1
    See also Johnston, Governor
Johnston, T., SG3Dec89:3
Johnston, Thomas, WC20Aug88:2, SG22Sep88:3,
    SG18Dec88:3, WC18Dec88:2, SG3Dec89:3
Johnston, W., SG3Dec89:3
Johnston, William, NCG29Jul84:3, NCGH2Feb86:3
Johnston County, N.C., NCG2Sep84:3, SG29Sep88:3,
    WC26Nov88:3, SG25Dec88:2
    taxes in, SG31Dec89:3
Jones, ____, SG1Oct89:2, SG3Dec89:3
Jones, Abraham, WC20Aug88:2
Jones, Allen, SG27Mar88:3
Jones, B., SG3Dec89:3
Jones, Betsy, WC29Jan89:2
Jones, Cad., NCGH19Jan86:4, NCGH2Feb86:4
Jones, E., WC2Jul88:3, SG3Dec89:3
Jones, Edward, NCG6Jan85:1, WC18Jun88:3,
    WC2Jul88:1,3, WC9Jul88:1,4, WC16Jul88:1,
    WC13Aug88:2, WC20Aug88:3, SG22Sep88:3—,
    SG17Nov88:4, WC26Feb89:3, SG30Jul89:3,
    SG6Aug89:4, SG10Sep89:3, SG3Dec89:3
Jones, Frederick, SG27Mar88:4
Jones, Friley, SG20Oct88:3, SG27Oct88:3
Jones, J. Paul, SG27Aug89:3
Jones, John, WC20Aug88:2, SG9Jul89:3
Jones, John Paul, WC17Sep88:2
Jones, Kilby, NCG6Jan85:1
Jones, Lovick, SG27Mar88:3
Jones, Mr., WC16Jul88:2, WC23Jul88:1, WC6Aug88:2,
    SG3Sep88:3, FG14Sep89:3
Jones, Nathaniel, WC20Aug88:2
Jones, Paul, WC15Oct88:1, WC5Nov88:2,

SG24Nov88:1, SG26Nov89:4, SG3Dec89:1
Jones, R., SG3Dec89:3
Jones, Rowland, WC13Aug88:3
Jones, Thomas, WC13Aug88:3
Jones, W., WC6Aug88:2
Jones, Wm., SG18Jan87:3
Jones, William, NCG6Jan85:1
Jones, Willie, SG7Feb88:3, WC20Aug88:2,
    SG20Oct88:3, SG27Oct88:1, SG1Oct89:2,3,
    SG8Oct89:4, SG15Oct89:4
    criticism of, SG27Oct88:1,2
Jonesborough, SG31Dec89:2
Jones County, N.C., NCG2Sep84:3, SG18Jan87:2,
    NCG15Aug87:3, SG18Dec88:3, WC18Dec88:2,3,
    SG25Dec88:2, SG15Jan89:3—, SG3Sep89:3
Jones & Neale, SG18Jan87:3, SG29Nov87:4,
    SG7Feb88:3
Jonican, ____, SG3Sep89:3
Jordan, James, SG17Dec89:3, SG31Dec89:4
Jordon, William, SG9Apr89:3—
Journeyman, wanted, NCGH6Oct85:4
Judges, N.C.
    act to increase number of, SG12Jan86:1,2
    controversy over, EI19Dec87:2
    decision of, NCG11Jul87:1
Judiciary
    commentary on, SG23Jul89:2
    nature of, SG2Jul89:3
Judiciary bill, SG30Jul89:3
Judson, Beach, SG9Jul89:3—
Juffy, Lois de, NCGH16Feb86:3, NCGH23Feb86:3
Juhan, James, NCG3Nov85:4
Jurors
    appointment of, SG31Dec89:3
    petit, SG25Dec88:3
"Juryman," SG7May89:1
"Juryman, A," EI9Apr88:3, SG27Oct88:1, SG11Jun89:2
Justice, nature of, EI4Jun88:3
Justice of the peace
    definition of misdemeanor of, WC19Nov88:3
    misdemeanor of, SG25Dec88:3

K

Kaign and Attmore, SG27Mar88:4
Kay, Rd., SG9Apr89:3—
Keais, Nathan, WC20Aug88:2
Keaton, Joseph, SG27Aug89:3, FG14Sep89:3
Keddie, James, SG20Oct88:3, SG27Oct88:3
Keddie, William, WC13Aug88:3
Keely, John, WC3Sep88:2
Keith, Robert, NCG29Jul84:2, NCG2Sep84:4
Kellyhan, Bryan, NCG6Jan85:1
Kenan, General, SG18Dec88:2—
Kenan, J., SG3Dec89:3
Kenan, James, WC20Aug88:2
Kenna Theatrical Company, WC18Jun88:3,4,
    WC17Sep88:3, WC24Sep88:2, WC19Nov88:3
Kenna, SG9Apr89:3—
Kennedy, Archibald, WC13Aug88:3
Kennedy, Col., SG11Dec88:3
Kennedy, George, SG7Feb88:3
Kennedy, George W., SG27Mar88:3
Kennedy, Henry, SG20Apr89:3—, SG13Aug88:3
Kenon, Mr., WC13Aug88:3

Kentucky, SG29Sep88:3, SG20Oct88:1,2,
    SG18Dec88:3, SG12Feb89:3, WC5Mar89:2,
    SG16Apr89:1, SG15Oct89:3
    alienation of from U.S., SG23Apr89:2
    convention in, SG29Oct89:3
    description of, WC2Jul88:1
    immigration to, SG26Feb89:3, WC5Mar89:2,
        SG12Nov89:3
    Indian attacks in, WC10Dec88:2, WC5Mar89:2,
        SG24Sep89:3, SG15Oct89:3, SG29Oct89:3
    letter from, SG18Jun89:3
    population of, SG10Sep89:2
    proposed statehood for, WC13Aug88:1
    report from, WC10Dec88:2
    sentiment for independence of, WC12Feb89:1,
        SG26Feb89:3, SG16Apr89:1
    separation from Virginia sought, SG29Oct89:3
    settlements of, SG27Mar88:4
    Spanish involvement in, SG26Feb89:3
    trade of with New Orleans, SG18Jun89:3
    volunteers from to fight Indians, SG24Sep89:3
Kentucky Gazette, extract from, SG16Apr89:1
Kenyan, General, SG17Sep89:3
Kenyon, James, SG22Sep88:3
Kerr, Archibald, NCG6Jan85:1
Kerr, Nath. John, SG27Mar88:3
Keys, James H., SG15Jan89:3, SG22Jan89:4,
    SG5Feb89:4, SG12Feb89:4, SG26Feb89:3,
    SG12Mar89:4
Kidd, ____, NCG3Nov85:2
Kidd, Joseph, SG2Sep84:4
Killester (slave), ran away, WC26Feb89:3, WC5Mar89:1
Kinchen, John, SG7Feb88:3, WC19Nov88:3,
    SG4Dec88:3
Kinchen, William, WC26Nov88:3
Kindal, William, WC20Aug88:2
Kindale, Mr., FG14Sep89:3
King, ____, SG3Dec89:3
King, James, SG6Jul86:4
King, John, SG20Oct88:3, SG27Oct88:3
King, Major, SG11Dec88:3
King, Myles, SG20Oct88:3, SG27Oct88:3
King, Thomas, WC20Aug88:2, SG29Jan89:3—
    death of, SG26Mar89:3
King, W., SG3Dec89:3
King, William, SG22Sep88:3, SG17Sep89:3
Kingsbury, J., WC10Sep88:3—
Kingsbury, John, WC26Feb89:3, WC5Mar89:1
Kingsbury, Major, WC20Aug88:3, WC27Aug88:3,
    WC10Dec88:3
Kingston, Jamaica
    death of David Douglass in, SG22Oct89:2
    hurricane in, WC10Sep88:2
    news from, NCGH16Feb86:2,3, SG7Feb88:2,
        WC25Jun88:2, WC27Aug88:3, WC10Sep88:2,
        SG29Sep88:2, SG20Oct88:2, WC8Jan89:4,
        WC15Jan89:2, WC22Jan89:2, SG28May89:3,
        SG25Jun89:2, SG10Sep89:1,2, SG8Oct89:2,
        SG22Oct89:2, SG3Dec89:1,2
    proceedings of court of vice admiralty in,
        SG3Dec89:1,2
    reception in for Prince William Henry, WC8Jan89:4
    royal navy in, WC10Sep88:2
    ship in destroyed, SG20Oct88:2
    shipping of, WC8Jan89:4, SG25Jun89:2,
        SG8Oct89:2

Kinnard, Michael, SG20Oct88:3, SG27Oct88:3
Kinston (Kingston), N.C., SG23Feb86:3,
    NCG29Mar86:1, SG6Jul86:3, 4, SG4Oct87:4,
    NCG19Dec87:4, SG17Dec89:2
    celebration in of anniversary of independence,
    SG6Jul86:3
Kirby, Hezekiah, SG9Jul89:3—
Kirk, Isaac, SG27Mar88:3
Kirk, Lewis, NCGH6Oct85:4
Knight, Peter, SG4Oct87:4
Knitting, WC5Nov88:2
Knowls, John, SG29Mar88:3
Knox, Ambrose, SG20Oct88:3, SG27Oct88:3,
    SG22Oct89:3, SG29Oct89:3, SG12Nov89:4,
    SG10Dec89:3, SG31Dec89:3
Knox, Andrew, SG17Dec89:4
Knox, General, seeks vice-presidency, SG10Nov88:3
Knox, Hugh, SG22Oct89:3, SG29Oct89:3,
    SG12Nov89:4
Knox, John, SG18Jan87:3
Knyphausen, Baron, death of, SG12Nov89:3
Kock, H. I., SG4Dec88:3
Kock, Hans I., SG11Dec88:3, SG18Dec88:3
Kock, Capt., SG25Dec88:3, SG8Jan89:3, SG15Jan89:4
Kocke, Capt., SG18Jun89:3—, SG9Jul89:3,4,
    SG16Jul89:4, SG23Jul89:4
Kowles, Phillip, NCG19Dec87:4
Kuhn, Daniel, SG27Mar88:3

L

Labrador, description of, WC8Jan89:1
Lacy, Thaddew, SG27Mar88:3
Ladner, George, EI4Jun88:3
Lady, epitaph of, SG29Nov87:4
Lady, English, seeks to entertain elderly gentlemen,
    SG22Jan89:2
LaFayette, Marquis, de, NCG2Sep84:2, SG13Oct88:2,
    SG17Nov88:1, WC19Nov88:2, SG8Oct89:2,
    SG5Nov89:2,3, SG10Dec89:1
    circular letter of, SG22Oct89:1,2
    destined for America, NCG2Sep84:2
Lake Ontario, letter from, WC12Feb89:1
Lalanna, Jack, SG27Mar88:3
Lallerstedt, FG12Oct89:4
Lambert, John, NCG29Jul84:3
Lamment, Thomas, NCG6Jan85:1
Lamond, William, NCG6Jan85:1
Lancaster, ____, SG24Sep89:3
Lancaster, John, NCG29Mar86:2
Lancaster, William, SG8Jan87:3, WC20Aug88:2
Land
    conveyance of, WC18Dec88:3
    exchange of, SG18Jan87:4
    lease of, NCG29Jul84:3
    recording transactions of, WC18Dec88:2
    relief for those in N.C. not registering or proving
        titles, WC18Dec88:3
    sale of, NCG29Jul84:3, NCG2Sep84:4,
        NCG9Dec84:4, NCGH6Oct85:4,
        NCG3Nov85:1,2, SG12Jan86:4,
        NCGH19Jan86:4, NCGH2Feb86:2,3,4,
        NCGH16Feb86:1,3,4, NCGH23Feb86:1,4,
        SG23Feb86:2,3,4, SG6Jul86:3, NCG15Aug87:4,
        SG7Feb88:3,4, SG27Mar88:4, WC18Jun88:1,
        WC2Jul88:3, WC9Jul88:3, WC23Jul88:3,4—,
        WC3Sep88:3, WC15Oct88:2—, SG15Jan89:3,
        WC29Jan89:3, WC5Feb89:3,4, SG2Apr89:4—,
        SG30Jul89:3, SG20Aug89:3, SG27Aug89:4,
        SG10Sep89:3, SG24Sep89:3, SG10Oct89:4
    settlement of disputes over, SG18Jan87:2
Land Office, SG23Feb86:1
Land Warrants, military, SG16Apr89:4
Lane, Col., SG17Sep89:3
Lane, H., SG3Dec89:3
Lane, Henry, SG17Sep89:3
Lane, Ja., SG3Dec89:3
Lane, Joel, WC20Aug88:2, SG29Sep88:3
Lane, John, WC20Aug88:2, SG9Jul89:3—
Lang, William, SG22Oct89:3, SG29Oct89:3,
    SG12Nov89:4
Lanier, Lewis, WC20Aug88:2
Lanier, Thomas, SG10Nov88:3
Lankester, Henry, SG20Oct88:3, SG27Oct88:3
Lankester, Henry & Co., SG9Apr89:3—
Lansingburgh, N.Y., news from, SG30Apr89:3
Lard, Capt., WC25Dec88:3
Laroque, Dr., SG9Jul89:3—
Lasiter, Jesse, SG23Feb86:2
Lasseter, ____, SG3Dec89:3
Lassiter, Nathan, SG3Sep89:3
Laths, sale of, WC3Sep88:3, WC10Sep88:4
Latimer, Capt., WC25Dec88:3
Latimore, Samuel, SG29Jan89:3—
Latin grammars, sale of, NCG9Dec84:4
Lavender, John, SG27Mar88:3
Lawrence, Doctor, SG20Oct88:3, SG27Oct88:3
Laws, N.C.
    proposal to print, SG6Oct88:4—
    subscriptions solicited for printing of, SG8Sep88:4—
Laws, William, NCG29Jul84:3
Lawson, Elizabeth, leaves husband, NCG2Sep84:4
Lawson, William, NCG2Sep84:4
Lawyers, NCGH16Feb86:2, SG13Aug89:3
Laymeur, Dr., NCGH19Jan86:4, NCGH2Feb86:4,
    NCGH16Feb86:4
Leach, B., WC10Sep88:1
Leach, J., SG3Dec89:3
Learning, promotion of, SG18Jan87:2, SG18Dec88:3,
    WC18Dec88:3
    See also Academy; Education
Leather goods, WC26Oct88:3, WC5Nov88:3
Leavens, Vine, SG20Oct88:3, SG27Oct88:3
Lectures, WC26Oct88:3, WC26Feb89:3, SG2Jul89:2
Ledbetter, George, WC20Aug88:2
Ledyard, John
    death of, SG6Aug89:4
    letter from, SG15Jan89:1
Lee, Daniel, SG27Mar88:3
Lee, James, SG4Dec88:3—
Leech, Joseph, NCG29Jul84:2, WC20Aug88:2,
    SG20Oct88:3, SG3Sep89:3
Leech, Mary, SG20Oct88:3
Leek, John, SG24Sep89:3
Leeward Islands, sugar exports from, WC25Dec88:2
Legett, David, SG6Jul86:3
Leggett, John, NCG29Mar86:2
Leghorn
    letter from, NCG2Sep84:2
    news from, NCGH23Feb86:2, EI4Jun88:2

Leigh, Elizabeth, SG3Dec89:3
Lemburg, letter from, SG3Nov88:2, WC5Nov88:2
Lenoir, ____, SG3Dec89:3
Lenoir, Col., FG14Sep89:3
Lenoir, William, WC20Aug88:2, SG17Dec89:3,
    SG31Dec89:3
Lenore, Col., WC10Dec88:3
Lenox, Robert, SG9Jul89:3—
Lent, Henry, SG18Jan87:3
Leonard, SG3Dec89:3
Leonard, J., WC27Aug88:3, WC10Sep88:4
Leonard, Jacob, WC20Aug88:2—, SG10Sep89:3
Leonard, James, SG27Mar88:3, WC27Aug88:3,
    WC3Sep88:4
Leonard, John, WC27Aug88:3
Leonard, Mr., WC10Sep88:3
LeRoy, Herman, SG27Mar88:3
Letter, love, WC2Jul88:4
Levi, Mr., SG29Nov87:4
Leviston, John, WC13Aug88:3
Levy, E., WC3Sep88:3, WC10Sep88:4
Lewes
    letter from, SG1Oct89:2,3
    storm in, SG1Oct89:2,3
Lewis, Howell, Jr., WC20Aug88:2
Lewis, Luke, SG29Nov87:1
Lewis, R., SG3Dec89:2,3
Lewis, W. J., WC26Nov88:3
Lewis, W. T., SG29Sep88:3
Lexington, Ky.
    celebration of anniversary of independence in,
      SG29Sep88:3
    news from, SG12Nov89:2
Lexington, Mass., Washington in, SG17Dec89:2
Libels, SG28May89:3
Life, views on, WC9Jul88:1
Lightfoot, Henry, SG17Dec89:3
Lightfoot, W., SG12Jan86:3
Lighthouse, SG24Sep89:2
    Charleston, S.C., harbor, WC22Jan89:3
Lighthouses, Beacons, Buoys, and Public Piers,
    SG10Sep89:4
Lightning
    death by, SG6Aug89:3, SG27Aug89:3
    effects of, NCG11Jul87:4, SG3Sep89:1
Lillibridge, Joseph, SG18Jan87:3, SG27Mar88:3
Limuel, Isabella, account of, WC9Jul88:1
Lincoln County, N.C., WC17Sep88:3, SG29Sep88:3,
    WC26Nov88:3, SG25Dec88:2, SG24Sep89:3
Lindley, ____, SG3Dec89:3
Lindley, J., SG17Sep89:3
Lindley, Jonathan, SG22Sep88:3
Lindsay, Mrs., NCG6Jan85:1
Linen
    manufacture of, WC5Nov88:2, WC19Nov88:3
    sale of, WC19Feb89:3
Linley, ____, SG3Dec89:3
Linley, Jonathan, WC20Aug88:2
Linley, Mr., SG3Dec89:3
Linton, James, SG26Mar89:3—
Linton, Lazarus, SG26Mar89:3—
Lisbon
    letter from, NCG29Jul84:2, SG6Oct88:3,
      SG11Dec88:3, SG28May89:3
    news from, NCG29Jul84:1, NCG9Dec84:3,
      WC15Oct88:1

Litchfield, Conn., SG26Mar89:2
    attempted robbery in, SG2Jul89:3
    jailbreak in, SG26Mar89:2
Literature, American, promotion of, SG13Oct88:2
Little, George, SG22Oct88:3, SG27Oct88:3,
    SG12Nov88:4
Little, W., WC20Aug88:2
Little, William, NCGH2Feb86:3, NCGH16Feb86:3,
    NCGH23Feb86:3
Littlejohn, Joseph, SG10Nov88:3
Littlejohn, Mr., SG23Apr89:3
Littlejohn, Thomas, SG10Nov88:3
Littlejohn, William, SG30Apr89:3—, SG24Dec89:3,
    SG31Dec89:3
Little River, S.C., WC12Nov88:4, WC10Dec88:3—
Liverpool
    exports to N.C. from, SG27Oct88:3—, SG3Nov88:4
    letter from, WC26Oct88:2,3, SG27Oct88:2,
      SG30Apr89:3
    newspaper of, SG4Dec88:4
Livingston, Samuel, SG18Jan87:3
Livingston, Susannah, death of, SG20Aug89:2
Lloyd, Roderick, SG9Apr89:3
Lock, ____, SG3Dec89:3
Lock, Gen., WC6Aug88:3, WC17Sep88:3,
    SG29Sep88:3, WC10Dec88:3,
    SG17Sep89:3,SG3Dec89:3
Lock, Mathew, WC20Aug88:2
Lock, Mr., SG3Dec89:4
Lockhart, Mrs., SG12Jan86:4
Locksmith
    See Gunsmith and Locksmith
Lockwood's Folly, WC10Sep88:3
Loftin, W., WC20Aug88:2
London
    accident in, SG19Nov89:1
    amphitheater in, SG20Aug89:1
    auction in, SG23Feb86:3
    bequest of wealthy widow of, SG10Nov88:2
    bet on horse in, WC3Sep88:1
    buildings in, NCGH19Jan86:2
    celebration of recovery of George III, SG30Jul89:2
    construction in, NCGH19Jan86:4
    deaths in, SG9Apr89:3
    fall of stock prices in, SG30Apr89:2
    false report of death in, WC3Sep88:1
    letter from, NCGH19Jan86:2, NCGH23Feb86:2,
      SG27Mar88:3, WC9Jul88:2, SG22Sep88:1,2,
      WC24Sep88:2, SG29Sep88:2, SG17Nov88:3,
      SG5Feb89:2, WC5Feb89:2, WC19Feb89:1,
      SG7May89:3, SG4Jun89:1,2, SG6Aug89:3,
      SG20Aug89:2, FG24Aug89:2, SG3Sep89:3,
      SG8Oct89:2
    life in, WC10Sep88:2, SG11Dec88:3
    marriage in, SG11Dec88:3
    mosque for, SG20Oct88:2
    news from, NCG29Jul84:2, NCG2Sep84:2,
      NCG9Dec84:3,4, NCG3Nov85:3,
      NCGH19Jan86:1,2, NCGH2Feb86:2,
      NCGH16Feb86:2, NCGH23Feb86:2,
      SG23Feb86:2, NCG29Mar86:2, SG6Jul86:2,
      EI19Dec87:2, SG7Feb88:1, WC18Jun88:2,
      WC25Jun88:2, WC2Jul88:2, WC9Jul88:2,
      WC30Jul88:2, WC13Aug88:1, WC3Sep88:1,
      SG8Sep88:1, WC10Sep88:2, SG15Sep88:1,
      SG22Sep88:1, WC24Sep88:1,2, SG6Oct88:1,2,

WC15Oct88:1, SG20Oct88:1,2, WC26Oct88:2,
SG27Oct88:2, SG3Nov88:2, WC5Nov88:2,
SG10Nov88:1,2, WC12Nov88:2, SG17Nov88:2,
WC19Nov88:1,2, SG24Nov88:1,2,
WC26Nov88:1,2, WC3Dec88:2, SG4Dec88:1,2,
WC10Dec88:2, SG11Dec88:1,2, WC18Dec88:2,
SG25Dec88:1,2, WC25Dec88:2,3,
SG8Jan89:2,3, WC8Jan89:2, SG15Jan89:1,
WC15Jan89:2, SG22Jan89:2,3, WC22Jan89:2,
WC29Jan89:2, WC5Feb89:1,2, SG12Feb89:2,
WC12Feb89:2, SG19Feb89:1,2, WC19Feb89:2,
SG26Feb89:1,2, WC26Feb89:2, SG5Mar89:2,
WC5Mar89:2, SG12Mar89:1,2, SG26Mar89:1,2,
SG2Apr89:1, SG16Apr89:1,2, SG30Apr89:2,
SG7May89:2, SG14May89:1, SG28May89:2,
SG18Jun89:1,2, SG25Jun89:2, SG16Jul89:1,2,
SG23Jul89:1, SG30Jul89:1,2, SG20Aug89:1,
FG24Aug89:2, SG27Aug89:1,2, SG3Sep89:2,
SG10Sep89:1, FG14Sep89:2, SG17Sep89:1,
SG24Sep89:2, SG1Oct89:1, SG8Oct89:1,2,
FG12Oct89:3, SG15Oct89:1,2, SG22Oct89:1,2,
SG29Oct89:1,2, SG5Nov89:1,2, SG12Nov89:2,
SG19Nov89:1,2, SG26Nov89:1, SG3Dec89:1,
SG10Dec89:1, SG17Dec89:1, SG24Dec89:1
newspaper advertisement of, NCG23Feb86:3
newspaper extract from, NCGH2Feb86:1,
SG29Nov87:3, WC16Jul88:1, WC18Dec88:3,
WC22Jan89:1, SG26Feb89:1, SG19Mar89:1,2,
SG26Mar89:4, SG9Apr89:3, SG30Apr89:1,
SG14May89:1, SG6Aug89:4, SG8Oct89:4,
SG20Oct88:2
prosperity of, SG3Sep89:3
royal religious procession in, SG23Jul89:1
shipping of, SG8Oct89:2
society of, SG8Sep88:2
sugar imported into, WC25Dec88:2
view of U.S. government, SG7May89:3
London (slave), ran away, FG12Oct89:4
London, John, WC16Jul88:3
London Gazette, extract from, WC26Oct88:1,
SG8Oct89:3
London General Advertiser, extract from,
NCGH6Oct85:1,2,3
London Review, extract from, SG22Jan89:1,2
Londonderry, news from, SG2Jul89:2
Long, ____, SG24Sep89:3
Long, James, SG31Dec89:3
Long, Lumford, SG11Dec88:3—, SG17Dec89:3
Long, Nicholas, Sr., SG11Dec88:3—
Longhead, James, SG7Feb88:3
Longhead, Robert and James (partnership), SG7Feb88:3
Long Island, on Holston, NCG11Jul87:2
Looms, NCGH19Jan86:3, NCGH2Feb86:3
Looney, David, WC20Aug88:2
Lord, W., SG3Dec89:3
Lord, William, SG10Sep89:3
Lord Lieutenant of Ireland, death of, SG7Feb88:1
L'Orient
letter from, NCG3Nov85:3, WC13Aug88:2,
SG6Oct88:3
news from, SG24Dec89:3, SG31Dec89:1
Lorimer, James, death of, SG15Oct89:3
Lots
exchange of, SG18Jan87:3
rent of, WC12Nov88:3, WC19Nov88:4,
SG4Dec88:3, SG11Dec88:4

sale of, SG12Jan86:3,4, SG23Feb86:2, SG6Jul86:3,
SG15Sep88:4, WC19Nov88:3, SG4Dec88:3—,
SG15Jan89:3, SG22Jan89:4, WC29Jan89:3,
WC5Feb89:3,4, WC19Feb89:3, WC26Feb89:3,
SG30Apr89:3—, SG25Jun89:3—,
SG30Jul89:3—
Lottery, WC29Jan89:2, FG24Aug89:3, FG14Sep89:4,
FG21Sep89:4
Loudon, John, SG22Oct89:2
Loudon, Lydia, death of in Conn., WC25Jun88:2
Loudon, Samuel, WC25Jun88:2
Louis XVI
birthday celebration of, SG12Nov89:1
declaration by, SG5Nov89:3
letter of, SG3Sep89:2, SG15Oct89:4,
SG22Oct89:1,3
possible attempted assassination of, WC3Sep88:1
speech of, SG20Aug89:1, SG22Oct89:2
Louisburg, N.C., NCG15Aug87:4, NCG19Dec87:4
Louisville, Ky., letter from, SG26Mar89:2,
SG24Sep89:3, SG29Oct89:3
Love, poetry extolling, SG4Oct87:4
Love, ____, SG3Dec89:3
Love letter, WC25Jun88:1, WC2Jul88:4
Lovell, ____, SG3Dec89:3
Lovell, Edward, SG24Sep89:3
Lovick, ____, NCG19Dec87:4
Lovick, John, NCGH16Feb86:3, NCGH23Feb86:3,
SG23Feb86:3
Loyalists, NCG9Dec84:2, NCGH16Feb86:2,3,
SG23Feb86:1,2, SG22Sep88:1, WC26Oct88:1,
SG7May89:3, SG18Jun89:3, SG27Aug89:3
address of agents of, SG20Oct88:1
British commissioner for, SG27Aug89:3
British consideration of, SG22Sep88:1,2
claims of, NCGH23Feb86:2
return of, SG12Jan86:2, SG18Jun89:3
Low, Thos., SG27Mar88:3
Lowder, Samuel, WC5Feb89:3—
Lowendall, Count, execution of, SG10Dec89:2
Lowrey, John, FG21Sep89:2
Lowther, William, SG2Jul89:3, SG23Jul89:4
Lowthrop, Francis, NCG3Nov85:2, SG7Feb88:4,
SG27Mar88:3
Lucas, George, NCGH6Oct85:4, WC20Aug88:2,
SG17Sep89:3
Lucas, Mr., WC13Aug88:3
Lucas, Sarah, SG22Jan89:3
Lumberton, N.C., establishment of,
WC18Dec88:3
Lunenburg Court House, Va., SG2Jul89:3
Lutterloh, ____, FG24Aug89:3
Lutterloh, Henry, SG10Sep89:3
Lutterlow, Henry, WC13Aug88:3
Luzerne, Chevalier de la, NCG29Jul84:2
Lyk, Archibald, NCG6Jan85:1
Lynn, Mass., manufacturing in, WC10Sep88:2
Lyon, John, SG23Feb86:2, WC16Jul88:3—,
WC5Feb89:3
Lyon, Mrs., WC25Jun88:3—
Lyons, David, NCG6Jan85:1
Lyons, Dr., anecdote of, WC16Jul88:4
Lytle, A., SG23Feb86:2
Lytle, Archibald, NCGH2Feb86:3, NCGH16Feb86:3,
NCGH23Feb86:3, SG23Feb86:3
Lytle, Hezekiah, SG31Dec89:3

Lytle, John, SG31Dec89:3
Lytle, Nancy, SG31Dec89:3
Lytle, Sarah, SG31Dec89:3

M

Mabson, William, WC13Aug88:3
McAllester, Alexander, SG10Sep89:3
McAllister, ____, FG24Aug89:3
McAllister, A., SG22Sep88:3
McAllister, Alexander, WC20Aug88:2
McAllister, John, WC20Aug88:2
McAlphine, James, SG20Oct88:3, SG27Oct88:3
McAnnelly, Charles, WC20Aug88:2
McArthur, Alexander, NCG6Jan85:1
McArthur, Neil, NCG29Mar86:2
MacBeth, WC19Nov88:3
McBryde, William, SG9Apr89:3—
McCabe, B., SG8Jan89:3—
McCann, James, SG20Oct88:3, SG27Oct88:3
McCarty, Florence, SG9Jul89:3—
McCauley, W., SG10Dec89:3
McCauley, William, WC20Aug88:2
McCauslan
    See Ewans and McCauslan
McCauslan, Alexander, NCG29Mar86:2, SG27Mar88:3
McCauslan, Duncan, FG24Aug89:3, FG14Sep89:4,
    FG21Sep89:4
McCawley, William, SG22Sep88:3
McCay, Alexander, NCG29Mar86:2
McComb, Joseph, SG22Oct89:3, SG29Oct89:3,
    SG12Nov89:4
McCommack, Mr., WC13Aug88:3
McCord, James, SG27Mar88:3
McCormack, William, NCG29Mar86:2
McCormick, Hugh, WC13Aug88:3
McCoy, Alexander, NCG29Mar86:2
McCoy, John, SG22Sep88:3
M'Claine, Joseph, SG9Jul89:3—
McClellan, George, SG20Oct88:3, SG27Oct88:3
McClellan, William, NCG29Mar86:2
McClish, John, NCG3Nov85:4
McCloud, John, NCG29Mar86:2
McClure, Dr., NCG29Jul84:3,4
McClure, John, NCG29Jul84:3
McClure, William, NCG29Jul84:3, NCG3Nov85:4
McCulloch, ____, WC18Jun88:3
McCulloch, B., SG12Jan86:2
McCulloch, Benjamin, SG23Feb86:4
McCulloch, Charles, SG23Feb86:3
McCulloch, Henry, SG29Mar86:2
McCulloch, H. E., NCGH23Feb86:3
McCulloch, Henry Eustace, NCGH2Feb86:3,4,
    NCGH16Feb86:3, SG23Feb86:3, NCG29Mar86:2
McCulloch, M., WC30Jul88:3
McCulloch, Michael, SG23Feb86:3
McCulloch, Mr., WC20Aug88:2, WC27Aug88:4—
McCulloch, Robert, NCGH2Feb86:3,
    NCGH16Feb86:3, NCGH23Feb86:3, SG23Feb86:3
McCulloch, Thomas, NCGH2Feb86:3,
    NCGH16Feb86:3, NCGH23Feb86:3, SG23Feb86:3
McDonald, ____, SG27Oct88:3
McDonald, John, SG9Jul89:3—, SG19Nov89:3,
    SG26Nov89:4
McDonald, William, SG13Oct88:3

McDonnell, John, SG6Jul86:3
M'Dougall, James, SG22Oct89:3, SG29Oct89:3,
    SG12Nov89:4
MacDougall, Rev. James, SG1Oct89:3
MacDougall, Rev. Samuel, SG8Oct89:4—,
    SG26Nov89:3
McDowal, Charles, WC20Aug88:2
McDowal, Joseph, WC20Aug88:2
McDowal, Joseph, Jr., WC20Aug88:2
McDowall, ____, SG3Dec89:3
McDowall, Gen., SG18Dec88:2—
McDowel, Joseph, WC10Dec88:3, SG17Dec89:3
McDowell, C., SG3Dec89:2
McDowell, J., SG3Dec89:3
McDowell, J., Jr., SG3Dec89:2
McDowell, John, SG6Jul86:3
McDowell, Joseph, SG7Feb88:3, SG17Dec89:3
McDowell, Mr., SG17Dec89:3
M'Dugal, Randal, SG6Jul86:3
M'Echran, Robert, SG22Oct89:3, SG29Oct89:3,
    SG12Nov89:4
M'Entire, Robert, NCGH2Feb86:2, NCGH16Feb86:4,
    NCGH23Feb86:4
McFarland, D., SG3Dec89:3
McFarland, Duncan, SG24Sep89:3
McFarland, Robert, WC13Aug88:3
McFarlane, John, WC13Aug88:3
M'Geachy, Neil, WC2Jul88:3
McGee, John, WC18Dec88:3
McGhee, Martha, NCG6Jan85:1
McGillivray (McGillivring; MacGilivery, McGilvray),
    ____, WC18Jun88:3, SG12Feb89:1,3, SG5Mar89:3,
    SG30Apr89:3, SG24Sep89:3, SG15Oct89:3,
    SG12Nov89:3
McGillivring (McGillivring, MacGilvery), Alexander,
    SG11Dec88:3, WC22Jan89:3, SG26Mar89:2,
    SG12Nov89:3
    letter from, SG27Oct88:3, WC5Mar89:2,
    SG30Jul89:2,3
    Spanish attention to, SG26Mar89:2
McGillivray, Mr., SG22Jan89:2,3, SG3Dec89:2
McGinnes, Charles, SG20Oct88:3, SG27Oct88:3
McGrath, Christopher, SG20Oct88:3, SG27Oct88:3
MacIntire, Donald, SG24Sep89:3
McIntosh, ____, SG3Dec89:3
McIver, Alexander, WC12Nov88:3—
McKay, ____, SG3Dec89:3
McKay, Donald, WC13Aug88:3
McKay, John, SG10Sep89:3
McKay, Margaret, WC2Jul88:3
McKeel, Michael, SG19Mar89:3—
McKellar, John, NCG6Jan85:1
McKenna, Charles, death of, WC29Jan89:2
McKennie, Richard, WC20Aug88:2
McKenzie, Andrew, WC13Aug88:3
Mackenzie, John, WC8Jan89:3
McKenzie, Mr., WC16Jul88:2, WC23Jul88:1,
    WC3Sep88:3
Mackenzie, William, WC20Aug88:2
McKernan, Charles, WC12Feb89:3—
McKetrick, ____, SG12Jan86:4
Mackee, Wm., SG18Jan87:3
Mackey, Enoch, SG9Jul89:3—
M'Kinlay, James, SG18Jan87:4
McKinnan, Fingal, WC13Aug88:3
McKinnie, ____, SG3Dec89:3

Macknight, Thomas, NCG29Mar86:2
M'Lane, Dr., WC17Sep88:3, SG29Sep88:3
McLane, Dr. William, SG24Sep89:3
Maclaine, ____, NCG9Dec84:2, WC6Aug88:2
Maclaine, A., SG23Feb86:2, WC18Jun88:3,4,
  WC25Jun88:3,4, WC2Jul88:3—, WC9Jul88:3,4,
  WC16Jul88:2,3, WC23Jul88:1, WC30Jul88:1,
  WC6Aug88:2,3, WC13Aug88:2,4, WC20Aug88:3,4,
  WC27Aug88:4, WC3Sep88:3,4, WC5Feb89:3
Maclaine, Arch., SG27Mar88:4
Maclaine, Archibald, SG27Mar88:4, WC25Jun88:3,
  WC2Jul88:3,4, WC30Jul88:4—
Maclaine, Thomas, WC2Jul88:2
Maclaine, William, WC20Aug88:2
McLaren, John, WC20Aug88:3, SG11Jun89:3
Maclean, ____, SG3Dec89:3
Maclean, W., SG3Dec89:3
McLeod, ____, SG3Dec89:3
MacLeod, Neil, SG24Sep89:3
M'Mains, James, SG6Jul86:4
McMorine, Charles, SG9Jul89:3—
M'Murphey, Daniel, WC6Aug88:3
McMurphey, James, WC13Aug88:3
McNair, ____, NCG29Mar86:2
McNair, John, NCG29Mar86:2, SG20Oct88:3,
  SG27Oct88:3
Macnaughton, A., WC2Jul88:3, WC20Aug88:2
McNeal, Donald, WC13Aug88:3
McNeale, James, NCG6Jan85:1
McNeil, Dan., NCG6Jan85:1
McNeil, James, NCG29Mar86:2
MacPherson, L., WC19Feb89:3, WC26Feb89:1
M'Pherson, Lewis, WC27Aug88:3—
MacRa, John, SG22Oct89:3, SG29Oct89:3,
  SG12Nov89:4
M'Ree, Griffith John, SG6Jul86:3
McRony, John, SG18Jan87:3
McTear, James, SG20Oct88:3, SG27Oct88:3
McVerrick, William, WC13Aug88:3
Machen, H., SG18Jan87:3, NCG19Dec87:4,
  SG27Mar88:3, SG26Feb89:3
Machin, Henry, SG12Jan86:3, SG8Sep88:4—,
  SG17Nov88:4, SG3Sep89:3
Macon, J., SG12Jan86:2
Macon, John, WC20Aug88:2, SG24Sep89:3
Macon, Mr., WC20Aug88:2
Mad dog, SG18Dec88:3
Madagascar, NCG9Dec84:4
Maddison, J., SG23Feb86:4
Madison, James, Jun., views of federal Constitution,
  SG23Apr89:1,2
Madras
  letter from, SG11Jun89:3
  news from, SG2Jul89:2
Madrid, SG30Apr89:2
  commercial houses in, NCG9Dec84:3
  news from, SG24Nov88:1
Magazine, selections from, SG10Nov88:4
Magee, John, SG18Dec88:3
Mahogany, SG18Dec88:3
Mahon, John, SG18Jan87:3
Mail, NCGH19Jan86:4, NCGH2Feb86:3, WC23Jul88:3,
  WC30Jul88:3, WC5Feb89:2, WC12Feb89:1,
  WC26Feb89:1, WC5Mar89:1
  route of, NCG29Mar86:1, NCG19Dec87:4
  schedule of, SG6Jul86:4

supposed theft of, WC8Jan89:3
  theft of, WC18Jun88:3, WC25Jun88:3,
    SG25Dec88:3, WC25Dec88:3
  See also Post; Stage
Mairs, William, SG22Sep88:3
Mallery, John, NCG2Sep84:4
Mallet
  See Mumford and Mallett
Mallet, Peter, WC16Jul88:3—, WC12Nov88:3,
  WC19Nov88:3
Mallet, Samuel, WC13Aug88:3
Malta, NCG2Sep84:2
Mangeon, P. & Co., WC5Feb89:3
Mankind, essay on, WC16Jul88:1
Manufactory
  cotton, financial report on, WC15Jan89:1,2
  paper, FG14Sep89:3
  wheat, SG9Jul89:3—, SG20Aug89:4, SG24Sep89:4
Manufacturing, WC10Sep88:2, WC24Sep88:2,
  WC5Nov88:2, WC19Nov88:3, SG29Jan89:2,
  WC12Feb89:1, SG19Mar89:2,3, SG2Apr89:3,
  SG21May89:3, SG10Sep89:2, FG21Sep89:2
  Boston, SG26Nov89:3
  Conn., SG23Apr89:3
  Great Britain, SG26Feb89:2
  invention for, SG5Mar89:3
  Mass., SG16Apr89:2
  N.C., SG9Jul89:3
  Philadelphia, WC29Jan89:2
  promotion of, SG11Jun89:1,4
  U.S., WC13Aug88:1, WC10Sep88:2,
    WC17Sep88:1, SG12Feb89:3—, SG16Jul89:3,
    SG10Sep89:1, FG21Sep89:2
  Worcester, SG19Mar89:2
Maps
  North American, sale of, SG8Jan89:1, SG15Jan89:3,
    SG29Jan89:4, SG5Feb89:3, SG26Feb89:3,
    SG5Mar89:3, SG26Mar89:3
  U.S., sale of, SG29Nov87:3, SG7Feb88:3
Marblehead, Mass., accident to fishing vessel of,
  SG27Aug89:2
Mare, J., SG7Feb88:3
Mare, John, FG14Sep89:3, SG17Sep89:3, SG6Aug89:3,
  SG13Aug89:3, SG27Aug89:3
Mare, Marion, death of, SG17Sep89:3
Marhouse, Abraham, NCG6Jan85:1
Marietta, Ohio, WC5Nov88:2, SG24Nov88:2,
  SG23Jul89:3, SG3Sep89:2
  ancient ruins in, WC26Nov88:2
  letter from, WC26Nov88:2, SG23Apr89:2
  passage to, SG23Apr89:2
  proposed settlement in, WC5Nov88:2,
    SG10Nov88:2
  report of death near, SG23Jul89:3
Marine List (ship entrances and clearances)
  Edenton, SG29Sep88:3—, SG11Dec88:3,
    SG1Jan89:3, SG22Jan89:3—, SG12Mar89:3,
    SG2Apr89:3—, SG25Jun89:3—, SG8Oct89:3,
    SG29Oct89:3—
  Wilmington, WC16Jul88:3, WC13Aug88:3—,
    WC15Oct88:1, WC26Oct88:3—, WC3Dec88:3,
    WC15Jan89:3
  See also Naval Office
Mariners, notice to, SG29Jan89:2
Market House, Wilmington, WC12Feb89:3—,
  rent of loft of, WC12Feb89:3—

Marnes, ____, SG3Dec89:3
Marns, William S., WC20Aug88:2
Marriage, WC2Jul88:1, WC13Aug88:4, WC27Aug88:4,
    WC3Sep88:4, SG26Mar89:4, SG2Apr89:4,
    SG1Oct89:3, FG12Oct89:4
    breach of promise of, SG6Jul86:2
    commentary on, WC9Jul88:1, SG15Sep88:4
    consideration of, WC26Nov88:1
    "creed" of, WC27Aug88:4
    decline of, WC26Nov88:1
    settlements of, SG23Feb86:2
    plural, SG25Dec88:3
    views on, WC9Jul88:1
    See also Bigamy and polygamy
Marriner, John, SG31Dec89:3
Marshal, Mrs., NCG3Nov85:4
Marshal, William, WC20Aug88:2
Martin, ____, NCG11Jul87:4, NCG1Aug87:4,
    SG22Sep88:2, SG26Feb89:2, WC5Mar89:2
Martin, A., SG1Jan89:4
Martin, Alexander, NCGH19Jan86:3, SG29Nov87:3,
    SG8Sep88:4, SG22Sep88:3—, WC12Nov88:3,
    WC10Dec88:3, SG19Feb89:2, SG9Apr89:3—,
    SG17Dec89:3
Martin, Catharine, WC30Jul88:3
Martin, Col., SG11Dec88:3
    letter from, SG4Dec88:3
Martin, F. X., SG1Jan89:3—, SG27Aug89:4—,
    SG24Sep89:4—
Martin, Francois Xavier, WC18Dec88:3, SG25Dec88:3,
    WC25Dec88:1, WC8Jan89:4—, SG20Aug89:4
Martin, General, SG20Oct88:2
Martin, Governor, NCG6Jan85:1
Martin, J., SG3Dec89:3
Martin, John, NCG29Jul84:4
Martin, Joseph, WC8Jan89:3, SG31Dec89:3
Martin, Josiah, NCG29Mar86:2
Martin, Luther, WC18Jun88:4
Martin, Mons., SG27Mar88:3
Martin, W., SG3Dec89:3
Martin, William, WC20Aug88:2, SG24Sep89:3
Martin County, N.C., EI9Apr88:4, WC26Nov88:3,
    SG25Dec88:2, SG9Apr89:3, SG3Sep89:3
Martin & Co., SG6Jul86:4
Martinborough, N.C., SG18Jan87:2
Martinico, WC26Nov88:3, WC10Dec88:3
    foreign shipping regulation by, WC15Oct88:1
    hurricane in, SG13Oct88:3, WC26Oct88:1,2
    letter from, WC15Oct88:1, SG27Oct88:2
    N.C. imports from, WC3Sep88:3
    regulation of foreign trade of, WC15Oct88:1,
        SG27Oct88:2,3
    slave insurrection in, SG29Oct89:2,3
    U.S. trade with, SG13Oct88:3
Martinique
    alliance of with U.S., SG17Dec89:2
    murderers executed in, SG20Oct88:2,3
    N.C. debt to, SG17Dec89:3
    regulation of importations of, SG26Feb89:4
    Roman Catholicism in, SG5Feb89:2
    support for French Revolution in, SG17Dec89:2
Martinsburgh, N.C., NCG29Mar86:1, SG18Jan87:2
Marue, Monsieur, SG20Oct88:3, SG27Oct88:3
Mary, Queen of Scots, SG2Apr89:2
    life of, SG27Oct88:2
Maryland, SG29Nov87:4

chancery court proceedings in, SG29Nov87:4
description of, SG28May89:4
elections in, SG12Feb89:3
electors of chosen, SG12Feb89:3
politics in, SG18Dec88:3, SG25Dec88:3
shipping of, EI4Jun88:2, WC16Jul88:3,
    WC24Sep88:1
Maryland Journal, extract from, SG1Jan89:3,
    SG23Apr89:1,2
Mason, Abraham, SG27Mar88:3
Mason, George, SG7Feb88:2
Mason, James, SG18Jan87:2, SG3Nov88:2
Mason, Mr., proposed amendments to Constitution of,
    FG24Aug89:1,2
Masons
    See Free Mason; Grand Lodge
Massachusetts
    address by governor and council of, SG10Dec89:4
    address of to President, SG6Aug89:3
    agriculture of, SG30Jul89:2
    antifederalist opposition in, EI9Apr88:4
    commerce of, SG12Jan86:2
    congressmen of, SG6Aug89:3
    consideration of federal Constitution, SG29Nov87:2
    consideration of separate state in, SG5Mar89:4
    constitutional convention in, SG25Dec88:3
    description of, SG28May89:4
    drilling militia in, WC25Jun88:2
    East India trade of, SG10Sep89:2
    elections of, WC18Jun88:3, SG11Dec88:2,
        WC25Dec88:3, SG1Jan89:2, SG22Jan89:3,
        WC19Feb89:2, WC26Feb89:2, SG18Jun89:2,
        SG2Jul89:3
    electors chosen for, SG12Feb89:2
    encouragement given to manufacturing,
        FG21Sep89:2
    exports of, SG19Mar89:2, SG7May89:3
    illegal shipping in, SG27Aug89:2, SG3Sep89:2
    increased trade of, SG7May89:3
    judiciary of, SG28May89:3, SG18Jun89:2
    legislation of, SG19Mar89:2
    legislature of, WC9Jul88:2
    letter from, EI9Apr88:4, SG4Dec88:2
    manufacturing in, WC12Feb89:1, SG16Apr89:2
    newspaper extract from, WC13Aug88:1
    politics in, SG12Jan86:2, EI9Apr88:2,4,
        WC18Jun88:3, WC9Jul88:2, SG11Dec88:2,
        SG18Dec88:2,3, WC25Dec88:3, SG1Jan89:2,
        WC15Jan89:3, SG22Jan89:3, WC29Jan89:1,
        SG12Feb89:2, SG19Feb89:2,3, WC19Feb89:2,
        SG26Feb89:2, WC26Feb89:2, SG12Mar89:3,
        SG9Apr89:3, SG23Apr89:2, SG2Jul89:3
    ratification of federal Constitution by, EI9Apr88:2,4
    reception of for British naval officers, SG18Jun89:2
    refugees in, SG12Jan86:2
    separatist sentiment in, SG12Jan86:2, SG5Mar89:4
    silver mine in, SG27Oct88:3
    U.S. senators from, SG30Apr89:3
Massachusetts Sentinel, extract from, SG17Nov88:1,
    SG30Jul89:4
Massachusetts Spy, extract from, WC2Jul88:1,
    SG26Feb89:4
Mathematics, solutions to problems of, SG18Jan87:1,2
Mathews, ____, SG3Dec89:3
Mathews, M., SG3Dec89:3
Mathews, Major, SG17Sep89:3

Matra, Consul, letter from, SG13Oct88:2
Maury, Mr., SG23Feb86:4
Maxims, SG8Oct89:3
Maxwell, James, SG6Jul86:3
Maxwell, Jas., SG9Apr89:3—
Maxwell, Peter, WC18Jun88:4, WC25Jun88:4,
  WC8Jan89:3
Maxwell, Robert, SG18Jan87:3, SG27Mar88:3
May, ____, SG3Dec89:3
May, John, WC20Aug88:2
May, Pleasant, SG24Sep89:3
Mayo, ____, SG3Dec89:3
Mayo, Nathan, WC20Aug88:2, SG3Sep89:3
Mayo, Thomas, SG20Oct88:3, SG27Oct88:3
Mazue, James, SG30Apr89:3, SG7May89:4,
  SG14May89:4
Meacon, John, SG23Feb86:4
Meadows, NCGH19Jan86:4
Mears, Thomas, SG9Jul89:3—
Meat
  price of in Wilmington, WC12Feb89:3
  spurious, WC18Jun88:3
Mebane, ____, SG3Dec89:3
Mebane, Alexander, WC20Aug88:2, SG22Sep88:3,
  SG17Sep89:3, SG10Dec89:3, SG31Dec89:3
Mebane, Mr., WC26Nov88:3
Mebane, Wm., WC20Aug88:2
Mechanical arts, promotion of, SG11Jun89:1,4
Mechanics, song of, SG19Feb89:4
Mecklenburg (Mecklimburgh, Mecklinburgh) County,
  N.C., NCG29Mar86:3, SG18Jan87:3,
  WC17Sep88:3, SG29Sep88:3, WC26Nov88:3,
  SG25Dec88:2, SG17Sep89:3
Mecklenburg (County?), Va., SG10Nov88:3
"Mediator," WC23Jul88:2
Medical Society of London, WC15Jan89:3
Medice, Captain, NCG2Sep84:2
Medicines, sale of, SG4Oct87:3, SG29Nov87:3,
  SG7Feb88:4, WC3Sep88:3—
  See also Drugs and Medicines
Mediterranean, plague in, NCG9Dec84:3
Meek, Mary, WC10Dec88:3, WC18Dec88:4
"Member, A," SG27Oct88:1
Mercantile goods, sale of, NCG29Jul84:4,
  NCG2Sep84:3,4, NCG3Nov85:2,4,
  NCGH19Jan86:3, NCGH2Feb86:4,
  NCGH16Feb86:4, NCGH23Feb86:3,4,
  SG23Feb86:2, NCG29Mar86:1, SG6Jul86:4,
  SG18Jan87:4, SG4Oct87:4, SG29Nov87:3,4,
  NCG19Dec87:4, SG7Feb88:3,4, SG27Mar88:4,
  EI9Apr88:4, EI4Jun88:4, WC18Jun88:4,
  WC25Jun88:4, WC27Aug88:3,4, WC17Sep88:3,
  WC24Sep88:1, WC26Oct88:3—, SG27Oct88:3—,
  WC19Nov88:3,4, WC26Nov88:3,4, WC3Dec88:1,3,
  WC10Dec88:3—, SG1Jan89:4, SG29Jan89:3,
  WC29Jan89:3, SG5Feb89:3,4, WC5Feb89:3,
  SG12Feb89:4, WC12Feb89:4, SG19Feb89:1,3—,
  WC19Feb89:1, WC26Feb89:1,3, SG5Mar89:1,
  SG6Aug89:3, SG13Aug89:4, FG24Aug89:3,
  FG14Sep89:4, FG21Sep89:4
  See also Dry Goods; Groceries
Mercantile Store, NCG29Jul84:3,4, NCG3Nov85:2,
  NCGH19Jan86:3, WC26Oct88:3,
  WC12Nov88:4—
Mercereau, John, SG12Feb89:3
Merchants, NCG29Jul84:4, NCGH16Feb86:3,

WC5Feb89:3, WC12Feb89:4
  Philadelphia association of, SG27Aug89:3
Meredith, David, SG20Oct88:3, SG27Oct88:3,
  SG29Jan89:1, SG9Jul89:3—, SG6Aug89:3—
Mero, Governor, SG22Jan89:3, SG1Oct89:3
  See also Miro, Governor
Mero District, SG18Dec88:3, SG22Jan89:3
Merrick, George, WC18Jun88:1
Merritt, William, NCGH23Feb86:3
Metcalfe, George, SG22Oct89:3, SG29Oct89:3,
  SG12Nov89:4
Methodist Episcopal Church, WC3Sep88:1
Middlesex County, Mass., SG5Mar89:2
Middletown, Conn.
  counterfeit dollars in, SG19Nov89:2
  news from, SG19Nov89:2
  newspaper extract from, SG16Apr89:3
Middletown, Mass., criminal convictions in,
  SG22Jan89:3
Middletown, (Mass.?), news from, WC26Nov88:2
Migration, westward, SG18Jun89:3
Miles, John, SG20Oct88:3, SG27Oct88:3
Milford, ____, SG27Oct88:3
Military bounties, SG9Apr89:4
Military claims, NCGH2Feb86:3,4, NCGH23Feb86:4,
  SG18Dec88:2
Military handbook, sale of, SG15Oct89:3—,
  SG12Nov89:3—
Military service, NCG29Mar86:1
Militia, WC19Nov88:3, SG25Dec88:3
  in Middlesex, Mass., WC25Jun88:2
  mustering of, NCGH19Jan86:2
  in N.Y., SG22Oct89:2
  in N.C., SG25Dec88:3
  in U.S., SG3Sep89:1
  use of, SG17Dec89:3
Miller
  See Young, Miller, and Co.
Miller, ____, NCGH16Feb86:3
Miller, Andrew, NCG29Mar86:2, SG27Mar88:3
Miller, George, NCG29Mar86:2
Miller, J., WC13Aug88:3
Miller, James, WC30Jul88:4
Miller, John, SG22Oct89:3, SG29Oct89:3,
  SG12Nov89:4
Miller, Robert, WC20Aug88:2
Millfield School, SG4Oct87:4
Millinery, SG7Feb88:3
Mills, grist and chocolate, WC15Jan89:3
Mills, James, WC16Jul88:3, WC23Jul88:1,
  WC6Aug88:3—
Mills, Joshua, NCG29Jul84:3
Mills, William, NCG29Jul84:3
Milner, James, NCGH2Feb86:3, NCGH16Feb86:3,
  NCGH23Feb86:3, SG23Feb86:3
Milton, ____, anecdote of, SG16Apr89:3
Ming, Mr., SG9Jul89:3—
Mingo (slave), SG4Dec88:3—
Minus, Drover, plight of, SG6Aug89:2
Mirick, ____, NCG6Jan85:1
Miro, Governor, SG16Apr89:2
  See also Mero, Governor
Miro, Madame, SG16Apr89:2
Miscellany, WC18Jun88:1,2, WC25Jun88:1,
  WC2Jul88:1, WC9Jul88:1,2, WC16Jul88:1,2,
  WC23Jul88:1,2, WC30Jul88:1—,

WC3Sep88:2, WC10Sep88:1, WC5Nov88:1,
WC26Nov88:1, WC29Jan89:1, SG2Apr89:1,
FG24Aug89:2, FG14Sep89:1, FG21Sep89:1,
FG12Oct89:1
Mississippi River
  trade on, SG22Jan89:3, SG26Mar89:2
  U.S. navigation of, SG18Jun89:3
Mitchell, Anthony, SG20Oct88:3, SG27Oct88:3
Mitchell, C., SG3Dec89:3
Mitchell, Elijah, WC20Aug88:2, SG29Sep88:3
Mitchell, Elisha, SG17Sep89:3
Mitchell, George, SG18Jan87:3, SG10Sep89:3
Mitchell, Nathan, SG9Apr89:3—
Molasses, sale of, SG30Jul89:3
Money, SG6Oct88:4
  antipathy to, WC2Jul88:1
  coppers, SG20Aug89:2, SG3Sep89:3
  counterfeit, NCG9Dec84:3, SG19Nov89:2
  emission of, SG6Jul86:1, NCG11Jul87:4
  explanation of N.C. public funds, SG18Jan87:3
  foreign, value of, FG24Aug89:2
  hard, SG13Oct88:3, SG10Nov88:4, SG20Aug89:2,
    SG3Sep89:3, SG10Sep89:2
  paper, NCG2Sep84:1, FG12Oct89:2,3,
    SG15Oct89:2, SG17Dec89:2
  redemption of, SG18Jan87:3, SG17Dec89:3,
    SG31Dec89:4
  Va., NCGH23Feb86:3
  wanted, SG18Jun89:3
Montego-Bay, Jamaica
  letter from, SG12Mar89:3
  news from, WC10Sep88:2, WC22Jan89:1,2
  shipping of, WC22Jan89:2
Montenegro, WC10Dec88:2
  war in, WC10Dec88:2
Montflorence, ____, SG3Dec89:3
Montflorence, James Cole, SG27Mar88:3
Montflorence, Mr., SG3Dec89:2
Montfort, H., SG23Feb86:4
Montfort, Henry, WC20Aug88:2
Montgomery, ____, SG3Dec89:3
Montgomery, J., SG3Dec89:3
Montgomery, R., SG3Dec89:3
  letter from, SG19Mar89:3
Montgomery, Robert, SG27Aug89:3, FG14Sep89:3
Montgomery, Sarah, SG22Oct89:3, SG29Oct89:3,
    SG12Nov89:4
Montgomery County, N.C., NCG15Aug87:4,
    SG29Sep88:3, SG11Dec88:4, SG18Dec88:4,
    SG25Dec88:2,3, FG14Sep89:3
Montgomery (County?), N.C., letter from, SG15Jan89:2
Montgomery County, Pa., SG24Sep89:2
Montmorin, Monsieur de, letter from, SG15Oct89:1
Mooklar, Mr., SG23Feb86:3,4
Mooney
  See Prentice & Mooney
Mooney, Mr., SG30Apr89:3—
Moor, John, SG2Sep84:4
Moor, Mr., WC19Nov88:3
Moore, ____, SG3Dec89:3
Moore, Alfred, NCG6Jan85:1, SG27Mar88:3,
    WC13Aug88:3, WC22Jan89:3,4
Moore, Edward, SG29Nov87:1
Moore, George, WC13Aug88:3, WC20Aug88:2
Moore, George Laine, SG18Jan87:3
Moore, J., SG3Dec89:3

Moore, James, SG10Sep89:3
Moore, John, NCG29Mar86:2, WC20Aug88:2,
    SG24Sep89:3
Moore, Maj., WC29Jan89:3, WC5Feb89:1,
    WC5Mar89:2
Moore, Maurice, EI9Apr88:4
Moore, Mrs., SG20Oct88:3, SG27Oct88:3
Moore, Rebecca, SG20Oct88:3, SG27Oct88:3
Moore, Richard, NCGH6Oct85:4
Moore, Robert, SG27Mar88:3
Moore, William, SG18Jan87:2, SG29Nov87:4
Moore County, N.C., SG23Feb86:2, SG22Sep88:3,
    SG25Dec88:2, SG17Sep89:3
Moore Shipyard, EI9Apr88:4
Mooring, ____, SG3Dec89:3
Mooring, Burwell, WC20Aug88:2
Moorish army, WC25Dec88:3
Moravian towns, NCG11Jul87:4
More, Thomas, anecdote about, NCG19Dec87:2
Morgan, John, SG11Jun89:1,4, SG18Jun89:4,
    SG12Nov89:3
Morgan, Peter, NCGH23Feb86:3
Morgan District, SG25Dec88:4
  addition judge for superior court in, WC18Dec88:2
  division of, SG31Dec89:3
Morganton, N.C., hanging in, SG30Apr89:3
Morin
  See Fontaine & Morin
Moring, William, SG3Sep89:3
Morocco
  animosity toward England, WC30Jul88:2
  British relations with, NCGH2Feb86:2,
    SG13Oct88:2
  Emperor of, SG13Oct88:3, WC8Jan89:3,
    WC5Feb89:1
  Empress of, WC5Feb89:1
  letter from Emperor of, WC12Nov88:2
  letter from Emperor's secretary of consuls at Tangiers,
    WC12Nov88:2
  navy of, WC30Jul88:2
  rebellion in, WC8Jan89:3
  seeks peace with England, SG22Jan89:2
  settlement with England, WC24Sep88:1
  unrest in, SG13Oct88:3
  U.S. relations with, NCGH2Feb86:2
Morris, George Anthony, WC18Jun88:4—
Morris, Governor, will of, SG17Nov88:3
Morris, James, WC18Jun88:4—
Morris, John, runaway, SG19Mar89:3—
Morris, Mr., WC19Nov88:3
Morris, Robert, SG16Apr89:3
Morris County, N.J., letter from, SG12Nov89:2
Morris Town, N.J., SG17Dec89:2
Morrison, Colin, WC13Aug88:3
Morrison, William, WC30Jul88:3
Morse, Jedediah, EI19Dec87:1
Mortality, NCGH2Feb86:2
Mortgages, redemption of, SG31Dec89:3
Morton, John, SG18Jan87:3
Moss, Emanuel, SG20Oct88:3, SG27Oct88:3
Mount Pleasant, WC25Jun88:4
Mountflorence, James Cole, NCG15Aug87:4
Mountmorris, Lord Viscount, lands of in Halifax,
    WC18Jun88:2
Mourning, plans for, SG8Oct89:3
Moustier, Count de, address to, response of,

SG11Dec88:2
Mouston, James, NCG6Jan85:1
Moye, Richard, WC20Aug88:2
Muir
 See Stuart & Muir
Muir, Mr., SG30Apr89:3
Muir, Wm., SG27Mar88:3
Muirhead, Robert, SG20Oct88:3, SG27Oct88:3
Mulattoes, SG7Feb88:2
Mulrain, James, SG22Oct89:3, SG29Oct89:3,
 SG12Nov89:4
Mumford, R., WC12Feb89:3—
Mumford, Robert, WC18Dec88:3
Mumford, Robinson, NCGH16Feb86:1,
 NCGH23Feb86:1
Mumford and Mallett, NCGH16Feb86:1,
 NCGH23Feb86:1
Munro, James, SG27Mar88:3
Murder, WC3Sep88:4, WC10Sep88:4, SG20Oct88:2,3
Murdoch, Mrs., NCG6Jan85:1
Murfree, H., SG3Dec89:3
Murfree, Hardy, NCG6Jan85:1, SG12Jan86:4
Murfree, William, SG18Jan87:2, SG29Jan89:1,
 SG27Aug89:3
Murfreesboro' (Murfreesboro, Murfreesborough),
 EI9Apr88:4, EI4Jun88:4, SG4Dec88:3—
Murley, Samuel, FG24Aug89:3, FG14Sep89:3,4,
 FG21Sep89:4
Murphy, Mr., SG27Oct88:1
Murray, John, NCG6Jan85:1
Murray, Robert, SG20Oct88:3, SG27Oct88:3
Mushrow, John, SG19Feb89:4—
Music
 influence of, WC16Jul88:1
 school for, SG18Jan87:3
Musket, lost or stolen, NCG19Dec87:4
Muskingum
 description of, SG29Sep88:2
 letter from, SG29Sep88:2
Mutiny, NCG2Sep84:2

N

Nache, Monsieur le President, SG20Oct88:3,
 SG27Oct88:3
Nails, manufacture of, SG7May89:3
Names, alteration of, SG18Jan87:2, SG31Dec89:3
Nantz, letter from consul in, NCG3Nov85:3
Naples, letter from, SG6Oct88:2
Narlcot, John, NCG29Jul84:3
Nash, ____, WC5Mar89:2, SG3Dec89:3
Nash, Abner, NCG6Jan85:1, SG6Jul86:3
Nash, Gov., SG20Oct88:3
Nash, Margaret, SG6Jul86:3
Nash, Mary, SG27Mar88:3, SG20Oct88:3
Nash, Mrs., SG23Jul89:3—
Nash, W., SG3Dec89:3
Nash County, N.C., SG25Dec88:2
Nashville (Tenn.), NCG11Jul87:4, SG20Oct88:1,
 SG18Dec88:3—, SG22Jan89:3, SG19Feb89:1,
 SG31Dec89:2
 description of, WC5Mar89:1
Nassau
 church and cemetery in, WC29Jan89:2
 crimes by slaves in, WC29Jan89:2

politics in, WC29Jan89:2
Nassau, Prince of, rewarded by Empress of Russia,
 WC26Nov88:1
National Assembly, France
 decrees of, SG12Nov89:1
 message to Louis XVI, SG12Nov89:1,2
 petition to, SG5Nov89:1,2
 proceedings of, SG22Oct89:2, SG12Nov89:1,
  SG10Dec89:1,2
 resolution of, SG22Oct89:1
Nathans, Abraham, SG7Feb88:4, SG27Mar88:3
Naval Office (entrances and clearances of ships)
 Edenton, EI9Apr88:3
 New Bern, NCG2Jul84:2, NCG9Dec84:3,
  NCG3Nov85:3
 Wilmington, WC18Jun88:3—, WC23Jul88:3—,
  WC5Feb89:3—
 See also Marine List
Naval Officer, duty of, SG18Dec88:3, WC18Dec88:2
Navigation
 improvement of, SG18Jan87:2, SG29Nov87:2,
  WC18Jun88:3, WC25Jun88:3, WC9Jul88:4,
  SG18Dec88:3, WC18Dec88:3, SG25Dec88:3,
  SG23Apr89:3—, SG9Jul89:3—
 promotion of, WC19Feb89:3
 See also Cape Fear River
Navy
 English, WC15Jan89:2
 Spanish, SG10Sep89:1
Neale
 See Jones & Neale
Neale, Abner, NCG29Jul84:2, NCG19Dec87:4,
 SG7Feb88:3,4
Neale, Thomas, WC23Jul88:3
Neale, Thomas, Jr., WC30Jul88:4—, WC29Jan89:3,
 WC5Feb89:4
Neckar, M., speech of, SG5Nov89:1
Neckar, Mr., letter from, SG15Oct89:4
"Ned Dub," WC27Aug88:4
Negroes
 able to carry burdens on heads, SG10Sep89:2
 employment for, SG4Oct87:4, SG29Nov87:4,
  SG7Feb88:4, WC30Jul88:3, WC6Aug88:1
 rights to confirmed, WC18Dec88:3
 sale of, FG14Sep89:4
 title to, SG7Feb88:3, SG18Dec88:3
 See also Slaves
Neil, William, SG27Mar88:3
Neilson, Alexander, SG20Oct88:3, SG27Oct88:3
Nelson, General, death of, SG19Feb89:2
Nelson, Mr., SG16Apr89:3
Nesbit, D., SG3Dec89:3
Nesbit, David, FG14Sep89:3
Nesbit, J., SG3Dec89:3
Nesbit, John, SG17Sep89:3
Nesbit, Mr., SG29Sep88:3
"Nestor," SG6Jul86:2
New Bern (Newbern), NCG29Jul84:2,3,4,
 NCG2Sep84:3, SG2Sep84:4, NCG9Dec84:4,
 NCG3Nov85:1,4, SG12Jan86:3, SG12Jan86:4,
 SG23Feb86:1,2,4, NCG29Mar86:2,4, SG6Jul86:4,
 SG18Jan87:2,3, SG1Aug87:4, SG4Oct87:3,4,
 SG29Nov87:4, EI19Dec87:2, SG7Feb88:4,
 SG27Mar88:2,3,4, WC18Jun88:3, WC6Aug88:2,3,
 SG8Sep88:4—, SG20Oct88:3,4, SG27Oct88:3,4,
 SG3Nov88:3—, WC26Nov88:3, SG4Dec88:3,

WC18Dec88:2, SG25Dec88:3, SG26Feb89:3,
WC26Feb89:3, WC5Mar89:1, SG23Jul89:3,
SG3Sep89:3, SG3Dec89:3, SG17Dec89:3
celebration of N.C. ratification, SG17Dec89:2,3
legislation for, SG17Dec89:3
meeting of Shandean Society in, SG11Jun89:1
New York imported goods, SG18Jan87:4
news from, NCG29Jul84:2, NCG2Sep84:3,
    NCG9Dec84:1,3, NCG3Nov85:3, SG12Jan86:3,
    SG23Feb86:3, NCG29Mar86:4, SG6Jul86:3,
    NCG11Jul87:4, NCG15Aug87:3,
    SG29Nov87:2,3, SG19Dec87:4, SG7Feb88:2,3,
    SG27Mar88:3, EI9Apr88:2, WC2Jul88:2,
    SG29Sep88:3, WC22Jan89:2, WC19Feb89:3,
    SG18Jun89:3, SG27Aug89:3, SG3Sep89:3,
    SG12Nov89:3, SG17Dec89:2
regulation of, SG18Jan87:3
schoolhouse in, SG18Jan87:2
theater in, SG27Mar88:3
New-Bern (Newbern) Academy, NCG29Jul84:3,
    NCG3Nov85:4, SG18Jan87:4
New-Bern Dancing-Assembly, NCG3Nov85:2
New Bern District, SG25Dec88:4
New Brunswick, Canada
    Quakers in, SG3Nov88:2
    settlement of, SG3Nov88:2
    shipbuilding in, SG3Nov88:2
New Brunswick, N.J., news from, SG7May89:3,
    SG17Dec89:2
New Durham, New Hampshire, dispute in, EI9Apr88:3
New England
    emigration from, SG10Nov88:2
    manufacturing in, WC19Nov88:3, SG10Sep89:1
New-Garden, SG31Dec89:3
New Hampshire
    description of, SG28May89:4
    elections in, SG23Apr89:2, SG25Jun89:2,
        SG16Jul89:3
    electors in, SG19Feb89:3
    fatal accident in, NCG11Jul87:2
    politics in, WC16Jul88:3, WC23Jul88:2,
        SG19Feb89:2,3, SG25Jun89:2
    president of, SG25Jun89:2
    ratification of federal Constitution by, WC16Jul88:3
    unexplained phenomena in, SG2Apr89:2,
        SG9Apr89:2
New Hanover County, N.C., SG23Feb86:2,
    NCG29Mar86:2, SG6Jul86:3, SG27Mar88:4,
    WC20Aug88:3, SG22Sep88:3, SG18Dec88:3,
    WC18Dec88:2, SG25Dec88:2, SG10Sep89:3
    inspectors appointed for, WC8Jan89:3
    proceedings of court of, WC8Jan89:3
New Haven, Conn.
    letter from, SG4Jun89:3
    news from, SG19Nov89:4
    suicide in, SG4Jun89:3
    visit of president to, SG19Nov89:4
New Jersey
    Cape May beacon, SG15Nov87:2
    description of, SG28May89:4
    consideration of constitutional amendments by,
        SG17Dec89:2
    election of Federalists in, WC19Feb89:2
    electors chosen for, SG5Feb89:2
    influence on Pennsylvania politics, SG7Feb88:2
    judges of, SG12Nov89:3

officers of courts take oath to support Constitution,
    SG12Nov89:2,3
paper money of, SG17Dec89:2
politics in, SG5Feb89:3, WC19Feb89:2
proceedings of legislature of, SG17Dec89:2
ratification of federal Constitution by, SG7Feb88:2
tender law in, SG12Nov89:3
New London, Conn., news from, WC30Jul88:2,
    WC6Aug88:2, WC26Nov88:2, SG19Feb89:1,
    WC5Mar89:1
New London Marine List, SG5Nov89:3
New Orleans
    commercial expedition to, SG26Mar89:2
    description of, SG16Apr89:2,3
    health of, SG15Jan89:2
    letter from, SG15Jan89:2, SG16Apr89:2,
        SG8Oct89:3
    life in, SG15Jan89:2
    Spanish in, SG15Jan89:2
    U.S. expedition to, SG26Mar89:2
New Providence, Nassau, NCG9Dec84:2
    exports of, WC25Jun88:2
    letter from, SG9Apr89:2,3
    news from, WC29Jan89:2
New River, N.C., SG18Jan87:4
New Year, observance of, SG19Feb89:2
New York
    accident to John London in, SG22Oct89:2
    agriculture in, SG17Sep89:3
    antifederal character of legislature of, WC8Jan89:2
    appointment of U.S. senators, SG19Mar89:2
    castor oil in, SG10Sep89:1
    chooses congressmen, SG26Feb89:2, SG30Apr89:3
    circular letter in, SG9Apr89:1,2, WC20Aug88:3
    defends failure to ratify federal Constitution,
        WC5Nov88:1,2
    description of, SG28May89:4
    disagreement over election of U.S. senators,
        WC5Feb89:2
    elections in, WC18Jun88:3, WC25Jun88:2,
        WC2Jul88:2, WC19Feb89:2, SG19Mar89:3,
        SG26Mar89:3, SG9Apr89:1,2, SG14May89:3,
        SG2Jul89:3
    Federal courts opened in, SG26Nov89:3
    General Assembly prescribes means of choosing U.S.
        congressman, WC12Feb89:1
    General Assembly requests amendments to federal
        Constitution, WC12Feb89:1, SG19Mar89:2
    Indian commissioners, WC17Sep88:2
    Indian negotiations of, SG3Nov88:2
    lack of grain in, SG16Jul89:2
    land reserved for federal government, SG13Aug89:2
    laws of, SG12Mar89:2
    legislative proceedings regarding Vermont,
        SG13Aug89:2,3
    legislature prepares address to president,
        SG6Aug89:3
    letter from, NCG2Feb86:2, NCG19Dec87:2,3,
        SG27Mar88:3, WC23Jul88:2, WC27Aug88:3,
        SG11Dec88:1,2, WC25Dec88:3, SG19Feb89:2,3,
        WC19Feb89:2, SG12Mar89:2, SG9Apr89:2,
        SG16Apr89:3, SG23Apr89:2, SG9Jul89:2,
        SG16Jul89:2, SG30Jul89:3, SG20Aug89:2,
        FG14Sep89:3, SG17Sep89:3, SG8Oct89:3,
        SG22Oct89:2
    manufacture of castor oil in, FG21Sep88:2

militia demonstration in, SG22Oct89:2
news from, NCG9Dec84:3, NCG3Nov[85]:3,
SG12Jan86:2,3, NCGH19Jan86:2,
NCGH2Feb86:2, NCGH23Feb86:2,
NCG11Jul87:2, SG15Nov87:1,2, SG20Nov87:2,
SG7Feb88:2, SG27Mar88:2,3, WC18Jun88:2,
WC25Jun88:2, WC23Jul88:2, WC30Jul88:2,3,
WC6Aug88:2, WC13Aug88:2, WC20Aug88:2,
WC3Sep88:3, SG8Sep88:2, WC10Sep88:2,3,
WC17Sep88:1,2, SG22Sep88:1,2,
WC24Sep88:2, SG29Sep88:2, SG6Oct88:3,
WC15Oct88:1, SG20Oct88:2, WC26Oct88:1,2,
SG10Nov88:2, WC12Nov88:2, SG17Nov88:3,
SG24Nov88:2, WC26Nov88:2, SG4Dec88:2,
WC10Dec88:2, SG18Dec88:2, WC8Jan89:2,3,
SG22Jan89:3, SG5Feb89:2, SG12Feb89:3,
WC12Feb89:1, WC19Feb89:1, SG26Feb89:2,
SG5Mar89:2, SG19Mar89:2, SG2Apr89:2,
SG9Apr89:1,2, SG30Apr89:3, SG7May89:3,
SG14May89:2, SG21May89:1,2,3, SG4Jun89:2,
SG11Jun89:2, SG18Jun89:2, SG25Jun89:2,
SG2Jul89:3, SG9Jul89:2, SG16Jul89:2,
SG23Jul89:2,3, SG6Aug89:2,3, SG13Aug89:2,
SG20Aug89:2, SG27Aug89:2,3, SG3Sep89:2,3,
SG10Sep89:2, FG14Sep89:2, SG17Sep89:1,2,3,
SG24Sep89:2, SG1Oct89:2, SG8Oct89:2,3,
SG15Oct89:2, SG29Oct89:2, SG5Nov89:2,3,
SG12Nov89:2, SG19Nov89:2, SG26Nov89:2,
SG3Dec89:2
opposition to federal Constitution in, SG30Apr89:3
party spirit in, SG12Mar89:2
politics in, NCG19Dec87:3, SG7Feb88:2,
WC18Jun88:3, WC25Jun88:2, WC2Jul88:2,
WC9Jul88:2, WC23Jul88:2, WC30Jul88:2,3,
WC6Aug88:2, WC13Aug88:2, WC20Aug88:3,
WC17Sep88:2, SG27Oct88:2, WC3Dec88:2,
WC8Jan89:2, WC22Jan89:1, SG5Feb89:3,
WC5Feb89:2, SG12Feb89:3, WC12Feb89:1,
SG19Feb89:2, SG26Feb89:2, SG12Mar89:2,
SG19Mar89:3, SG26Mar89:3, SG9Apr89:1,2,
SG16Apr89:2, SG23Apr89:2,3, SG30Apr89:3,
SG14May89:3, SG11Jun89:3, SG2Jul89:3,
SG16Jul89:2, SG6Aug89:3,4, SG13Aug89:2
proceedings of General Assembly of, SG9Apr89:2
proceedings of state constitutional convention,
WC23Jul88:2, WC30Jul88:2,3, WC6Aug88:2,
WC13Aug88:2
proclamation by governor of, SG10Nov88:2
ratification of federal Constitution by,
WC20Aug88:3, WC27Aug88:3
retaliation for criticism of ratification celebration,
WC20Aug88:3
robbery in Westchester County, WC12Feb89:1
seeks new constitutional convention, SG5Feb89:3
taxation to construct statehouse, SG26Feb89:2
weather in, SG17Sep89:3
See also New York, town of
New York, town of
attempted robbery in, WC12Feb89:1
capitol building of, SG29Jan89:3, WC5Feb89:2,
SG26Feb89:2, SG9Apr89:2
celebration of anniversary of evacuation of British
troops, WC8Jan89:2
celebration of birthday of George III, WC9Jul88:2
celebration of birthday of queen of England,
SG5Mar89:2

celebration of Fourth of July, SG23Jul89:3
celebration of Mass. ratification of federal
constitution, SG27Mar88:3
celebration of ratification of federal Constitution,
WC20Aug88:2
comedic performance in, SG5Nov89:3
commencement of U.S. government in, SG2Apr89:2
construction of capitol building in, WC5Feb89:2
construction of city hall in, WC8Jan89:2
criminal activity in, SG22Jan89:3, WC29Jan89:2
exports to New Bern, N.C., SG18Jan87:4
federal court in, SG26Nov89:3
George Washington arrives in, SG21May89:1
health of persons in, SG17Sep89:3
India trade of, SG22Jan89:3
ladies of, SG17Dec89:2
levee by president in, SG8Oct89:2
meeting of citizens in, SG9Apr89:1
North Carolina imports from, SG7Feb88:4
meeting of legislature of, SG10Nov88:2,
SG16Jul89:2, SG6Aug89:2,3
merchants' remittances, SG23Jul89:1
newspaper extracts from, WC3Sep88:2,
SG6Oct88:1, SG15Jan89:3, SG19Feb89:3,
SG14May89:3, SG1Oct89:4, SG22Oct89:2
preparations to honor president, SG30Apr89:3,
SG14May89:2
preparations to institute federal government,
WC5Feb89:2
robbery, SG5Feb89:2, SG5Mar89:2
ship to convey president in, SG19Mar89:2
shipbuilding in, SG20Oct88:2
shipping of, WC18Jun88:2, WC17Sep88:2,
SG12Feb89:3, WC19Feb89:1, SG26Feb89:2,
SG12Mar89:2
sickness in, SG17Sep89:3
society for manumission of slaves in, SG8Jan89:3
storm in, WC10Sep88:2
See also New York
New York Daily Advertiser, extract from, SG6Jul86:2,
WC10Sep88:1, WC5Nov88:1, SG24Dec89:4
New York Daily Gazette, extract from, SG14May89:3
New Zealand, adventure in, SG2Apr89:1
Newbern Academy, SG18Jan87:4
Newbern District, SG6Jul86:3
Newbern Volunteers, SG27Aug89:3, SG12Nov89:3,
SG17Dec89:2
Newby, Exum, SG9Apr89:3—
Newgate, female convicts in, SG24Nov88:1
Newman, William, NCGH19Jan86:3, NCGH2Feb86:3
Newport, R.I.
letter from, WC22Jan89:3, SG28May89:3,
SG23Jul89:3
meeting of Society of Cincinnati in, SG6Aug89:2,
SG13Aug89:2
news from, NCG9Dec84:3, WC25Jun88:2,
WC27Aug88:3, WC26Oct88:2, SG26Mar89:2,
SG23Apr89:2, SG23Jul89:2,3, SG6Aug89:2,
SG29Oct89:2
seeks state constitutional convention, SG26Nov89:3
shipping to, SG19Feb89:2
Newspaper, SG2Sep84:4, SG22Jan89:3, WC12Feb89:1
expense of printing, SG3Sep89:3
French, NCG29Jul84:2, SG2Sep84:4
number of copies printed in U.S., SG5Nov89:2
patronage of, NCG3Nov85:3

printers of, NCGH19Jan86:2
prospectus of, FG24Aug89:1
size of, NCGH6Oct85:3
subscriptions to, NCG1Aug87:3, WC18Dec88:3
supplement to, NCG15Aug87:3
terms of advertisements in, WC18Jun88:3—
    U.S., SG22Jan89:3, SG5Nov89:2
Niel, G., SG21May89:3, SG28May89:4, SG18Jun89:4
Nihell, Mr., SG4Oct87:4
Nicholas, Sarah, SG31Dec89:3
Nicholson
    See Hartley & Nicholson
Nicholson, James, SG6Jul86:3
Nixon, Richard, WC20Aug88:2, SG3Sep89:3
Nixonton, N.C., SG22Sep88:3, SG26Mar89:3—,
    SG10Dec89:3—
Noller, Richard, SG18Dec88:2—
Nonimportation, difficulty of, SG5Mar89:3
Norcom, Frederick, SG10Nov88:3, SG9Jul89:3—
Norfleet, ___, SG24Sep89:3, SG3Dec89:3
Norfleet, Abraham, SG29Nov87:1
Norfleet, E., SG11Dec88:3—
Norflet, Reuben, SG20Oct88:3, SG27Oct88:3
Norfolk, NCG2Sep84:3, SG21May89:3, SG28May89:4,
    SG18Jun89:4
    address of mayor, recorder, and aldermen,
        SG10Dec89:2
    fire in, NCG11Jul87:4
    letter from, SG3Sep89:3
    news from, NCG11Jul87:4, WC13Aug88:2,3,
        SG6Oct88:3, WC10Dec88:2,3,
        WC25Dec88:3, SG10Sep89:3, SG12Nov89:3,
        SG10Dec89:2
    newspaper extracts from, EI4Jun88:1
    public lecture in, WC25Dec88:3
    storm in, WC13Aug88:2,3
Norfolk and Portsmouth Journal, extract from,
    SG17Nov88:3
North, Lord, WC12Feb89:2
North America
    exploration of, FG21Sep89:2
    proposed tour of, SG26Mar89:2
    trade of, NCGH2Feb86:2
North Carolina
    act to appoint Indian agent for, SG31Dec89:3
    agriculture in, SG1Oct89:2, SG5Nov89:3
    amendments to federal Constitution of,
        WC20Aug88:1
    approval of federal Constitution forecast,
        SG3Nov88:2
    attitude toward national government, SG3Nov88:2
    backcountry of, SG11Dec88:2,3, SG29Jan89:2,
        WC5Mar89:1,2
    bills considered by General Assembly,
        WC19Nov88:3
    capital of, WC6Aug88:3, WC13Aug88:3,
        SG8Sep88:3, WC19Nov88:3, SG3Dec89:3
    celebration of ratification of federal Constitution,
        SG3Dec89:2
    cession of western lands, SG31Dec89:3
    commentary on legislation concerning Davidson
        County, 1786, WC23Jul88:2, WC30Jul88:1,2,
        WC6Aug88:1,2
    commerce of, SG23Feb86:4
    commissioners of confiscated property of,
        SG18Jan87:3

commissioners of supplies in, SG18Jan87:3
consequences of rejection of federal Constitution,
    SG15Sep88:1
constitution of, NCG15Aug87:1,2
constitutional convention in, SG29Sep88:3,
    SG1Oct89:2
Council of State, SG4Dec88:3
criticism of judges of, EI19Dec87:2
criticism of legislature of, EI9Apr88:2,3
crops in, SG1Oct89:2, SG5Nov89:3
debt of, SG18Dec88:2,3
Declaration of Rights of, WC20Aug88:1,
    WC5Nov88:2, SG19Nov89:2
defense of failure to ratify federal
    Constitution, SG6Oct88:1
deficiency of records of, SG25Dec88:3
delays in courts of, WC12Nov88:3
delegates to Constitutional Convention,
    SG18Jan87:3
description of, SG28May89:4
difficulty of securing justice in, WC12Nov88:1
diminution of revenue of, WC18Dec88:2
economic conditions in, SG11Jun89:1
elections in, NCG2Sep84:3, SG18Jan87:3,
    SG27Aug89:3
erection of fort in western territory of,
    WC18Dec88:3
examination of legislation to grant five percent tax
    to Congress, WC16Jul88:2
exports of, SG3Dec89:3
and federal Constitution, SG8Sep88:2, SG6Oct88:1,
    SG26Nov89:3, WC22Jan89:3, SG3Dec89:2
federalism in, SG29Sep88:3
financial accounts with U.S., SG1Jan89:4
financial support of U.S., SG17Dec89:3
fiscal support of government of, SG18Jan87:3
frosts destroy crops in backcountry of, FG12Oct89:3
and Georgia, WC22Jan89:2
government finances of, SG3Dec89:3
government salaries of, WC18Dec88:3
governor of, NCG19Dec87:4
gubernatorial proclamation in, SG23Feb86:4,
    SG6Jul86:4
healthfulness of, SG5Nov89:3
independence of, SG16Apr89:2
Indian commissioners of, SG22Jan89:3,
    SG26Nov89:3
Indians relations of, SG29Sep88:1, SG30Jul89:2,
    SG13Aug89:1
Indians in western territory of, WC5Mar89:2
influence on location of national capital,
    SG12Nov89:3
intemperance in, SG5Nov89:3
land acreage of, SG25Dec88:2
judiciary of, SG2Jul89:3
letter from, SG20Aug89:2·
legislation for election of congressmen from,
    SG31Dec89:2,3
legislation to impose taxes in, SG31Dec89:4
legislative session, 1788, SG26Feb89:2,3
letter from, SG20Aug89:2
location of capital of, WC26Nov88:3
monetary claims against, SG10Dec89:3
need to ratify federal Constitution, WC12Nov88:3,
    WC3Dec88:1, WC10Dec88:1, FG14Sep89:3
N.Y. imports to, SG27Mar88:4

opposition to federal Constitution, SG27Mar88:1,2,
   FG21Sep89:1,2, SG24Sep89:3
patriotism of, SG4Jun89:3
payment of domestic debt of, SG31Dec89:4
payment of taxes in, EI9Apr88:1
pilots of, SG4Jun89:3
politics of western counties of, WC17Sep88:3
polls in, SG25Dec88:2
proposed purchase of Indian lands by, SG26Feb89:3
propriety of calling a constitutional convention in,
   WC5Nov88:2,3
public officers of, SG18Dec88:3
qualification of governor of, SG17Dec89:3
raising revenue of, SG3Dec89:3, SG31Dec89:3
reconsideration of federal Constitution,
   SG4Dec88:2,3
rejection of federal Constitution, SG8Sep88:2
resolution of General Assembly, WC10Dec88:3
revenue of, SG18Dec88:1,2
revision of laws, WC18Dec88:3
and Revolutionary War, WC5Nov88:1
salaries of public officials of, SG18Dec88:3,
   WC18Dec88:3
shipping of, SG3Nov88:3, SG12Nov89:3
and State of Franklin, SG29Nov87:3
support for federal Constitution, SG20Aug89:2,
   SG1Oct89:2, SG26Nov89:3
and Tariff of 1789, FG12Oct89:3
taxation in, NCG9Dec84:2, WC19Nov88:3,
   SG18Dec88:3, WC18Dec88:2
thievery in, SG9Apr89:3
trade of, SG4Jun89:3
trade with Martinico, WC26Nov88:3
and U.S., SG6Oct88:1, SG4Jun89:3, SG1Oct89:3
U.S. Senators for, SG17Dec89:3, SG31Dec89:3
and George Washington, SG9Jul89:2,3
western claims of, SG29Sep88:1
North Carolina Gazette, publication schedule of,
   SG12Jan86:3
North River, Mass., accident on, SG19Mar89:2
Northampton, Mass., proceedings of supreme court in,
   SG18Jun89:2
Northampton County, N.C., SG18Jan87:2,
   WC18Dec88:3, SG25Dec88:2, SG24Sep89:3
Northcott, John, NCG6Jan85:1
Northumberland County, Pa., letter from, SG20Aug89:2
Northumberland County, Va., SG25Dec88:3—
Northwest Territory, SG23Apr89:2
   government of, SG24Sep89:4
   Indians in, SG12Mar89:2, SG26Mar89:2
   trade of, SG26Mar89:2
Norwood, John, WC20Aug88:2
Norwood, William, SG10Nov88:3
Notes, SG18Dec88:4
   final settlement, wanted, SG4Oct87:4,
      SG29Nov87:3
   of hand, WC16Jul88:3
   personal, SG23Feb86:4, WC26Oct88:3, SG1Jan89:3,
      SG5Feb89:3, SG13Aug89:3—
Notes on the State of Virginia, extract from, SG10Sep89:3
Nougier, Peter, SG24Sep89:3
Nova Scotia, SG8Jan89:3
   Benedict Arnold in, WC26Oct88:2
   importations of, SG8Jan89:3
   Negroes brought from to N.C., SG12Jan86:3,
      SG23Feb86:4

Novel, WC12Feb89:1
Nugent, Earl of
   burial of, WC5Feb89:1
   death of, WC29Jan89:1
"Numerous," NCG9Dec84:2
Nutbush Seminary, SG10Nov88:3
Nutt, John, WC23Jul88:3—
Nutt, William, WC18Jun88:4—, WC19Feb89:3,
   WC26Feb89:1

O

O'Bryen, John, misfortunes of, SG8Oct89:4
*Observations on the New Constitution and on the Federal
   and State Constitutions.* By a Columbian Patriot, sale
   of, WC18Jun88:4, WC25Jun88:4
"Observator," SG30Jul89:3
O'Connor, Mr., SG29Sep88:3
Ocracoke Bar
   accidents to shipping at, SG10Dec89:3
   shipping at, SG12Nov89:3
Ocracoke Island, lighthouse on, SG31Dec89:3
Office and Authority of a Justice of the Peace, The,
   subscriptions sought for new edition of,
   NCG11Jul87:4, NCG1Aug87:4
Office seekers, SG28May89:3
Officeholders, necessary qualifications of,
   WC12Nov88:2
Ogden, T., SG7Feb88:3
Ogden, Thomas, NCG15Aug87:3
Ogden, Titus, NCG1Aug87:3, NCG15Aug87:4
Ogden, T. and T., NCG6Jan85:1
Ogden, Thomas and Titus, NCG29Jul84:2,
   NCG2Sep84:2
Oggs, John, SG31Dec89:3
Oggs, Prudence, SG31Dec89:3
Ohio Company, WC5Nov88:2, SG23Apr89:2,
   SG30Apr89:3, SG3Sep89:2,3
   directors of, SG30Apr89:3
Ohio, Falls of, letter from, SG24Sep89:3
Ohio Territory
   description of, SG29Sep88:2, SG23Apr89:2,
      SG28May89:3
   fertility of soil in, SG28May89:3
   immigration to, SG3Nov88:2
   Indian troubles in, SG12Nov89:2
   letter from, SG24Sep89:3, SG12Nov89:2
   negotiations with Indians in, SG23Apr89:2
   robberies in, NCG29Jul84:2
   settlement in, SG3Nov88:2, SG3Sep89:2,3,
      SG10Sep89:2
   silk growth in, SG28May89:3
Old Abraham, WC24Sep88:2
Old Bailey, SG4Dec88:2
   proceedings at, NCGH16Feb86:2
   trial at, SG22Jan89:3
"Old Batchelor," FG12Oct89:4
"Old Honesty," WC10Sep88:3
Old Maid, SG11Dec88:4
Old Tassell, WC24Sep88:2
Oldham, Thomas, NCG29Mar86:2
O'Leary, Father, writing by, SG10Dec89:2
Oliver, Andrew, WC20Aug88:2
Oliver, Benjamin L., SG9Apr89:3—
Oliver, Francis, WC20Aug88:2

Oliver, Joseph, NCG2Sep84:4
Olives, preserving of, SG18Jun89:4
O'Malley, Myles, SG5Feb89:3—, SG23Jul89:3
"One of the People," NCG2Sep84:1, NCG9Dec84:2
Onsby, Clement, WC16Jul88:3
Onslow County, N.C., NCG15Aug87:3, SG22Sep88:3,
    WC26Nov88:3, WC18Dec88:2, SG25Dec88:2,
    SG10Sep89:3
    court of, NCGH19Jan86:3
Orange County, N.C., NCG2Sep84:2, NCGH2Feb86:3,
    NCGH16Feb86:3, NCGH23Feb86:3, SG23Feb86:3,
    SG22Sep88:3, SG25Dec88:2, SG17Sep89:3,
    SG31Dec89:3
Oratory, SG13Oct88:2,3
Orillac, Monsieur Roy, SG22Oct89:3, SG29Oct89:3,
    SG12Nov89:4
Orillat, Mons. Roy, SG27Mar88:3
Orme, Mr., historian of India, SG22Oct89:3
Orme, William, SG27Mar88:3
Ornsby, Clement, death of, WC16Jul88:3
Orphans, Craven County, N.C., SG18Jan87:3
Orrenton, William, SG29Jan89:3—
Osborn, ____, SG24Sep89:3
Osborn, A., SG3Dec89:3
Osborn, Col., SG17Sep89:3
Osborn, Henry, SG13Aug89:1
Ostend
    exports to N.C., SG27Oct88:3—
    festival in, WC24Sep88:2
    letter from, SG10Dec89:1
Otsiquette, Peter, arrival of in Boston, WC3Sep88:2
Ottoman Empire
    death of ruler of, SG13Aug89:3, SG20Aug89:3
    reception given to English diplomat, WC25Jun88:2
    rule of emperor of, WC8Jan89:2
    sultan of, SG3Sep89:2
Ouitleau, Col., SG16Apr89:3
Outer Banks, inhabitants of, SG4Jun89:3
Outerbridge, Stephen, SG30Jul89:3, SG3Sep89:4—
Outlaw, ____, SG3Dec89:3
Outlaw, Mr., SG17Dec89:3
Overseer, wanted, WC10Dec88:3—
Overton, ____, SG22Sep88:3
Overton, Col., SG24Sep89:3
Overton, J., SG3Dec89:3
Owen, Col., WC18Jun88:3, WC25Jun88:3
Owen, T., SG3Dec89:2
Owen, Thomas, WC20Aug88:2, SG10Sep89:3
Owens, John, NCG29Jul84:2
Owens, Thomas, SG20Oct88:3, SG27Oct88:3
Oxford, NCG19Dec87:4
Oyer and Terminer, Court of, Boston, SG26Nov89:2

P

Pacha, Captain, speech of to Turkish fleet,
    WC19Nov88:1,2
    See Pasha, Captain
Packet boats, SG30Jul89:4
Painter, gilder, glazier, EI4Jun88:3
Palmer, Col., NCG2Sep84:3
Palmer, Lemuel, SG27Mar88:3
Palmer, Philip, SG27Mar88:3
Palmer, Robert, NCG3Nov85:1, NCG29Mar86:2
Palmer, William, SG12Jan86:3, SG27Mar88:3

Paper currency, FG12Oct89:2,3
    emission of, SG13Aug89:3
    sinking of, WC19Nov88:3, SG25Dec88:3
Paper manufacturing
    See Manufacturing, paper
Paper products, sale of, SG12Jan86:4, WC26Oct88:3—,
    WC8Jan89:4—
Pardon, Act of, SG18Jan87:2, WC18Dec88:3
Pardon and Oblivion, Act of, WC18Dec88:3
    partial repeal of, SG31Dec89:3
Pardon, legislation for, SG18Jan87:2
Paris, WC5Nov88:3
    aged man inherits estate in, SG16Apr89:1
    anarchy in, SG17Dec89:1
    banks in, NCG2Sep84:2
    execution in, SG10Dec89:2
    fashions in, SG29Jan89:3
    hospitals and orphanages of, SG6Aug89:4
    hunger in, SG17Dec89:1
    insurrection in, SG30Jul89:2
    letter from, SG10Nov88:1, SG29Jan89:3,
        WC5Feb89:1, WC26Feb89:2, SG19Mar89:3,
        SG7May89:3, SG18Jun89:2, SG25Jun89:2,
        SG29Oct89:3, SG26Nov89:2, SG24Dec89:3,
        SG31Dec89:1
    meeting of parliament in, WC3Dec88:3
    mob in, WC3Dec88:3, SG29Oct89:1
    news from, NCG29Jul84:2, NCG2Sep84:2,
        NCG9Dec84:3, WC15Oct88:1, SG18Jun89:1,
        SG20Aug89:1, SG3Sep89:2, SG24Sep89:2,
        SG1Oct89:1, SG8Oct89:1, SG15Oct89:1,
        SG22Oct89:1, SG29Oct89:1, SG12Nov89:1,2,
        SG10Dec89:1, SG17Dec89:1
    politics in, SG20Aug89:1
    revolution in, SG15Oct89:1
    riots in, FG14Sep89:2
    storm in, WC5Nov88:3
    threats of destruction in, FG12Oct89:3
    scarcity of bread in, SG17Dec89:1
    wood in, NCGH19Jan86:1
Parker (slave), ran away, WC15Jan89:4—
Parker, Elias, SG30Apr89:3, SG7May89:4
Parker, James, NCG29Mar86:2
Parker, Job, SG12Jan86:4
Parker, Jonathan, SG18Jan87:2
Parker, Robert, SG29Oct88:3, SG27Oct88:3
Parkinson, James, NCGH2Feb86:2, NCGH16Feb86:4,
    NCGH23Feb86:4
Parliament, British
    address to by Lords Commissioners, SG28May89:2,3
    legislation of, NCG9Dec84:4, SG29Oct89:3
    meeting of, NCG29Jul84:2, WC25Dec88:2,
        SG19Feb89:3
    proceedings of, NCG19Jan86:1, NCGH23Feb86:2,
        WC3Sep88:1, SG22Sep88:1,2, SG12Mar89:1,
        SG30Apr89:1, SG7May89:2, SG28May89:2,3
    resolutions of, NCGH6Oct85:1,2,3
    See also House of Commons; House of Lords
Parliament, Irish, SG3Sep89:2
Parnassian Loom, WC20Aug88:4—, WC26Oct88:4—,
    WC3Dec88:4—, WC29Jan89:4—
    See also Poetry; Poet's Corner
Parrott, ____, SG3Dec89:3
Parsons, General, WC10Dec88:3
Pasha, Captain, NCGH19Jan86:2
    See Pacha, Captain

Pasha, Turkish, character of, NCGH19Jan86:2
Pasquotank County, N.C., NCG29Mar86:2,
    SG25Dec88:2, SG15Jan89:4, SG27Aug89:3,
    FG14Sep89:3
    court of, SG1Jan89:3, SG8Jan89:4, SG22Jan89:4
Pasteur
    See Halling and Pasteur
Pasteur, Mrs. J., SG6Jul86:3
Pasteur, W., SG6Jul86:3
Patent, U.S., SG16Jul89:1
Paterson, James, WC12Nov88:3—
Patillo, Henry, SG7Feb88:4
Patrick, Alexander, WC13Aug88:3
Patrick, Mary, NCG6Jan85:1
Patriotism, SG9Jul89:4
Patterson, Samuel, NCG6Jan85:1
Patterson, William, SG20Oct88:3, SG27Oct88:3
Pattillo, Anderson, SG10Nov88:3
Pattillo, Henry, SG10Nov88:3, SG24Dec89:3,
    SG31Dec89:4
Pattillo, Richard, SG10Nov88:3
Pattillo, William T., SG10Nov88:3
Paul
    See Stuart and Paul
Paul, James, SG18Jan87:3
Paul, Robert, SG18Jan87:3
Payne, ____, SG17Sep89:3
Payne, James, WC20Aug88:2
Payne, Michael, SG12Jan86:2, NCG19Dec87:4,
    WC20Aug88:2, WC26Nov88:3, SG4Dec88:3
Payne, R., SG3Dec89:2
Payne, Robert, SG22Sep89:3
Peale's American Museum, WC19Feb89:1
Pearsall, ____, SG3Dec89:3
Pearson, T., WC20Aug88:2
Pearson, Thomas, NCG6Jan85:1
Pearson, Thomas W., SG9Apr89:3—
Peas, wanted, WC25Dec88:3
Peebles, ____, SG24Sep89:3, SG3Dec89:3
Peebles, Robert, WC20Aug88:2
Peete, ____, SG24Sep89:3, SG3Dec89:3
Pelham, Mr., NCG9Dec84:4
Pembroke, Earl of, anecdote of, FG12Oct89:4
Pendleton, ____, NCG6Jan85:1
Penn, William, maxims of, SG8Oct89:3
Pennsylvania
    attitude toward federal Constitution, SG29Nov87:2,
        SG27Mar88:3
    cession of land to U.S. for capital, SG1Oct89:3
    circuit court proceedings in Chester County,
        SG4Jun89:2
    deaths in western area of, SG20Aug89:2
    description of, SG28May89:4
    disturbances in, WC3Sep88:1
    elections in, SG20Oct88:2, SG15Jan89:2,
        SG29Jan89:2
    electors in, SG12Mar89:2
    Federalist sentiment in, EI4Jun88:2
    frontier of, SG18Jun89:3
    judiciary of, SG4Jun89:2
    legislation of, SG19Mar89:2,3
    legislature of, SG26Mar89:3
    manufacturing in, WC5Nov88:2
    message to General Assembly of, WC25Dec88:4
    newspaper extract from, SG3Nov88:3
    paper mills in, SG10Sep89:1

    petition to allow dramatic entertainments in,
        SG12Mar89:2
    politics in, SG15Nov87:2, NCG19Dec87:3,
        SG13Oct88:2, SG20Oct88:2, WC26Oct88:2,
        SG27Oct88:2, SG18Dec88:3, SG15Jan89:2,
        SG29Jan89:2, SG5Feb89:2, WC19Feb89:3,
        SG12Mar89:2, SG19Mar89:3, SG26Mar89:3,
        SG16Apr89:2, SG23Apr89:2, SG1Oct89:3
    preparations of for presidential visit, SG23Apr89:2,
        WC27Aug89:3
    proceedings of General Assembly of, SG13Oct88:2,
        SG16Apr89:2
    proposed meeting of convention to alter state
        constitution, SG2Apr89:2, SG1Oct89:3
    provides seat of government for U.S., WC19Feb89:3
    western settlements of, SG18Jun89:3, SG20Aug89:2
Penobscot, letter from, SG22Sep88:2
Pensioner, Scottish, SG12Nov89:2
Pensioners, U.S. payment to, SG12Nov89:4,
    SG19Nov89:4
Pensions, army, SG4Oct87:4, SG29Nov87:4
Peppen, Augustus Mons., NCG6Jan85:1
Performances, dramatic, SG25Dec88:3, SG12Mar89:2
    See Kenna and Company
Perkins, ____, SG3Dec89:3
Perkins, H., SG17Sep89:3
Perkins, Mr., WC17Sep88:3, SG29Sep88:3
Perquimans County, N.C., EI19Dec87:1,
    SG25Dec88:2,3, SG8Jan89:3, WC15Jan89:3,
    SG22Jan89:3—, SG16Jul89:4—, SG27Aug89:3,
    FG14Sep89:3, SG5Nov89:3
Perry, ____, SG3Dec89:3
Perry, B., SG3Dec89:3
Perry, Benjamin, SG27Aug89:3, FG14Sep89:3
Perry, Jacob, SG8Jan89:3
Perry, Joseph, SG29Nov87:1
Perry, Peter, FG24Aug89:3, FG14Sep89:4, FG21Sep89:4
Person, ____, SG3Dec89:3
Person, General, SG17Sep89:3
Person, Mr., SG3Dec89:4
Person, T., SG29Sep88:3, SG3Dec89:3
Person, Thomas, NCGH19Jan86:3, WC20Aug88:2,
    SG17Dec89:3, SG31Dec89:3
Persons, ____, WC6Aug88:2
Persons, Capt., SG18Jan87:3
Persons, Osborne, SG20Oct88:3, SG27Oct88:3
Peru, WC30Jul88:4
Petchy, John, SG22Oct89:3, SG29Oct89:3,
    SG12Nov89:4
Peter (slave), SG4Oct87:4, SG30Apr89:4—
    execution of, WC13Aug88:3
Peter the Great, anecdotes of, SG8Jan89:4
Peters, ____, SG3Dec89:3
Peters, Michael, SG3Sep89:3
Petersburg (Petersburgh), Russia, WC30Jul88:2
    flooding in, WC22Jan89:2
    letter from, WC15Oct88:1, SG27Oct88:2
        SG19Nov88:1,2, SG15Jan89:1, SG19Nov89:2,
        SG24Dec89:1
    news from, NCG29Jul84:1, WC30Jul88:2,
        SG3Nov88:2
Petersburg (Petersburgh), Va., NCGH23Feb86:3,
    WC24Sep88:2, SG27Oct88:3, SG3Nov88:4—,
    SG4Dec88:3—, SG7May89:4, SG14May89:4
    celebration of Washington's birthday in,
        WC5Mar89:2

damage by storm in, WC13Aug88:2, WC20Aug88:3
news from, SG15Nov87:2, WC2Jul88:2,
WC13Aug88:2, WC20Aug88:3, WC3Sep88:1,
SG3Nov88:2, WC3Dec88:2,3,
WC19Feb89:1,2,3, WC5Mar89:2, SG16Apr89:3,
SG16Jul89:3, SG3Sep89:3, SG10Dec89:2
price of tobacco in, NCGH23Feb86:3
Petersburg Gazette (Russia), extract from,
WC19Nov88:1,2
Petty, William, SG18Jan87:2
Peyrinnaut, F., WC19Nov88:3—, SG30Jul89:3—
Peyrouse, Comte de, account of circumnavigation of
world by, WC5Feb89:1
Pfifer, ____, SG3Dec89:3
Pfifer, Caleb, WC20Aug88:2, WC17Sep88:3,
SG29Sep88:3, SG17Dec89:3
Pfifer, Col., SG17Sep89:3
Phelps, Oliver, SG18Jan87:3, SG9Apr89:3
Philadelphia, SG27Mar88:4, SG29Sep88:3
celebration of Mass. ratification of federal
Constitution, SG27Mar88:3
cotton manufactory in, FG21Sep89:2
court session of, SG15Nov87:2
criticism of, SG19Feb89:3
dramatic entertainments in, SG19Mar89:3
elections in, SG29Nov87:2, SG5Feb89:2
federal procession of shoemakers in, SG10Sep89:1
fire in, SG29Nov87:2
free school in, SG19Mar89:3
governance of, SG15Nov87:2
health in, SG17Sep89:3
jailbreak in, SG5Mar89:2
legislation for, SG26Mar89:3
letter from, WC27Aug88:3, SG10Sep89:1,2
mail robbery near, WC25Dec88:3
Manufactory Society of, SG10Sep89:1,2
markets of, SG11Dec88:2
merchant's association of, SG27Aug89:3
merchants and traders of to abide by U.S. law,
SG1Oct89:3
murder in, SG29Nov87:2
news from, NCG29Jul84:2, NCG2Sep84:2,
NCG9Dec84:2, NCGH19Jan86:2,
NCGH23Feb86:2, NCG29Mar86:1,
NCG11Jul87:2,3, NCG15Aug87:2,
SG15Nov87:2, SG29Nov87:2, NCG19Dec87:3,
EI4Jun88:2, WC9Jul88:2, WC23Jul88:2,
WC13Aug88:2, WC3Sep88:1, SG15Sep88:1,
WC24Sep88:2, SG29Sep88:2, SG6Oct88:3,
SG13Oct88:1,2, SG20Oct88:2, WC26Oct88:2,3,
SG27Oct88:2, SG3Nov88:2, WC5Nov88:2,
WC19Nov88:2,3, SG24Nov88:2, SG11Dec88:2,
SG18Dec88:3, WC25Dec88:3, SG1Jan89:2,
SG8Jan89:3, SG15Jan89:2, WC15Jan89:1,
SG22Jan89:3, SG29Jan89:2, WC29Jan89:2,
SG5Feb89:2, WC5Feb89:2, SG12Feb89:3,
SG19Feb89:2, SG5Mar89:2,3, SG12Mar89:2,
SG19Mar89:2,3, SG2Apr89:2, SG9Apr89:2,3,
SG16Apr89:2,3, SG23Apr89:2, SG30Apr89:3,
SG7May89:3, SG14May89:2, SG28May89:3,
SG4Jun89:3, SG11Jun89:3, SG18Jun89:2,3,
SG2Jul89:3, SG9Jul89:2, SG16Jul89:2,
SG23Jul89:3, SG6Aug89:3, SG13Aug89:2,
SG20Aug89:2, FG24Aug89:2,3, SG27Aug89:3,
SG3Sep89:3, SG17Sep89:3, SG24Sep89:2,3,
SG1Oct89:2,3, SG8Oct89:3, SG29Oct89:2,3,

SG5Nov89:3, SG12Nov89:2,3, SG19Nov89:2,3,
SG26Nov89:2, SG17Dec89:2
newspaper extract from, SG7Feb88:2,3
politics in, SG29Nov87:2, WC5Feb89:2,
SG19Feb89:3, WC19Feb89:2, SG12Mar89:2
prices in, WC29Jan89:2
proposed ban on dramatic entertainments in,
SG12Mar89:2
proposed capital for U.S., SG2Apr89:3
public buildings of, SG16Apr89:2
school in, SG26Mar89:3
schoolmasters' meeting in, FG21Sep89:2
shipping of, SG29Jan89:2, SG5Feb89:2
steel importation into, SG10Sep89:2
steel manufacturing in, WC29Jan89:2
support for federal Constitution in, WC9Jul88:2
theater in, SG26Mar89:3
thefts in, SG4Oct87:4, SG5Mar89:2
trade association of, SG8Oct89:3
tribute to Washington, SG14May89:2
weather in, SG17Sep89:3
witchcraft in, SG15Nov87:2
Philanthropy, English, SG20Aug89:1
Philip, Lewis, Duke of Orleans, death of,
NCG29Mar86:4
Philips, Abraham, SG24Sep89:3
Philips, Mr., SG29Sep88:3
Philips, Robert, SG22Oct89:3, SG29Oct89:3,
SG12Nov89:4
Phillips, A., SG3Dec89:3
Phillips, Abraham, WC20Aug88:2
Phillips, E., SG3Dec89:3
Phillips, Ethelred, SG3Sep89:3
Phillips, James, WC20Aug88:2
Phillips, John M., SG25Dec88:3—
Phillips, Nancy, SG20Oct88:3, SG27Oct88:3
Phillis (slave), emancipation of, SG18Dec88:3,
WC18Dec88:3
"Philomathes," SG18Jan87:2
Physicians, SG11Dec88:3
fees of, WC9Jul88:2
ridicule of, SG5Nov89:3
Pickens, ____, SG24Sep89:3
Pickens, Davis, WC20Aug88:2
Pickens, Thomas, SG13Aug89:1
Pierce, Aaron, WC13Aug88:3
Pierce, Evert, WC20Aug88:2
Pierce, John, SG22Sep88:2
Pierson, Thomas W., SG6Jul86:4
Pig, WC15Jan89:4
Pilkington, Edward, SG29Nov87:4
Pilkington, Thomas, SG29Nov87:4
Pilotage, Cape Fear River, regulation of, SG18Jan87:3
Pilots, WC30Jul88:3, WC5Nov88:3, WC12Nov88:4,
SG10Dec89:3
Pimental, Aaron, WC2Jul88:3—
Pine Long, Cherokee Nation, letter from, SG9Apr89:3
Pinkstone, Thomas, WC15Jan89:3—
Pintard, John Marsden, U.S. agent to Madeira,
SG7Feb88:2
Piracy, SG25Dec88:3, WC25Dec88:3, SG19Mar89:3,
SG27Aug89:3, SG3Sep89:3, SG10Sep89:2,3
escape of, SG15Oct89:2
punishment of, WC2Jul88:2, WC19Nov88:3,
SG25Dec88:3
Pirates, SG11Dec88:3, SG15Oct89:2

Pitcairne, Dr., NCGH23Feb86:1
Pitch, WC17Sep88:4
Pitt, Mr., NCGH16Feb86:2, SG4Jun89:4, SG23Jul89:1
    French compliment to, SG16Jul89:3
Pitt, W., communication of to Prince of Wales,
    SG30Apr89:1
Pitt, William, SG26Mar89:1,2, SG4Jun89:4
Pitt County, N.C., SG18Jan87:2, SG25Dec88:2,
    SG9Apr89:3, SG3Sep89:3, SG31Dec89:3
Pittsborough, N.C., SG18Jan87:2
Pittsburg (Pittsburgh), Pa., SG27Mar88:4
    Conn. troops arrive in, WC19Feb89:2
    letter from, SG28May89:3, SG1Oct89:3,
        SG8Oct89:3
    news from, WC19Feb89:2, SG26Mar89:2,
        SG1Oct89:3, SG8Oct89:3
Plantation
    rent of, SG4Dec88:3, SG11Dec88:4, WC29Jan89:3,
        WC5Feb89:1
    sale of, EI9Apr88:1, WC23Jul88:1—,
        WC10Dec88:3—, WC5Feb89:4, SG27Mar88:4
"Planter, A," WC9Jul88:3
Platt, Mrs., WC26Oct88:3, WC5Nov88:3
Plummer, Aaron, WC26Oct88:3
Plummer, K., SG22Oct89:3
Pocketbook
    found, WC8Jan89:3—
    lost, SG6Jul86:3
    stolen, SG30Apr89:3—
Poems by Robert Burns, SG8Jan89:1—, SG26Feb89:3,
    SG12Mar89:3—, SG23Apr89:3—
    sale of, SG18Jun89:4—, SG23Jul89:3,4,
        SG6Aug89:4, SG10Sep89:3,4,
        SG17Sep89:3,4, SG24Sep89:3,4, SG15Oct89:4,
        SG29Oct89:4, SG19Nov89:3, SG26Nov89:3
Poetry, NCG11Jul87:4, SG15Oct89:3
    See also Parnassian Loom; Poet's Corner
Poet's Corner, NCG29Jul84:4, NCG2Sep84:4,
    NCGH6Oct85:4, NCG3Nov85:4, SG12Jan86:4,
    NCGH19Jan86:4, NCGH2Feb86:4,
    NCGH16Feb86:4, NCGH23Feb86:4, SG23Feb86:4,
    SG6Jul86:4, SG18Jan87:4, NCG11Jul87:4,
    SG4Oct87:4, SG29Nov87:4, SG7Feb88:4,
    SG27Mar88:4, EI9Apr88:4, EI4Jun88:4,
    WC18Jun88:4, WC2Jul88:4, WC16Jul88:4,
    WC30Jul88:4—, SG8Sep88:4—, WC17Sep88:4,
    WC24Sep88:2,4, WC15Oct88:2, WC26Oct88:4,
    FG24Aug89:4, FG14Sep89:4, FG21Sep89:2,
    FG12Oct89:4
    See also Parnassian Loom; Poetry
Point Petre, Guadalupe, letter from, SG18Dec88:3
Poland
    condition of, WC15Oct88:1
    meeting of diet of, WC19Feb89:2
    news from, SG4Jun89:1
Political Magazine, extract from, SG4Jun89:3
Politicians, British, character of, NCGH2Feb86:1,
    SG10Sep89:1
Polk, J., SG9Apr89:3—
Polk, William, SG8Sep88:4—, SG17Dec89:3
Pollock, Cullen, SG7Feb88:3
Pollock, George, SG7Feb88:3
Pollock, Hugh, SG27Mar88:3
Pollock, Thomas, SG7Feb88:3
Pons, Mr., SG20Oct88:3, SG27Oct88:3
Ponsonby, Richard, SG20Oct88:3, SG27Oct88:3

Pool, John, SG9Apr89:3—
Pool, Thomas, NCGH19Jan86:4, NCGH2Feb86:4
Poor, Wardens of, SG18Jan87:3, SG18Dec88:3
Poor house, SG18Jan87:2
Pope
    circular from, SG2Apr89:2
    effect of the French Revolution on, SG10Dec89:1
    intends to visit France, SG24Dec89:1
    sends representative to Prussia, WC10Sep88:2
Popularity, ode to, SG13Aug89:4
Port-au-Prince
    hurricane in, SG29Sep88:3, SG6Oct88:3
    shipping to America, SG28May89:3
Port Beaufort, N.C., SG18Jun89:3
Port Brunswick, N.C., vessels cleared from,
    SG14May89:3
Port Roanoke, N.C., exports from, SG15Jan89:2,3
Port Swansborough, N.C., SG18Jan87:2
Porter, EI4Jun88:4
Porter, ___, SG3Dec89:3
Porter, Captain, SG17Sep89:3
Porter, Daniel, SG27Mar88:3
Porter, David, WC13Aug88:3
Porter, J., SG3Dec89:3
Porter, Thomas, NCG6Jan85:1
Porter, William, WC20Aug88:2, SG31Dec89:3
Porterfield, Col., WC2Jul88:3
Porterfield, James, WC20Aug88:2, WC18Dec88:3
Portland, Mass. (New England)
    naval officer of, SG27Aug89:2
    news from, SG17Nov88:2,3, WC26Nov88:2,
        SG3Sep89:2, SG24Sep89:2
    newspaper extract from, SG27Aug89:2
    petition from, SG5Mar89:4
    trade to, SG10Sep89:2
Portland Point, Mass., erection of lighthouse on,
    SG24Sep89:2
Ports of Entry and Delivery, bill for considered by
    Congress, SG2Jul89:1
Portsmouth, England
    letter from, WC22Jan89:2, WC5Feb89:2
    enlistment of seamen in, WC25Dec88:2
Portsmouth, N.H., SG20Oct88:2, WC19Nov88:2,
    SG24Nov88:2
    jailbreak in, SG16Apr89:2
    news from, SG23Apr89:2, SG25Jun89:2
Portsmouth, Va., SG12Feb89:3—
    storm in, WC13Aug88:3
Portugal
    commerce of, SG10Dec89:1
    death of Don Joseph Francisco Xavier in,
        WC3Dec88:3
    line of royal succession in, WC3Dec88:3
    politics in, WC3Dec88:3, SG11Dec88:3
    promotion of commerce in, SG10Dec89:1
    U.S. trade with, SG30Apr89:2
Positions, wanted, SG18Jan87:4
Post, Samuel, SG6Jul86:3
Post, SG12Jan86:3, NCG1Aug87:3, WC30Jul88:3,4,
    WC3Sep88:2, WC24Sep88:2, WC18Dec88:3,
    WC15Jan89:3, SG15Oct89:3
    Continental, NCG19Dec87:4
    route of, NCG19Dec87:4, WC2Jul88:3,
        WC23Jul88:3, SG20Oct88:4, SG27Oct88:4
    See also Mail; Stage
Post and Cady, SG18Jan87:4

Post Office
  Edenton, letters left in, SG20Oct88:3,
    SG27Oct88:3, SG8Jan89:3, SG15Jan89:4,
    SG9Apr89:3—, SG9Jul89:3—, SG22Oct89:3,
    SG29Oct89:3, SG12Nov89:4
  New Bern, letters left in, NCG29Jul84:2,
    NCG6Jan85:1, NCG19Dec87:4, SG18Jan87:3,
    SG27Mar88:3
  Philadelphia, SG11Dec88:3, SG25Dec88:3,
    WC8Jan89:3
  U.S., SG20Oct88:4, SG27Oct88:4
  Wilmington, letters left in, WC20Aug88:3
Post Stages, SG6Jul86:4
Potash, SG22Jan89:3, WC29Jan89:2, SG3Jul89:3
  export of, WC25Jun88:2
  manufacture of, WC25Jun88:2, SG2Jul89:3,
    SG31Dec89:3
Potts, Joshua, WC12Nov88:3—, WC19Feb89:3,
  WC26Feb89:1,3
Potts, Mr., WC16Jul88:2, WC23Jul88:1
Poughkeepsie (Poukeepsie)
  letter from, WC6Aug88:2, SG30Apr89:3
  news from, WC17Sep88:2, SG24Nov88:2,
    SG2Apr89:2
  witchcraft in, SG30Apr89:3
Powel, William, WC29Jan89:3, WC5Feb89:4
Powell, John, SG22Oct89:3, SG29Oct89:3,
  SG12Nov89:4
Prat, ____, NCG3Nov85:2
Prentice, Henry, death of, WC9Jul88:2
Prentice, James, WC13Aug88:3
Prentice & Mooney, SG20Oct88:3, SG27Oct88:3
President, U.S., SG4Dec88:2, SG16Jul89:2
  address to, SG11Jun89:2,3, SG6Aug89:3
  appointments by, FG12Oct89:3
  election of, SG6Jul86:1, WC27Aug88:3,
    WC15Oct88:1, SG15Jan89:2, WC22Jan89:2,
    SG29Jan89:2, SG5Feb89:2, WC5Feb89:2,
    SG12Feb89:2,3, WC12Feb89:1, SG19Feb89:2,3,
    WC19Feb89:2, SG26Feb89:3, WC26Feb89:2,
    SG5Mar89:3, SG12Mar89:2,3, SG16Apr89:2,
    SG30Apr89:2
  illness of, SG9Jul89:2, SG16Jul89:2
  ode to, SG10Dec89:4
  proclamation of, SG29Oct89:4
  reception of, SG14May89:2
  salary of considered by Congress, SG2Jul89:1
  tour of, SG5Nov89:2, SG12Nov89:3, SG3Dec89:2,4,
    SG10Dec89:2, SG17Dec89:2
  trip to New York, SG30Apr89:2
  See also Washington, George
Press, freedom of, WC9Jul88:2, SG3Sep89:3,
  SG10Sep89:3, SG10Dec89:4
Price, Dr.
  approval of federal Constitution by, WC25Jun88:2,
    SG29Sep88:3
  letter from, SG29Sep88:3, SG18Jun89:2
Prices current
  Fayetteville, FG24Aug89:3, FG14Sep89:3,
    FG21Sep89:3
  Wilmington, WC18Jun88:3—, WC23Jul88:3—,
    WC5Nov88:3—, WC18Dec88:3,
    WC25Dec88:3, WC8Jan89:3, WC22Jan89:3,
    WC29Jan89:3, WC12Feb89:3, WC26Feb89:3
Prichard, T., SG8Jan89:3, SG15Jan89:4
Prichard, William, SG29Sep88:3

Pride, ____, SG24Sep89:3, SG3Dec89:3
Pridgen, David, WC20Aug88:2
Prince of Wales, NCG9Dec84:4, SG9Apr89:3,
  SG7May89:2, SG14May89:1
  address, SG30Apr89:1
  anecdote about, NCGH23Feb86:1
  response to Mr. Pitt, SG30Apr89:1
  See also Prince William Henry
Prince William Henry, NCGH19Jan86:2,
  WC25Jun88:2, WC8Jan89:4, WC15Jan89:3,
  WC22Jan89:2, SG30Apr89:2, SG27Aug89:2,3
  address to, WC22Jan89:1
  answer of, WC22Jan89:1
  concern for father, WC12Feb89:2
  honored in Jamaica, WC22Jan89:2
  response to Jamaican Council, WC22Jan89:1
  See also Prince of Wales
Princess Ann(e) County, Va., SG29Jan89:3,
  SG5Feb89:4, SG19Feb89:4, SG26Feb89:4,
  SG21May89:3, SG28May89:4, SG18Jun89:4
Princess Elizabeth, intrusion upon, WC10Sep88:2,3,
  SG22Sep88:2,3
Prindle, David, SG9Jul89:3
Printer's blanks, sale of, NCG29Jul84:4, SG2Sep84:4,
  NCG9Dec84:4, NCGH6Oct85:4, SG18Jan87:4,
  NCG1Aug87:3, NCG15Aug87:4, NCG19Dec87:4,
  EI4Jun88:4, WC18Jun88:4—, WC8Jan89:4—,
  SG12Feb89:3, SG19Feb89:4, SG4Jun89:4,
  SG9Jul89:4—, SG6Aug89:4, SG27Aug89:4,
  SG24Sep89:4, SG19Nov89:3,4
Printing, FG24Aug89:1
  political importance of, SG5Feb89:3
Printing office, Wilmington, WC20Aug88:3,
  WC27Aug88:3, WC18Dec88:3
Prison, SG18Jan87:3
  erection of, WC18Dec88:2
  escape from, SG26Mar89:2
Privateers, NCG29Mar86:4
Privy Council, SG8Oct89:3
  proceedings of, SG1Oct89:3
Proceedings and Debates of the Late Convention of North
  Carolina, sale of, SG18Jun89:3—, SG23Jul89:3,
  SG6Aug89:4, SG20Aug89:4, SG24Sep89:4—,
  SG12Nov89:3, SG26Nov89:3, SG10Dec89:4,
  SG17Dec89:3
Produce, country, sale of, WC3Sep88:3, WC10Sep88:4,
  WC19Feb89:3,4
Professions, characterization of, WC10Sep88:1
Property, N.C.
  confiscated, NCG6Jan85:1,2
  taxation of, SG18Jan87:4
Protestant Episcopal Church, U.S., meeting of,
  SG12Nov89:2
Providence, R.I.
  bell for meeting house in, NCG9Dec84:3
  celebration of election of artillery officers in,
    WC2Jul88:2
  counterfeit money in, SG20Aug89:2
  elections in, SG24Sep89:3
  letter from, SG15Oct89:2
  manufacturing in, WC10Sep88:2
  militia musters in, WC2Jul88:2
  news from, WC2Jul88:2, SG10Nov88:2,
    WC29Jan89:2, SG12Feb89:2, SG26Feb89:2,
    SG16Apr89:2, SG4Jun89:2, SG10Dec89:2
Providence College, SG13Oct88:2

Providence Gazette, extract from, SG5Mar89:3, SG18Jun89:3
Provoost, Rev. Dr., WC5Feb89:2
Provost, Right Rev. Dr. SG22Jan89:3
Prussia, WC15Oct88:2
    anecdote of corporal of the King's Life Guards, WC15Oct88:2
    dispute with Russia, WC22Jan89:2
    emperor of, WC19Feb89:3
    English treaty with, WC10Sep88:2, SG2Jul89:4
    king of, WC18Dec88:4, SG5Mar89:2
    letters from king of to Madame de Camas, SG5Mar89:1,2
    politics in, SG8Sep88:1
    U.S. treaty with, NCG29Mar86:1
Pryor, William, SG6Jul86:3
Psalmody, WC5Feb89:2
Public entertainment, SG27Mar88:3
Public printer, SG3Dec89:3
Public records, WC19Nov88:3
Publications, sale of, WC18Jun88:4—
"Publicola," SG27Mar88:2
Pugh, Francis, SG27Aug89:3, FG14Sep89:3
Pugh, Mr., SG3Dec89:3
Pugh, Thomas, SG16Apr89:3
Pugh, Thomas, Sr., SG9Apr89:3
Puritan, dialogue with Quaker, WC10Dec88:4
Pursell, James, SG17Sep89:3
Purss, Henry, NCG3Nov85:2, NCG19Dec87:4
Putnam, Capt., SG25Dec88:3—

Q

Quack, Will, ran away, NCG2Sep84:4
Quadrant, stolen, EI4Jun88:4
Quadruple Alliance, SG27Aug89:1,2
Quakers, WC3Sep88:4, SG24Nov88:2, SG10Dec89:2, SG31Dec89:3
    anecdote about, WC26Nov88:1,2
    charity of, SG3Nov88:2
    dialogue with Puritan, WC10Dec88:4
    opposition to slave trade, SG24Nov88:2
    treatment of, WC26Nov88:1,2
Qualls, ____, SG24Sep89:3, SG3Dec89:3
Quebec, SG12Jan86:2
    government of, SG12Jan86:2
    governor of, NCGH23Feb86:2, SG22Sep88:1
    news from, NCGH16Feb86:3, NCGH23Feb86:2,3, WC12Feb89:1
    trade of with U.S., SG23Jul89:1
    weather in, NCGH16Feb86:3
Queen of England, SG7May89:2
Quick, Will, ran away, NCG2Sep84:4
"Quieting Act," NCG11Jul87:1
Quills, SG23Feb86:3
Quilting, WC17Sep88:2
Quince, Mrs., WC12Nov88:3, WC19Nov88:3
Quince, Parker, WC8Jan89:3, WC15Jan89:3, WC26Feb89:3, WC5Mar89:1, SG31Dec89:3
Quince's Alley, WC26Oct88:3, WC5Nov88:3
Quincey, Richard, SG3Sep89:3

R

"R," NCG3Nov85:3

Raford, Captain, WC22Jan89:4
Rags, wanted, EI19Dec87:1, SG8Sep88:4—, SG15Jan89:3
Raleigh Canal, SG23Apr89:3—, SG23Jul89:4
Raleigh Inlet, SG9Jul89:3
Ralph, Thomas, SG8Jan89:3, SG15Jan89:4
Ramke, F., SG8Jan89:3—, SG12Mar89:3
Ramke, Frederick, NCG29Jul84:3, SG2Sep84:4
Ramsay, Ambrose, WC20Aug88:2, SG22Sep88:3
Ramsay, David, SG8Jan89:3—
Ramsay, J., SG3Dec89:3
Ramsey, John, SG17Sep89:3
Randal, William, WC20Aug88:2
Randall, William, SG3Sep89:3
Randolph County, NCGH16Feb86:3, NCGH23Feb86:3, SG23Feb86:3, SG29Sep88:3, WC26Nov88:3, SG18Dec88:3, WC18Dec88:2, SG25Dec88:2,3, SG1Jan89:3, SG5Feb89:3, FG14Sep89:3
Rangle, Mr., SG20Oct88:3, SG27Oct88:3
Rapids of the Ohio, letter from, SG24Sep89:3
Rascoe, James, SG29Nov87:1
Ratley, Mr., SG13Aug89:3
Rawhides, exportation of, SG31Dec89:3
Rawlings, Asahel, WC20Aug88:2
Ray, ____, SG3Dec89:3
Rayborn, John, SG18Jun89:3—
Razor, Mrs., SG12Jan86:4
Rea, William, SG20Oct88:3, SG27Oct88:3, SG9Apr89:3—
Read, Col., WC18Jun88:3, WC25Jun88:3, WC9Jul88:4
Read, James, WC19Feb89:3, WC26Feb89:1
Read, Thomas, SG17Nov88:3
Reading, ____, SG3Dec89:3
Reading, Thomas, WC20Aug88:2, SG27Aug89:2, FG14Sep89:3
Reading, Pa., letter from, SG12Mar89:2
Real estate, descent of, SG31Dec89:3
Reardon, D. & Co., WC3Sep88:3
Reardon, Dennis & Co., WC9Jul88:3
Reasonover, Joseph, NCG15Aug87:3
Recognizances, forfeited, SG25Dec88:3
Reddick, J., SG3Dec89:3
Reddick, Joseph, WC20Aug88:2
Reding, Benjamin, NCG6Jan85:1
Reflection, pleasure of, SG4Dec88:1
Regan, John, WC20Aug88:2
Regency, Great Britain, SG9Apr89:3
Reilly, Philip, NCG9Dec84:4
Reilly and Tuton, NCG9Dec84:4
Relfe, Enoch, WC20Aug88:2, SG1Jan89:3—, SG27Aug89:3, FG14Sep89:3, SG22Oct89:3, SG29Oct89:3, SG12Nov89:4
Religion, WC3Sep88:1, WC26Oct88:4, WC19Nov88:4, SG14May89:3
    encouragement of, WC5Feb89:2
    establishment of, FG21Sep89:1, FG12Oct89:1
    Hindu, SG19Feb86:3
    observations on, FG14Sep89:1
"Reporter, A," NCG11Jul87:4
"Republican, A," SG6Oct88:1, WC5Nov88:2
Revenue
    diminution of, WC18Dec88:2
    raising of, SG3Dec89:3, SG31Dec89:3
Revolutionary War, veterans of, SG6Aug89:2
Reynolds
    See Hepburn and Reynolds

Rhea, ____, SG3Dec89:3
Rhea, John, SG29Nov87:3
Rhea, Mr., SG17Dec89:3
Rhode Island, SG30Apr89:3, SG11Jun89:2,
    SG15Oct89:2, SG3Dec89:2
    antifederalism in, SG26Feb89:2
    benefits of new government for, SG26Feb89:2
    commerce, WC19Feb89:2, SG18Jun89:3,
        SG8Oct89:2
    considers constitutional convention, SG23Apr89:3,
        SG23Jul89:2
    and Constitutional Convention, NCG11Jul87:4
    debate in over federal collection of impost,
        SG4Jun89:2
    denunciation of, SG22Sep88:2, SG3Dec89:4
    description of, SG28May89:4
    elections in, WC18Jun88:3
    and federal Constitution, WC22Jan89:3,
        SG29Jan89:3, SG26Nov89:3, SG3Dec89:4
    Federalists in, SG8Oct89:2
    independence of, SG16Apr89:2
    letter from, NCG11Jul87:4, SG8Oct89:2,
        SG19Nov89:2,3
    meeting of General Assembly of, WC19Feb89:2
    need to resort to smuggling, SG8Oct89:2,3
    N.C. association with, WC12Nov88:3
    opposition to federal Constitution in, SG8Sep88:2,
        WC22Jan89:3, SG19Nov89:2,3
    paper currency in, FG12Oct89:3, SG15Oct89:2
    parody on opposition of to federal Constitution,
        SG3Dec89:4
    pirates in, SG26Feb89:2
    politics in, WC18Jun88:3, WC20Aug88:3,
        SG11Dec88:3, WC22Jan89:3, SG29Jan89:3,
        SG12Feb89:2, WC12Feb89:3, WC19Feb89:2,
        SG5Mar89:3, SG26Mar89:2, SG23Apr89:3,
        SG28May89:3, SG4Jun89:2, SG23Jul89:2,3,
        SG24Sep89:3, SG15Oct89:2, SG19Nov89:2,3,
        SG26Nov89:2, SG10Dec90:2
    proceedings of General Assembly of, SG4Jun89:2,
        SG10Dec89:2
    refusal of General Assembly to call constitutional
        convention, SG10Dec89:2, SG12Feb89:2,
        WC12Feb89:3, SG5Mar89:3
    seeks exemption from U.S. tonnage duties,
        SG24Sep89:3
    Society of Cincinnati in, SG29Oct89:2
    Tender Law in, WC22Jan89:3
    and U.S. SG30Apr89:3, SG18Jun89:3, SG2Jul89:2,
        SG23Jul89:2, SG24Sep89:3, SG1Oct89:3,
        SG8Oct89:2, SG26Nov89:2
Rhodes, Benjamin, SG27Mar88:3
Rhodes, J., WC13Aug88:3
Rhodes, William, NCG6Jan85:1
Rice, ____, SG3Dec89:3
Rice, D., SG3Dec89:3
Rice, David, SG22Oct89:3, SG29Oct89:3,
    SG12Nov89:4
Rice, J., SG3Dec89:3
Rice, John, NCG29Jul84:3
Rice, Mr., SG17Dec89:3
Richards, H. J., WC23Jul88:1, WC30Jul88:4,
    WC20Aug88:3, WC3Sep88:4, WC26Nov88:3
Richardson, John, NCG6Jan85:1, SG9Jul89:3—
Richardson, Thomas, SG3Nov88:2
Richmond, Va.

Indian chieftains in, SG5Nov89:3
letter from, SG14May89:3
news from, NCG29Jul84:2, NCG2Sep84:2,
    NCG9Dec84:3, SG29Nov87:2, WC13Aug88:1,
    SG17Nov88:3, SG24Nov88:3, SG11Dec88:2,3,
    SG15Jan89:2, SG29Jan89:2, SG12Feb89:3,
    WC19Feb89:2, SG26Feb89:2,3, WC5Mar89:2,
    SG12Mar89:3, SG16Apr89:3, SG30Apr89:3,
    SG4Jun89:3, SG1Oct89:3, SG15Oct89:3,
    SG29Oct89:3, SG5Nov89:3, SG26Nov89:3,
    SG17Dec89:2
shipping of, SG26Nov89:3
Richmond County, N.C., NCG15Aug87:4,
    WC26Nov88:3, SG18Dec88:3, WC18Dec88:2,
    SG25Dec88:2, SG24Sep89:3
    academy in, SG18Dec88:3
Richmond Garden, poem, sale of, SG23Apr89:3—
Riddick, Joseph, SG12Jan86:2
Ridgely, Richard, SG29Nov87:4
Riding, Benjamin, NCG29Jul84:3
Riding chair, WC23Jul88:4
Ried, John, SG20Oct88:3, SG27Oct88:3
Righten, William, SG27Aug89:3, SG3Sep89:4,
    FG14Sep89:3
Righton, ____, SG3Dec89:2
Righton, William, SG29Nov87:1, SG30Jul89:3,
    SG10Sep89:3—, SG22Oct89:4
Ringworm, remedy for, SG12Nov89:3
Ripley, Eliphalet, WC18Dec88:3, SG25Dec88:3—,
    WC25Dec88:1, WC8Jan89:4—, SG20Aug89:4—,
    SG24Sep89:4—, SG8Oct89:4—
Ripley, James, SG10Nov88:3
Ritchie, William & Co., NCG29Mar86:1
Rittenhouse, ____, SG12Jan86:3
Road
    opening of in western N.C., SG18Dec88:3—
    stoppage of, SG10Dec89:1
Roanoke, Port of, SG18Dec88:3
Roanoke Inlet, channel of, SG29Nov87:2
Roanoke Island, SG26Mar89:3—
    letter from, SG23Apr89:3
    shipping at, SG23Apr89:3
Robbery, NCGH23Feb86:2, SG22Jan89:3,
    WC12Feb89:1
Roberson (Robertson, Robinson) County, N.C.,
    SG22Sep88:3, SG18Dec88:3, WC18Dec88:3,
    SG25Dec88:2, SG17Sep89:3
    taxes in, SG31Dec89:3
    town in, SG18Dec88:3
Roberts, George, WC20Aug88:2
Roberts, James, NCG29Mar86:2
Roberts, Willis, SG9Jul89:3—
Robertson, Charles, WC20Aug88:2
Robertson, Col., SG22Jan89:3
Robertson, James, SG20Oct88:1, SG18Dec88:3—
Robeson, ____, SG3Dec89:3
Robeson, Wm., SG27Mar88:3
Robespierre
    anecdote about, WC15Jan89:1
    speech of, SG10Dec89:4
Robinson, Charles, SG29Nov87:3
Robinson, Peter, SG20Oct88:3, SG27Oct88:3
Robinson, W., SG24Sep89:3
Robinson, William, WC29Jan89:3, WC5Feb89:4
Rochambeau, Count de, WC26Nov88:1
Rockingham County, N.C., SG29Sep88:3,

SG25Dec88:2, SG24Sep89:3
  court of, SG18Dec88:3, WC18Dec88:3
  tax levy in, WC18Dec88:3
Rock-Landing, Ga.
  Indian negotiations at, SG15Oct89:3, SG12Nov89:3
  Indian treaty at, SG24Sep89:3
  letter from, SG15Oct89:3
  meeting with Indians at, SG30Jul89:2,3
Roddy, James, WC20Aug88:2
Rogers, Joseph, SG2Sep84:4
Rogers, Miriam, SG2Sep84:4
Rogers, Mr., SG4Oct87:4
Rogers, William, SG29Nov87:2
  executed for piracy, WC2Jul88:2
Rolando, A. D. Henrique, SG22Oct89:3, SG29Oct89:3,
  SG12Nov89:4
Rolando, Henry, SG22Oct89:3, SG29Oct89:3,
  SG12Nov89:4
Roman Catholic Church, NCGH19Jan86:2,
  SG29Oct88:2, SG5Feb89:2, SG10Dec89:2,
  SG17Dec89:1
  Pope of, SG3Sep89:2
Roman Empire, decline of, SG10Dec89:2
Rome, census taken in, SG15Jan89:2
Ronaldson, A., WC19Feb89:3, WC26Feb89:1
Rose, William, NCG29Mar86:2
Ross, James, SG27Mar88:3
Ross, John, WC13Aug88:3
Rotterdam Gazette, extract from, SG7Feb88:2
Rountree, Thos., SG22Oct89:3, SG29Oct89:3,
  SG12Nov89:4
Rouson, James, SG31Dec89:3
Rousseau, John James, FG14Sep89:1
Roussel, Mons., SG9Apr89:3—
Routledge, Thomas, SG7Feb88:3
Row, James, WC13Aug88:3
Rowan, John, NCG29Jul84:3, WC13Aug88:3,
  SG20Oct88:3, SG27Oct88:3
Rowan, Robert, NCGH19Jan86:3, NCGH2Feb86:3,
  NCGH16Feb86:1, NCGH23Feb86:4, SG23Feb86:2,
  WC23Jul88:1, WC30Jul88:4, WC20Aug88:3,
  WC3Sep88:3, FG21Sep89:2, WC24Sep88:2,
  WC15Oct88:2—
Rowan County, N.C., NCGH19Jan86:4,
  NCGH2Feb86:4, NCG29Mar86:2, SG18Jan87:2,3,
  WC23Jul88:3—, WC17Sep88:3, SG29Sep88:3,
  WC26Nov88:3, SG18Dec88:3, WC18Dec88:2,
  SG25Dec88:2, FG24Aug89:3, FG14Sep89:3,
  SG17Sep89:3, FG21Sep89:4, SG31Dec89:3
  letter from, WC23Jul88:2,3
Rubbish, WC5Feb89:3
Rulers, drinking to the health of, SG26Mar89:1
Rum, sale of, SG6Jul86:4, WC3Sep88:3—,
  WC19Feb89:4, SG30Jul89:3, SG13Aug89:4,
  SG20Aug89:4
Rum and molasses, sale of, SG23Jul89:3—
Rum and sugar, sale of, WC3Sep88:3
Rumsey, James, NCG9Dec84:3
Rush, Dr., observations of, SG7Feb88:2
Russel, Edward, WC15Oct88:2—
Russel, Samuel, WC13Aug88:3
Russel, William, SG23Feb86:4
Russell, Ann, SG29Nov87:4
Russell, Elizabeth, SG22Oct89:3, SG29Oct89:3,
  SG12Nov89:4
Russell, Habakuk, SG29Nov87:4

Russia, WC18Dec88:2
  anecdotes of the empire of, SG19Mar89:4
  attacked by Sweden, WC15Jan89:1
  compared to U.S., SG3Dec89:1
  condition of, WC15Oct88:1
  declaration of Empress of, NCG29Jul84:1,
    WC3Dec88:3
  description of, SG15Jan89:1
  dispute with Prussia, WC22Jan89:2
  discourse on foreign politics stopped, SG13Oct88:2
  Empress of, SG1Jan89:3, SG19Mar89:4
  fleet of, SG5Nov89:3
  government regulation of trade of, NCG29Jul84:1
  naval engagement with Sweden, WC12Nov88:2
  navy of, WC19Nov88:2,3, WC18Dec88:2
  negotiations with Sweden, WC19Feb89:2
  news from, SG4Jun89:1
  politics in, WC2Jul88:2, SG13Oct88:2,
    SG29Oct89:1
  preparations for war by, WC30Jul88:2
  privateer of seizes French vessel, WC25Dec88:2
  refuses volunteers of other countries in army,
    WC25Jun88:2
  relations with Ottoman Empire, WC9Jul88:2
  reported revolution in, WC25Jun88:2
  sailing of naval squadron of, WC3Sep88:1
  Sweden plots revolution in, WC26Nov88:2
  U.S. trade with, NCG9Dec84:2,3
  Vice-admiral of, SG19Nov89:2
  wars of, WC10Sep88:2, WC26Oct88:2,
    WC19Nov88:1,2, WC26Nov88:1,
    WC3Dec88:2,3, SG26Nov89:4
Rutherford, Gen., WC17Sep88:3, SG29Sep88:3
Rutherford, Griffith, WC20Aug88:2, SG31Dec89:3
Rutherford, John, WC13Aug88:3
Rutherford, Lieutenant, SG9Apr89:3—
Rutherford, Thomas, NCG29Mar86:2, WC29Jan89:3,
  WC5Feb89:1
Rutherford County, N.C., SG18Jan87:3, SG18Dec88:3,
  WC18Dec88:2, SG25Dec88:2
Ryan, Ann, SG22Oct89:3, SG29Oct89:3,
  SG12Nov89:4

S

Sabbath Day, WC26Nov88:4
Sacheverell, Dr., anecdote of, NCGH16Feb86:1
Saddlebags, lost, SG10Sep89:4, SG17Sep89:4
Sailors, SG12Jan86:4, WC12Feb89:3
  death of, SG27Aug89:3
  fighting of, SG26Mar89:2,3
  friendship of, SG12Jan86:4
  marital life of, NCGH19Jan86:2
  scarcity of in England, WC25Jun88:2
  travels of, WC19Nov88:2
  trial of, SG19Feb89:3
  See also Seamen
St. Andrew's, Scotland, damage in by storm,
  WC2Jul88:2
St. Andrew's Day, celebration of, WC3Dec88:3
St. Augustine, East Florida
  letter from, SG26Mar89:2
  protection given in to runaway slaves, WC9Jul88:2
St. Clair, Arthur, WC17Sep88:3
  arrival of at Muskingum, WC17Sep88:3

letter from, SG15Oct89:3
proclamation of, SG26Mar89:2
report of, SG15Oct89:3
St. Clair, Governor, SG12Mar89:2
St. Domingo, demand for flour in, SG28May89:3
St. Eustatius
    letter from, SG25Dec88:3
    prices in, WC27Aug88:3
St. George, Grenada
    account of ratification of U.S. constitution in,
        WC13Aug88:2
    news from, WC13Aug88:2
    trade of, WC13Aug88:2
St. James Chronicle, extract from, SG15Jan89:4
St. John's, Antigua
    news from, SG3Dec89:1, SG10Dec89:2
    ship sails from, WC17Sep88:2
St. John's, New Brunswick
    emigration from to U.S., SG22Jan89:3
    news from, SG22Jan89:3
St. John the Evangelist, festival of, WC8Jan89:1,
    WC19Feb89:1
St. John's Day, WC25Dec88:3
St. John's Lodge, No. 2 (New Bern), SG18Jun89:3,
    SG12Nov89:3, SG17Dec89:2
    officers of, WC8Jan89:3
St. John's Parish, N.C., disposal of glebe land in,
    SG18Jan87:2
St. Kitts, sugar crop in, WC13Aug88:2
St. Merry, Moreau de, speech of, SG5Nov89:4
St. Paul's, England, SG23Jul89:1
St. Paul's Church, SG25Jun89:2
St. Petersburg, Russia
    See Petersburg, Russia
St. Tammany, character of, SG24Sep89:4
St. Thomas, exports of to N.C., SG6Jul86:4
Salem, Mass.
    accident in, SG19Mar89:2
    news from, NCG9Dec84:2,3, WC3Sep88:2,
        SG17Nov88:2, SG22Jan89:3, SG19Mar89:2,
        SG23Apr89:2
    trade of, WC10Sep88:2
    Washington's tour through, SG10Dec89:2
Salem, N.C., FG14Sep89:3, SG3Dec89:3
Salisbury, N.C., NCGH19Jan86:4, SG18Jan87:2,3,
    NCG15Aug87:2, WC23Jul88:3—, SG29Sep88:2,
    WC29Jan89:3, WC5Feb89:1, SG26Feb89:3,
    WC5Mar89:2
    letter from, SG28May89:3
    regulation of, SG18Jan87:2
    tobacco inspectors at, SG18Jan87:3
Salisbury District, S18Jan87:3, SG25Dec88:4
    taxes in, SG18Jan87:2
Salt, WC22Jan89:4
    sale of, SG6Jul86:4, WC22Jan89:4
Salt springs, sale of, SG31Dec89:3
Sam (slave), WC26Feb89:3
Sampson (slave), runaway, WC12Feb89:3—
Sampson, Michael, NCGH6Oct85:4, NCGH19Jan86:2,
    NCGH2Feb86:2, NCGH16Feb86:4,
    NCGH23Feb86:4
Sampson County, N.C., SG22Sep88:3, WC26Nov88:3,
    SG25Dec88:2, SG17Sep89:3
Sanders, ____, SG3Dec89:3
Sanders, B., SG17Sep89:3, SG3Dec89:3
Sandford, Darius, SG6Jul86:4

Sandy, James, SG18Jan87:4
Sandy-Hook, N.J., drowning in, SG17Sep89:3
Santeuil, anecdote of, NCGH16Feb86:1
Sappinfield, Matthias, NCG29Mar86:2
Sappinfield, Tobias (?), NCGH19Jan86:4
Sardinia, letter from King of, SG5Nov89:2
Saunders, Britain, WC20Aug88:2
Saunders, J., SG7Feb88:3
Saunders, Mr., SG29Sep88:3
Savage, D. W., SG20Oct88:3, SG27Oct88:3
Savage & Westmore, SG20Oct88:3, SG27Oct88:3
Savannah
    dramatic performances in, WC19Feb89:1
    duel in, WC10Sep88:3
    letter from, NCGH2Feb86:2
    Masons in, WC19Feb89:1
    news from, WC9Jul88:2, SG24Nov88:3,
        WC22Jan89:2, SG12Feb89:2,3, WC19Feb89:1,
        SG6Aug89:3, SG27Aug89:3, SG12Nov89:3
Saw mills, SG27Mar88:3
    sale of, WC12Nov88:3—
    tender for wanted, SG29Nov87:4
Sawyer, ____, SG3Dec89:2,3
Sawyer, Enoch, WC20Aug88:2, SG3Sep89:3
Scantling, sale of, SG7Feb88:4
Scarborough, Benjamin, SG9Jul89:3—
Schaw, Robert, WC18Jun88:4, WC25Jun88:4
Schomberg, Dr. J., NCG29Jul84:1
School, NCG9Dec84:4, NCG23Feb86:4, SG23Feb86:4,
    SG6Jul86:3, SG18Jan87:3, NCG1Aug87:3,
    SG4Oct87:4, SG7Feb88:4, WC30Jul88:3,
    WC15Oct88:2—, WC19Nov88:3,4,
    WC26Nov88:3—
    Fencing and Dancing, NCG29Jul84:4
    French instruction, NCG1Aug87:3
    Vocal music, SG18Jan87:3
    See also Academy; Education
Schoolhouse, erection of, SG18Jan87:3
Schoolmaster, NCG3Nov85:4, SG18Jan87:4
Science, promotion of, EI19Dec87:1
Scotland, SG12Feb89:2
    divorce in, SG12Feb89:2
    dukes of, NCG29Jul84:2
    efforts to combat bankruptcies in, WC3Sep88:1
    emigrants from, SG10Nov88:2
    eroding prejudices against, SG31Dec89:2
    fire in, SG22Sep88:1
    Highland dress in, NCGH23Feb86:2
    history of, SG24Nov88:2
    land in, SG29Nov87:3
    letter from, SG19Nov89:2
    news from, NCG9Dec84:4
    politics in, NCG29Jul84:2, NCG9Dec84:4
    potatoes in, WC9Jul88:2
    reform in, SG8Sep88:1
    unrest in, NCGH23Feb86:2
Scots, reputation of, SG31Dec89:2
Scott, ____, SG3Dec89:3
Scott, John, WC20Aug88:2
Scott, Joseph, SG20Oct88:3, SG27Oct88:3
Scott, Robert, SG7Feb88:2
Scott, William, SG18Dec88:3, WC18Dec88:2
Scull, J. G., SG3Dec89:3
Scull, John, SG10Sep89:3
Scuppernong, N.C., letter from, SG11Jun89:2
Seamen

fund for, SG31Dec89:3
misfortune of, WC19Nov88:2
See also Sailors
Searle, D., SG22Jan89:3—
Secretary, J. B., WC26Oct88:4
Secretary of the Treasury, appointment of, SG9Jul89:2
Securities
    legislation to make negotiable, SG18Jan87:2
    Continental, WC17Sep88:2
    public, cancellation of, SG11Dec88:3
Selby, Col., SG13Aug89:3
Sellers, John, WC13Aug88:3
Selwyn, George, SG18Jun89:2
Senate, N.C.
    dissent in, SG12Jan86:2
    proceedings, SG12Jan86:2, SG3Dec89:4
Senate, U.S.
    address of, SG11Jun89:2
    classification of members of, SG4Jun89:3
    members of, WC8Jan89:3
    proceedings of, SG4Jun89:3
Seneca, S.C., letter from, SG30Jul89:2
Sergeant at arms, discourse on office of, SG11Jun89:2
Servant, runaway, SG19Mar89:3—
Sessions, Isaac, WC19Nov88:3—
Sevier, ____, WC23Jul88:2, SG11Dec88:3,
    SG29Jan89:2, SG12Feb89:3, WC19Feb89:2,
    SG26Feb89:3, WC5Mar89:2
Sevier, Gen., SG16Apr89:3, SG30Apr89:3
Sevier, Governor, WC6Aug89:3, SG8Sep88:3,
    WC5Mar89:2
Sevier, J., SG3Dec89:3
Sevier, John, SG29Nov87:3, SG29Sep88:1,
    WC8Jan89:3, WC19Feb89:2, SG30Jul89:2
    imprisonment of, WC8Jan89:3
    letter from, SG30Jul89:2
Sewall, Thomas, WC13Aug88:3
Sexton, Absalom, SG3Nov88:2
Shakespeare, WC3Dec88:4
Shallotte, N.C., WC30Jul88:3
Shandean Society of New Bern, N.C., SG11Jun89:1,4,
    SG17Dec89:2
    proceedings of, SG18Jun89:4
Sharpe, Edward, WC13Aug88:3
Sharpe, John, WC20Aug88:2
Sharpe, William, WC13Aug88:3
Shauls, stolen, WC19Feb89:3
Shaw, Col., WC26Feb89:3, WC5Mar89:1
Shaw, Colin, NCG29Mar86:2
Shaw, Hugh, SG20Oct88:3, SG27Oct88:3
Shaw, John, SG30Apr89:3—
Shaw, Samuel, NCG23Feb86:3
Shaw, Wm., SG18Jan87:3
Shawick, Mr., NCGH29Jul84:3
Shawls
    See Shauls
Shays, Daniel, NCG15Aug87:1
Shearman, Gideon, SG9Jul89:3—
Shebeare, Dr., anecdote of, SG1Jan89:4
Sheddan, John, SG20Oct88:3, SG27Oct88:3
Shelburne
    news from, SG2Apr89:2
    exports of, SG2Apr89:2
Shelburne, Lord, republican sentiment of, SG28May89:3
Shelby, Evan, SG19Nov87:3
Sheppard, B., SG3Dec89:3

Sheppard, William, SG22Sep88:3
Shepperd, Benjamin, SG2Jul89:3, SG9Jul89:4,
    SG23Jul89:3, SG3Sep89:3
Shepperd, William, WC20Aug88:2
Sheridan, Mr., speech of in Parliament, SG17Nov88:1
Sheridan, Thomas, dictionary of, SG4Dec88:1
Sheriffs
    relief of, SG18Dec88:3
    settlement of accounts, SG29Jan89:1
    tax collections by, SG18Jan87:2
Sherrod, ____, SG3Dec89:3
Sherrod, T., SG3Dec89:3
Sherrod, Thomas, WC20Aug88:2
Sherwood, Albert, SG9Apr89:3—
Sherwood, Col., SG24Sep89:3
Sheut, Joseph, SG9Apr89:3—
Ship
    charter of, WC2Jul88:3—
    cargo of sold at public auction, WC15Oct88:1
    damaged by storm, SG25Dec88:2
    distress of, NCG9Dec84:3, WC25Dec88:3,
        SG6Aug89:3, SG8Oct89:2,3
    explosion of, WC27Aug88:3, SG20Oct88:2
    launch of, SG20Oct88:2
    lost, WC30Jul88:3
    poor construction of, SG5Feb89:2
    sailing of, WC18Jun88:3, WC25Jun88:3,
        WC9Jul88:3—, WC30Jul88:1,3, WC20Aug88:3,
        WC3Sep88:3—, WC5Nov88:3, WC12Nov88:4,
        WC3Dec88:3—, WC19Feb89:3
    sale of, SG6Jul86:3, NCG1Aug87:3,
        NCG15Aug87:4, WC25Jun88:3, WC2Jul88:3,
        EI9Apr88:4, SG22Jan89:3—, WC5Feb89:3,
        WC12Feb89:3,4, WC19Feb89:1, WC26Feb89:1,
        SG10Dec89:3, SG17Dec89:4, SG31Dec89:3
    sale of cargo of, WC15Oct88:1
    stolen, SG6Jul86:4, SG29Nov87:4
    struck by lightning, WC2Jul88:2
    threatened by storm, WC3Sep88:2
    wanted for charter, SG26Mar89:3—
    wreck of, WC19Feb89:1
Shipbuilding, SG6Jul86:3, SG5Feb89:2
Shipping, NCG2Sep84:1,2
    accidents to, WC5Nov88:3, WC26Nov88:3,
        WC25Dec88:3, WC22Jan89:3, SG29Jan89:2,
        WC12Aug89:3, SG6Aug89:3
    attacks on, NCG2Sep84:2
    British, SG12Mar89:2
    English, SG22Jan89:3
    European, SG22Oct89:2
    French, WC3Sep88:2
    insurance for, NCGH2Feb86:2
    New York, SG19Mar89:2
    N.C., SG29Nov87:2,3
    Portuguese, NCG29Jul84:2
    regulation of British, WC3Sep88:1
    U.S., EI4Jun88:2, WC18Jun88:2, WC2Jul88:2,
        WC20Aug88:3, WC27Aug88:3, WC3Sep88:2,
        WC24Sep88:1,2, SG6Oct88:3, WC26Oct88:2,3,
        WC5Nov88:3, SG17Nov88:2,3, WC26Nov88:3,
        WC3Dec88:3, WC10Dec88:2, SG25Dec88:2,
        SG22Jan89:3, WC22Jan89:3, SG29Jan89:2,3,
        WC29Jan89:2, WC12Feb89:3,
        WC19Feb89:1,2,3, SG26Feb89:2, SG5Mar89:2,
        SG12Mar89:2, SG19Mar89:2, SG6Aug89:3,
        SG13Aug89:2, FG14Sep89:3, SG8Oct89:3,

SG10Dec89:3
    accident in, SG26Nov89:2
    British definition of, WC10Dec88:2
    British restrictions on, WC24Sep88:2
    capture of, WC16Jul88:3
    distress of, WC3Sep88:2
    facilitation of, SG15Nov87:2
    French regulation of, WC26Feb89:2
    imports, SG22Sep88:1
    Martinique restrictions on, SG22Jan89:3
    mutiny in, SG3Sep89:2
    protection of, WC24Sep88:2
    regulation of, SG12Jan86:2
Shipwreck, SG29Jan89:2
Shipwright, WC25Jun88:3
Shoes, manufacture of, WC10Sep88:2
Sholer, Gotlieb, FG14Sep89:3, FG21Sep89:4
Shoot, Joseph, SG8Jan89:3, SG15Jan89:4
Shubrick, Mr., WC12Feb89:3—
Shullheis, John Peter, SG8Jan89:3, SG15Jan89:4
Shute, Captain, SG27Aug89:3
Sibley, John, FG24Aug89:3, FG14Sep89:4,
    FG21Sep89:4
Sibley & Howard, SG3Dec89:3
Sierra Leone, survivors of settlement in, SG8Jan89:3
Silk, NCGH2Feb86:2, WC17Sep88:2,3
    speculation in, WC15Oct88:1
Silver mine, SG18Dec88:3
Simmons, James, NCG1Aug87:4
Simont, Edward, WC13Aug88:3
Simpson, Gen., SG27Mar88:3
Simpson, John, NCG6Jan85:1, NCG29Mar86:1
Simpson, Rossiter, SG27Mar88:3
Simpson, S., SG3Dec89:3
Simpson, Samuel, SG3Sep89:3
Simson, Jean, WC29Jan89:3, WC5Feb89:1
Singletary, Mrs. Alevy, NCG29Jul84:3
Singleton, Mr., SG6Jul86:4
Singleton, Richard, WC29Aug88:3
Singleton, Spyers, NCG2Sep84:3, NCG29Mar86:1
Sitgreaves, John, NCG29Jul84:3, NCG3Nov85:4,
    SG18Jan87:4, SG29Nov87:3, SG27Mar88:3,
    WC20Aug88:2, SG8Sep88:4—, WC12Nov88:3,
    SG4Dec88:3, WC10Dec88:3, SG18Dec88:2—
Skellbeck, Van, NCG6Jan85:1
Skerret, Issidore, SG27Mar88:3
Skillins, William, SG8Jan89:3, SG15Jan89:4
Skinner, J., SG3Dec89:3
Skinner, John, SG7Feb88:3, WC20Aug88:2,
    WC19Nov88:3, WC26Nov88:3, SG4Dec88:3,
    SG29Jan89:1, SG9Jul89:3—, SG6Aug89:3,
    SG20Aug89:4, SG27Aug89:3, FG14Sep89:3,
    SG24Sep89:4
Skinner, Joshua, WC20Aug88:2, SG20Aug89:4,
    SG24Sep89:4
    See also Skinner, John and Joshua
Skinner, Mr., SG3Dec89:4
Skinner, Sarah, SG6Aug89:3
Skinner, W., EI9Apr88:1
Skinner, William, WC20Aug88:2
Skinner, John and Joshua, SG9Jul89:3
Slade, Emelia
    See Slade, John and Emelia
Slade, John, SG18Jan87:3
Slade, John and Emelia, SG8Jan89:3, SG15Jan89:4
Slade, William, WC20Aug88:2

Slave code, WC15Jan89:2
    Jamaican, WC22Jan89:2
Slaver
    conditions on, SG15Oct89:2
    letter from, SG15Oct89:2
Slavery, observations on, SG10Sep89:3
Slaves, NCG3Nov85:2
    abolition of trade in, SG29Sep88:3
    act to prevent trading with, WC18Dec88:3
    allowances for masters of those executed,
        SG18Jan87:3
    apprehended, NCG19Dec87:4, WC15Oct88:2—,
        SG4Dec88:3—, SG26Mar89:3—, SG13Aug89:3,
        SG5Nov89:3
    auction of, WC16Jul88:3—
    British attempt to abolish trade in, SG30Jul89:1
    British trade in, SG24Nov88:1, SG27Aug89:2
    compensation for execution of, SG25Dec88:3
    confirmation of titles to, WC18Dec88:3
    crimes of, WC29Jan89:2
    death of, SG27Aug89:3
    description of trade of, SG15Oct89:2
    duty on importation of, SG18Jan87:3
    emancipation of, SG8Jan89:3, SG23Apr89:3,
        SG31Dec89:3
    exchange of, SG18Jan87:3
    execution of, SG18Jan87:3, WC13Aug88:3,
        WC10Sep88:3, WC19Nov88:3
    French trade in, SG27Aug89:4
    gift and sale of, SG31Dec89:3
    Havana opens trade in, FG21Sep89:2
    hire of, WC23Jul88:4, SG4Dec88:3, WC8Jan89:3,
        WC29Jan89:3, WC5Feb89:4, WC19Feb89:3,
        WC26Feb89:1
    illicit trade by, SG29Nov87:4, WC18Dec88:3,
        SG30Jul89:3, SG6Aug89:4, SG13Aug89:3
    importation of, SG12Jan86:3, SG23Feb86:4,
        WC19Nov88:3, SG18Dec88:3, SG25Dec88:3,
        WC5Feb89:3
    insurrection by, NCG29Jul84:1, SG29Oct89:2
    life of, SG10Sep89:4
    outlawry of, NCG29Jul84:2
    protection of runaways, WC2Jul88:2
    runaway, NCG29Jul84:2,4, NCG2Sep84:3,4,
        NCG3Nov85:4, NCG15Aug87:3, SG4Oct87:4,
        SG7Feb88:3,4, EI4Jun88:3, WC18Jun88:3,4,
        WC25Jun88:3,4, WC2Jul88:2, WC9Jul88:2,3,
        WC27Aug88:3—, SG4Dec88:3—,
        WC8Jan89:3—, WC22Jan89:3,4, SG29Jan89:3,
        WC29Jan89:3,4, SG5Feb89:4, WC5Feb89:1—,
        SG19Feb89:4, SG26Feb89:4, WC26Feb89:3,4,
        WC5Mar89:1, SG2Apr89:3—, SG21May89:4,
        SG28May89:4, SG25Jun89:3, SG2Jul89:3,4,
        SG9Jul89:4, SG23Jul89:3,4, SG13Aug89:3,
        FG12Oct89:4, SG17Dec89:3, SG31Dec89:4
    sale of, NCGH6Oct85:4, NCGH19Jan86:3,
        NCGH2Feb86:3, NCGH16Feb86:3,
        NCGH23Feb86:3, SG4Oct87:4,
        SG29Nov87:3,4, SG7Feb88:4, WC25Jun88:3,
        WC12Feb89:4, SG26Feb89:3—, SG5Mar89:3,
        SG23Jul89:3, SG6Aug89:4, SG13Aug89:4,
        FG24Aug89:3, FG14Sep89:4, SG24Dec89:3,
        SG31Dec89:3
    taken in Revolution and coming back from Nova
        Scotia, SG12Jan86:3, SG23Feb86:4
    trade of, NCG29Jul84:1, SG12Feb89:3,

WC19Feb89:1, SG23Jul89:1, SG27Aug89:4
trial of, WC13Aug88:3, WC19Nov88:3
wanted, WC19Nov88:3, WC26Nov88:4
in Wilmington, WC5Feb89:3
Slaves, free Negroes, and mulattoes, legislation
concerning, SG7Feb88:2
Sloan, John, WC20Aug88:2
Sloop, for sale, SG22Jan89:3, SG5Feb89:4,
SG12Feb89:4
Slup, Polly, SG8Jan89:3, SG15Jan89:4
Smith
See Hewes, Smith and Allen
Smith, ____, SG30Jul89:3, SG6Aug89:4
Smith, Agness, NCG29Jul84:3
Smith, B., SG3Dec89:2,3
Smith, Benjamin, NCG29Jul84:3, WC2Jul88:3,
WC9Jul88:3, WC23Jul88:4, WC6Aug88:4,
WC20Aug88:2, WC3Sep88:3, WC15Oct88:2,
WC5Nov88:4, WC3Dec88:4, WC29Jan89:2,
WC5Feb89:4, SG30Apr89:3—, SG10Sep89:3,
SG3Dec89:2, SG31Dec89:3
Smith, Col., WC18Jun88:2, WC2Jul88:2, SG22Jan89:3
Smith, D., SG3Dec89:3
Smith, Francis, NCG29Jul84:3
Smith, James, Sr., SG22Oct89:3, SG29Oct89:3,
SG12Nov89:4
Smith, Jane, WC23Jul88:3
Smith, John, NCG29Jul84:3, NCG2Sep84:4,
NCG3Nov85:4, SG27Mar88:3, EI4Jun88:4,
SG8Jan89:3, SG15Jan89:4
Smith, Joseph, NCG29Jul84:3, SG2Jul89:3
Smith, Mrs., SG17Dec89:3
Smith, Nathan, NCG15Aug87:4
Smith, Robert, NCG29Jul84:3, NCG6Jan85:1,
WC13Aug88:3, SG20Oct88:3, SG27Oct88:3
Smith, S., SG29Nov87:3, SG3Dec89:3
Smith, Samuel, SG18Jan87:3, SG29Nov87:3,
WC13Aug88:3, SG9Jul89:3—
Smith, Thomas, SG27Mar88:3
Smithfield, N.C., WC6Aug88:3
Smuggling, prevention of, SG8Oct89:3
Smyrna, letter from, SG20Aug89:1
Snead, ____, SG3Dec89:3
Snead, Robert W., SG10Sep89:3
Snodgrass, Neal, NCG29Mar86:2
Society, reform of, NCG2Sep84:1
Society of Cincinnati, SG6Aug89:2, SG13Aug89:2
celebration of July 4 in N.Y., SG23Jul89:2,3
R.I., address by G. Washington to, SG29Oct89:2
"Soldier and Citizen," SG27Oct88:1
Soldiers
payment of, SG31Dec89:3
Prussian, anecdote about, SG1Jan89:4
relief of, SG25Dec88:3
settlement of accounts of, SG23Feb86:4
Solomon, Mr., SG3Nov88:3
comedian, SG29Nov87:4
Soulange, M., letter from, NCG3Nov85:3
South Carolina, WC12Feb89:3—
constitutional convention in, SG7Feb88:2,
WC25Jun88:2
debt of to France, WC12Nov88:3
defeats promotion of inland navigation in,
WC19Feb89:3
description of, SG28May89:4
elections in, WC15Jan89:3, SG12Feb89:3,

WC12Feb89:2
execution of murderers in, WC18Jun88:2
forbids importation of slaves, SG18Dec88:3
Indian affairs of, SG2Apr89:2,3
manufacture of silk in, WC17Sep88:2,3
members of U.S. House of Representatives,
WC19Feb89:1
militia of, SG2Apr89:3, SG7May89:3
politics in, WC25Jun88:2, WC4Dec88:4,
WC15Jan89:3, WC12Feb89:2, WC19Feb89:1,3,
SG12Mar89:3
ratification of federal Constitution by,
WC25Jun88:2
replacement of judge in, WC19Feb89:1
robbery in, SG12Nov89:3
silk in, NCGH2Feb86:2
state constitution of, SG4Jun89:3
South Sea Islands, discovery of, SG6Oct88:3
Southampton County, Va., SG4Oct87:4
Southerland, Daniel, SG6Jul86:3
Sowell, Charles, SG12Jan86:4
Sp____, William, SG6Jul86:3
Spaight, ____, SG27Mar88:2
Spaight, R. D., SG27Mar88:3
Spaight, Richard D., SG18Jan87:3, WC20Aug88:2,
SG3Sep89:3
Spaight, Richard Dobbs, NCGH19Jan86:4,
SG23Feb86:4, SG18Jan87:3, NCG19Dec87:4,
SG20Oct88:3, SG17Dec89:3
Spain, NCG9Dec84:3, SG23Apr89:2
abolition of Inquisition by, WC25Dec88:2,
WC12Feb89:1
attempt to settle Mississippi and Masure (Missouri)
region, SG10Sep89:3
attitude of toward Kentucky, SG26Feb89:3
disavows encouraging Indians in Cumberland,
SG20Oct88:2
failure to take Gibraltar, SG17Dec89:1
government of, SG30Apr89:3, SG7May89:3
Inquisition of, WC25Dec88:2
interest in western U.S. settlements, WC18Jun88:1,
SG24Sep89:3, SG1Oct89:3
military preparations of, WC25Jun88:2
minister of to U.S., SG5Nov89:2
naval preparations of, WC18Jun88:2, WC3Sep88:1,
WC25Dec88:2, SG12Feb89:3
opposition to Russia, WC3Sep88:1
politics in, SG8Sep88:1
power of, SG10Dec89:1
reaction to events in France, SG5Nov89:2
regulation of U.S. trade on Mississippi River,
SG1Oct89:3
reported death of king of, SG7Feb88:2
ships of, SG12Feb89:3
toleration in, SG6Oct88:3
treaty of with Great Britain, NCG2Sep84:2
U.S. relations with, WC18Jun88:1, SG24Sep89:3
Spain, Thomas, SG30Apr89:3—
Spanish Town, Jamaica, SG8Oct89:2
Spalding, Luther, SG27Mar88:3
Spaulding, Mr., SG4Oct87:4
Spaulding, Philip, WC18Jun88:3, WC25Jun88:3,
WC17Sep88:3, WC24Sep88:1, WC5Feb89:3
Speculators, WC17Sep88:2
Speed, Joseph, SG10Nov88:3
Speight, ____, WC6Aug88:2

Spelling books, sale of, SG7May89:3—, SG4Jun89:4, SG9Jul89:3, SG16Jul89:4, SG6Aug89:4, SG27Aug89:3—, SG15Oct89:4, SG29Oct89:3, SG12Nov89:4, SG31Dec89:3
Spencer, ____, SG3Dec89:3
Spencer, James, SG6Jul86:4
Spencer, Joseph, death of, SG12Mar89:2
Spencer, Judge, EI4Jun88:3, SG27Oct88:1, SG24Sep89:3
Spencer, Samuel, EI9Apr88:3, WC20Aug88:2
Spencer, Thomas, SG8Jan89:3, SG15Jan89:4
Spergen, William, NCG29Mar86:2
Spicer, ____, SG3Dec89:3
Spicer, John, WC20Aug88:2, SG10Sep89:3
Spiller, ____, SG3Dec89:3
Spiller, James, SG17Sep89:3, SG17Dec89:3
Spiller, Mr., SG17Dec89:3
Spoon, silver, WC18Dec88:4
    found, SG23Jul89:3—
Spratt, James, NCG6Jan85:1
Sprewill, Benjamin, SG20Oct88:3, SG27Oct88:3
Springfield, Mass., news from, SG23Jul89:2
Springs, Sedgick, WC19Feb89:3, SG26Feb89:1
Springs and Harris, WC19Feb89:3, WC26Feb89:1
Sprow, Andrew, NCG3Nov85:1
Spruill, Benjamin, SG9Apr89:3—
Spruill, S., SG3Dec89:3
Spruill, Simeon, FG14Sep89:3
Spruill, Simon, SG27Aug89:3
Stage, route of, NCGH19Jan86:4, NCGH2Feb86:3, SG29Nov87:4, SG8Jan89:3—, SG18Jun89:3—
    Suffolk, SG2Apr89:3
    See also Post; Mail
Standin, L., SG9Apr89:3—, SG22Oct89:3, SG29Oct89:3, SG12Nov89:4
Standin, Lemuel, SG27Oct88:3, SG15Jan89:4, SG16Jul89:4, SG23Jul89:4
Stanley, Ann, death of, SG23Jul89:3
Stanley, John Wright, SG23Jul89:3
Stanly, John Wright, death of, SG18Jun89:3
Stark, George, WC13Aug88:3
Starkey, Edward, NCG15Aug87:3
State Gazette, The
    appreciation to subscribers of, SG3Sep89:3
    expense of publication of, SG3Sep89:3
    publication schedule of, SG12Jan86:3, SG24Nov88:3
    subscription payments for, SG26Feb89:3
States (U.S.), characterization of, SG12Feb89:3
States General, SG27Aug89:4, SG3Sep89:2
    instructions to, SG20Aug89:1
    meeting of, WC5Feb89:1
    proceedings of, FG12Oct89:3
    speech to, SG20Aug89:1
Staton, Charles, SG9Apr89:3
Staton, John, SG9Apr89:3
Staunton, Augustine, WC12Feb89:3—
Staves, WC3Sep88:3, WC17Sep88:4
Stead, N., SG3Dec89:3
Steamboat, NCG9Dec84:3
Steed, Jesse, WC18Dec88:3
Steel, John, SG13Aug89:2
Steel, Thomas, SG27Mar88:3
Steel, ____, SG17Sep89:3, SG24Sep89:3
Steele, Col., SG26Feb89:3, WC5Mar89:2
Steele, J., SG3Dec89:3

Steele, John, SG13Aug88:1, WC20Aug88:2, SG29Sep88:3, WC15Jan89:3—, SG22Jan89:3, SG13Aug89:1
Steele, Mr., WC17Sep88:3, SG29Sep88:3, WC29Jan89:3, WC5Feb89:1, SG3Dec89:2
Steele, William, WC22Jan89:2
Stephens, James, WC25Jun88:3
Stevens and Telfair, WC19Feb89:3, WC26Feb89:1
Stevenson, Silas, NCG29Jul84:2
Stewart, Capt.. WC25Jun88:3
Stewart, D., SG3Dec89:3
    letter from, SG24Nov88:3
Stewart, Daniel, SG20Oct88:3, SG27Oct88:3
Stewart, Dougal, WC13Aug88:3
Stewart, Duncan, SG10Sep89:3
Stewart, Finley, SG20Oct88:3, SG27Oct88:3
Stewart, J., SG3Dec89:3
Stewart, James, SG27Mar88:3, WC20Aug88:2, SG20Oct88:3, SG27Oct88:3, SG8Jan89:3, SG15Jan89:4, SG9Jul89:3—
Stewart, John, SG20Oct88:3, SG27Oct88:3, SG8Jan89:3, SG15Jan89:4, SG9Apr89:3—, SG30Apr89:3—, SG3Sep89:3
Stewart, Joseph, WC20Aug88:2, SG17Sep89:3
Stewart, Rev., WC15Oct88:2—
Stewart, T., SG3Dec89:3
Stewart, Thomas, WC20Aug88:2, SG8Sep88:3, SG29Jan89:1, SG9Jul89:3, SG27Aug89:3, FG14Sep89:3
Stewart, Thos., SG9Apr89:3—
Stewart, William, WC20Aug88:2, WC27Aug88:4—
Stillwell, Obadiah, SG9Apr89:3—
Stimson, Joshua, SG20Oct88:3, SG27Oct88:3
Stiron, Capt., SG17Dec89:2,3
Stockholm
    letter from, SG18Jun89:2
    news from, SG22Sep88:1, SG4Dec88:1
Stocks, price of, NCGH2Feb86:2
Stokes, ____, SG3Dec89:3
Stokes, J., SG3Dec89:3
Stokes, John, SG7Feb88:3, SG3Dec89:3, SG17Dec89:3, SG31Dec89:3
Stokes, Mr., SG3Dec89:4, SG17Dec89:3
Stokes, William, WC20Aug88:2
Stokes County, N.C., SG31Dec89:3
Stone, D., SG3Dec89:3
Stone, David, SG27Aug89:3, FG14Sep89:3, SG22Oct89:3, SG29Oct89:3, SG12Nov89:4
Stone, Fergus, SG31Dec89:3
Stone, Zedekiah, SG9Apr89:3—, SG22Oct89:3, SG29Oct89:3, SG12Nov89:4
Storch, Rev., SG22Oct89:3, SG29Oct89:3, SG12Nov89:4
Store
    commission, WC18Dec88:3, WC25Dec88:3
    John Campbell's, WC26Oct88:3
    medical, SG27Mar88:4
    mercantile, NCGH2Feb86:4, NCGH16Feb86:4, NCGH23Feb86:3,4, SG29Nov87:3, SG7Feb88:3, WC10Sep88:4—, WC18Dec88:3, WC25Dec88:3, WC29Jan89:3, WC5Feb89:3—, FG14Sep89:4, FG21Sep89:4
    rent of, WC17Sep88:3, WC24Sep88:1, SG4Dec88:3
Storehouse, building of, SG31Dec89:3
Storm, WC6Aug88:2, WC13Aug88:2,3, WC20Aug88:3, SG8Sep88:2, WC10Sep88:2, WC10Dec88:2,

WC8Jan89:2, SG23Apr89:3, SG18Jun89:3,
SG1Oct89:2
See also Hurricane
Stors, Frederick, SG9Jul89:3—
Stott, Watson, SG27Oct88:3—, SG30Apr89:3—
Stott and Donaldson, SG27Oct88:3—
Strasburg, violence in, SG15Oct89:2
Stratford, Conn.
    accident in, SG16Apr89:3
    arrival of President Washington in, SG19Nov89:2
    letter from, SG19Nov89:2, SG26Nov89:2
Stringer, Francis, SG4Oct87:3, SG27Mar88:3
Strudwick, William, SG17Sep89:3
Stuart, John, SG18Jan87:3
Stuart & Muir, SG9Apr89:3
Stuart & Paul, SG18Jan87:3
Stubbins, Joseph, NCGH16Feb86:1, NCGH23Feb86:1
Sturges, Josiah, SG20Oct88:3, SG27Oct88:3
Styron, ____, SG3Dec89:2
Styron, Wallis, WC20Aug88:2
Styron, William, SG24Sep89:3
"Subscriber, A," SG5Feb89:1, SG20Aug89:2
Suffolk, Va., SG6Jul86:4, SG27Oct88:3—,
    SG25Feb89:3,4, SG5Mar89:3, SG12Mar89:3,
    SG30Apr89:3—, SG18Jun89:3—
    letter from, SG23Apr89:3
Suffresin, Bailli de, exile of, WC12Nov88:2
Sugar, WC3Sep88:3—
    British speculation in, SG27Oct88:2
    sale of, NCG29Mar86:1, WC3Sep88:3—,
    SG29Jan89:3
Suicide, SG6Oct88:2, SG20Oct88:2, SG3Nov88:3,
    SG11Dec88:2, WC12Feb89:1, SG4Jun89:3
Sullivan, John, letter from, WC18Jun88:1
Sullivan, Mr., WC10Sep88:4, WC17Sep89:4
Sullivan County, N.C., SG18Jan87:2,3, SG18Dec88:2,3,
    WC18Dec88:2,3, SG25Dec88:2, SG26Feb89:3,
    SG16Apr89:3
    court of, SG18Jan87:3, SG18Dec88:3
    letter from, WC5Mar89:2
Summer, James, EI19Dec87:1
Sumner, General, NCG6Jan85:1
Sumner, Rufus, EI4Jun88:4
Sumner County, N.C., SG20Oct88:1, SG18Dec88:3,
    WC18Dec88:2, SG25Dec88:2,4, SG1Jan89:4,
    SG22Jan89:3
Sunflower oil, WC13Aug88:1
Superior Court, WC18Dec88:3
    act to divide into circuits, SG12Jan86:1
    establishment of, WC18Dec88:2
    Halifax District, SG3Nov88:2
    Hillsborough District, SG3Nov88:2
    judges for, WC18Dec88:2
    Wilmington District, WC18Jun88:3
Surry County, N.C., NCGH19Jan86:4, NCGH2Feb86:4,
    NCG29Mar86:2, WC17Sep88:3, SG29Sep88:3,
    WC26Nov88:3, SG25Dec88:2, SG24Sep89:3,
    SG31Dec89:3
    division of, SG31Dec89:3
Sutherland, John, WC13Aug88:3
Sutton, ____, SG3Dec89:3
Sutton, Ashberry, SG27Aug89:3
Sutton, Ashbury, FG14Sep89:3
Swain, Capt., WC25Dec88:3
Swainey, Darby, SG24Sep89:3
Swan, John, FG14Sep89:3

Swann, J., SG3Dec89:3
Swann, John, SG27Aug89:3, SG22Oct89:3,
    SG29Oct89:3, SG12Nov89:4
Swann, Mildred, SG27Mar88:4
Swann, Mr., WC16Jul88:3—, WC20Aug88:4—
Swann, Samuel, SG27Mar88:4
Swannanoe, WC22Jan89:4
Swansborough (Swanborough), NCG29Jul84:2,3
    Port of, SG18Jan87:2
Sweden, WC18Dec88:2
    attack on by Russia, WC15Jan89:1
    commerce of, SG19Mar89:2
    confusion in, WC8Jan89:2
    constitution of, SG5Feb89:1, SG12Feb89:3
    duties on imports of, SG19Mar89:2
    government in, SG18Jun89:1
    king of, SG24Nov88:2
    naval officers of in America, SG24Nov88:2
    navy of, WC15Oct88:1, WC19Nov88:2,3
    naval engagement of with Russia, WC12Nov88:2
    negotiations with Russia, WC19Feb89:2
    penal reform in, SG27Oct88:2
    politics in, SG22Jan89:2, SG18Jun89:2
    reply of king of to Russia, WC3Dec88:3
    reported revolution in, SG11Jun89:3
    speech by king of, SG5Feb89:1, SG12Feb89:1
    truce of with Denmark, WC12Feb89:2
    war with Russia, WC19Nov88:1,2, WC26Nov88:1,
    WC3Dec88:2,3, WC22Jan89:2
Sweney, John, NCG6Jan85:1
Swift, Dean, anecdote of, WC12Nov88:4, SG12Mar89:4
Swift Creek, Craven County, NCG29Jul84:4
Symmes, Judge
    letter from, SG3Nov88:2
    obtains land from Congress, SG3Nov88:2

T

Tablespoon, silver, WC10Dec88:3
Tagert Ross & Co., SG18Jan87:4
Tagert Ross & Tagert, SG18Jan87:4, NCG19Dec87:4
Tailor
    See Taylor; Taylor and Habit-Maker
Tailoresses, SG7Feb88:3
Talbot County, Md., fishing in, SG1Oct89:3
Tallow, NCGH19Jan86:3, NCGH2Feb86:4,
    NCGH16Feb86:4, NCGH23Feb86:4,
    SG13Oct88:3—, SG10Nov88:4
Tangiers
    letter from, SG13Oct88:2
    news from, SG25Jun89:1
Tanner
    See Currier and Tanner
Tanner, David, WC20Aug88:2
Tar, wanted, WC17Sep88:4, WC25Dec88:3
Tar and pitch, wanted, WC3Sep88:3
Tarbe, Peter, FG12Oct89:4
Tarborough, NCG9Dec84:4, NCG29Mar86:1,
    SG29Nov87:3,4, NCG19Dec87:4, SG7Feb88:3,
    SG27Mar88:4, WC6Aug88:3, SG8Sep88:3,
    WC17Sep88:3, SG27Oct88:3, SG10Nov88:3,
    WC26Nov88:3, SG4Dec88:3, SG29Jan89:1,
    SG7May89:4, SG20Aug89:3, SG27Aug89:4,
    SG10Sep89:3, SG24Sep89:3, SG1Oct89:4,
    SG3Dec89:3

address from inhabitants of, WC17Sep88:3
inhabitants of, WC26Oct88:3
letter from, NCG19Dec87:4
letter to inhabitants of, SG20Oct88:3
petition of inhabitants of, SG8Sep88:3
regulation of, SG18Dec87:2
support for federal Constitution in, SG8Sep88:3
survey of, SG18Jan87:2
Tariff, U.S., SG7May89:3, SG14May89:3,
    SG21May89:3, SG28May89:1,2, SG11Jun89:2,
    SG25Jun89:1,3, SG9Jul89:1,2, SG16Jul89:3,
    SG23Jul89:3, SG30Jul89:4, SG6Aug89:1,2,
    FG24Aug89:2,3,4, SG31Dec89:3
congressional consideration of, SG2Jul89:1,2,
    SG9Jul89:1,2
effect of on N.C., FG12Oct89:3
revenue from, SG15Oct89:3
Tarkington, Joseph, SG22Oct89:3, SG29Oct89:3,
    SG12Nov89:4
Tartars, assessment of, SG15Jan89:1
Tarven, ____, SG24Sep89:3
Tarver, ____, SG3Dec89:3
Tassel, Chief, SG27Oct88:3
Tatam, Absalom, SG18Jan87:3
Tatham, William, WC6Aug88:2, WC13Aug88:2
Tatom, A., WC20Aug88:2
Taton, Absalom, SG22Sep88:3
Tavern, EI4Jun88:4, WC2Jul88:2, WC9Jul88:3,
    WC23Jul88:4, WC3Sep88:3, WC15Oct88:2,
    WC5Nov88:4, WC26Nov88:3, WC3Dec88:4,
    SG4Dec88:3, WC18Dec88:3, SG25Dec88:3,4,
    WC25Dec88:3, SG8Jan89:3, SG15Jan89:4,
    WC29Jan89:2, SG12Feb89:3, SG19Feb89:4,
    SG26Feb89:3,4, SG5Mar89:3,4, SG12Mar89:3,4,
    SG25Jun89:2, FG14Sep89:3, FG21Sep89:2,4,
    SG24Dec89:3, SG31Dec89:3
Taxable property, returns of, SG31Dec89:3
Taxes, WC25Jun88:3
assessment of, SG18Jan87:2
British return of, WC10Dec88:2
imposition of, SG18Jan87:3, WC18Dec88:2
N.C., NCG9Dec84:1,2, SG12Jan86:1,2,
    SG23Feb86:1, SG18Jan87:2, EI9Apr88:1
U.S., WC17Sep88:1,2
Wilmington, WC19Feb89:3, WC26Feb89:1
Taylor (tailor), seeks employment, WC20Aug88:3—
Taylor and Habit-Maker, SG6Jul86:4, SG29Nov87:4,
    SG27Mar88:3
Taylor, E., SG17Sep89:3, SG3Dec89:3
Taylor, James, SG20Oct88:3, SG27Oct88:3,
    SG9Jul89:3—, SG3Dec89:2, SG31Dec89:3
Taylor, John, NCGH16Feb86:3, SG27Mar88:3,
    SG20Oct88:3, SG27Oct88:3
Taylor, Joseph, WC20Aug88:2
Taylor, Thomas, NCGH16Feb86:4, NCGH23Feb86:4,
    SG29Nov87:1
Taylor, William, WC20Aug88:2
Tea, Hyson, WC3Sep88:3—
Teeth
cleaned, NCG1Aug87:3
wanted, NCGH19Jan86:4, NCGH2Feb86:4,
    NCGH16Feb86:4
Telfair
See Stevens and Telfair
Telfair, Alexander, NCG29Mar86:2
Telfair, Hugh, NCG29Mar86:2

Telfair, John, WC8Jan89:3
Telfair, Mr., NCGH2Feb86:2
Temple, John, SG12Jan86:3
Temple, William, NCG29Jul84:3
Teneriffe Island, Spanish protest to English fleet at,
    SG4Jun89:2
Tennessee
government of, SG16Apr89:3
guard for, SG18Dec88:3
war with Indians in, WC24Sep88:2
Tennessee County, N.C., SG18Dec88:3, WC18Dec88:2,
    SG22Jan89:3
Tennison, Abraham, Jr., SG9Apr89:3
Tennison, Abraham, Sr., SG9Apr89:3
Tennison, Absalom, SG9Apr89:3
Tennison, Jacob, SG9Apr89:3
Terrell, Aaron, NCGH19Jan86:3, NCGH2Feb86:3
Thalley, John, NCG29Jul84:3
Thanksgiving, SG22Jan89:3, SG22Oct89:4
presidential proclamation for national day of,
    SG29Oct89:4
Theater, SG29Nov87:4, SG27Mar88:3, WC18Jun88:3,
    WC24Sep88:2, WC19Nov88:3, WC26Feb89:3
"Theatricus," WC26Feb89:3
Theft, SG4Oct87:4, EI4Jun88:4, WC10Dec88:3,
    WC18Dec88:4, SG22Jan89:3
N.C. legislation concerning, SG7Feb88:2
Thicknesse, Mr., anecdote of, SG18Jun89:2
Thieves, band of, SG9Apr89:3
Thomas, Caleb, WC12Feb89:3
Thomas, Charles, NCGH16Feb86:4, SG4Oct87:4,
    SG30Apr89:3, SG20Aug89:2
Thomas, Coal, NCG6Jan85:1
Thomas, Elias, SG22Oct89:3, SG29Oct89:3,
    SG12Nov89:4
Thompson, Col, WC29Jan89:3, WC5Feb89:1
Thompson, James, SG17Sep89:3
Thompson, John, NCG29Mar86:2, SG17Sep89:3
Thompson, Philip, SG20Oct88:3, SG27Oct88:3
Thompson, William, WC30Jul88:3
Thomson, Charles, NCGH19Jan86:4, SG4Oct87:4,
    SG29Nov87:4, WC25Jun88:1, SG6Oct88:3,
    WC10Dec88:2,3, SG23Apr89:3, SG14May89:2,
    SG20Aug89:2
Thomson, Capt. Daniel, letter from, WC24Sep88:2
Thomson, J., SG3Dec89:3
Thornbury, Joseph, SG8Jan89:3, SG15Jan89:4
Thoulouse (Toulose), France, SG16Jul89:1
Thuller, Swedish, value of, SG17Nov88:3
Thurston, William, WC13Aug88:3
Tier, Richard, NCG3Nov85:1
Timber, preservation of, WC10Sep88:1
Tindale, ____, SG3Dec89:3
Tindale, James, FG14Sep89:3
Tindall, Mr., SG29Sep88:3
Tiner, Kezie, SG8Jan89:3, SG15Jan89:4
Tinker, Euphamia, SG27Mar88:3
Tinker, Stephen, SG6Jul86:3, SG18Jan87:3
Tinnen, Carnes, NCGH16Feb86:4, NCGH23Feb86:4
Tinning, Charles, WC13Aug88:3
Tipton, Col., WC8Jan89:3
Tipton, John, WC20Aug88:2
Tipton, Joseph, WC20Aug88:2
Tisdale, William, NCG6Jan85:1, SG18Jan87:3
Titles
essay on, SG30Jul89:4

observations on, SG20Jul89:4
for state governors, SG27Aug89:3
and U.S. Congress, SG11Jun89:3
Toasts, WC2Jul88:2, WC23Jul88:3, WC3Sep88:4,
WC10Sep88:1, WC26Nov88:3, WC3Dec88:3,
SG23Jul89:4, SG3Dec89:2, SG17Dec89:2,3
Tobacco, NCGH2Feb86:3, NCGH23Feb86:3,
SG8Sep88:4—, SG25Dec88:3
classifying of, WC19Nov88:3
commissioners of for purchase of, NCGH19Jan86:3,
NCGH2Feb86:4, NCGH16Feb86:3,
NCGH23Feb86:4
cultivation of, SG10Sept89:2
English regulation of imports of, SG29Oct89:3
English trade in, WC9Jul88:2, SG10Dec89:1
inspection of, NCG29Jul84:4, SG18Jan87:2,3,
WC26Nov88:3, SG31Dec89:3
price of, NCGH16Feb86:3
sale of, SG8Sep88:3, SG22Sep88:4, SG29Sep88:4
wanted, NCGH19Jan86:3, NCGH2Feb86:4,
NCGH16Feb86:4, NCGH23Feb88:4
Tobacco notes, SG30Apr89:3, SG14May89:4
Tobey, Samuel, SG6Jul86:4
Toby (slave), apprehended, SG4Dec88:3—
Todd, Joseph, NCG2Sep84:4
Todd, Mallery, NCG2Sep84:4
Tom (slave), SG7Feb88:3, WC10Sep88:4
reward for, WC27Aug88:3
Tombstones, origin of, SG24Nov88:3
Toms, Foster, SG29Nov87:1
Toney (slave), SG29Jan89:3—
Tonnage duties, SG20Aug89:3, FG12Oct89:3
Tony (slave), WC25Jun88:4
Tooley, William, SG7Feb88:3
Toomer, H., WC19Feb89:3, WC26Feb89:1
Toomer, Henry, WC18Jun88:3—, WC5Nov88:3,
WC12Nov88:4, WC8Jan89:3—
Toomer's Alley, WC12Nov88:3, WC19Nov88:4
Toomer's Bridge, WC8Jan89:3
Torrens, Elizabeth and children, SG18Jan87:2
Tow, ____, SG25Dec88:3, WC15Jan89:3
Towmer, Richard Z., SG22Oct89:3, SG29Oct89:3,
SG12Nov89:4
Town
establishment, SG18Jan87:2, SG18Dec88:3,
WC18Dec88:2,3, SG31Dec89:3
proposed, EI9Apr88:1
Town commissioners, Edenton, SG12Feb89:4—,
SG13Aug89:3
Townes, Richard, SG18Jun89:3
Townsend, Chancey, NCG29Mar86:2
Tradesmen and manufacturers, meeting of in Baltimore,
SG12Mar89:3
Treason, SG25Dec88:3
definition of, WC19Nov88:3
Treaty of Paris, ratification of, NCG2Sep84:3
Trenton, N.C., NCG15Aug87:3
Trenton-Bridge, N.J., ladies at honor President
Washington, SG17Sep89:3
Trial by jury, NCG15Aug87:1, EI9Apr88:3,
WC16Jul88:2
Trinity Church, N.Y., construction of, WC10Sep88:2
Tripoli
news from, NCGH2Feb86:2
plague in, NCGH2Feb86:2
Trippe, Betty, and daughter, SG7Feb88:3

Troak, Jacob, NCGH19Jan86:4
Troops, N.C., raising of, SG18Jan87:2
Trotter, Richard, SG8Jan89:3, SG15Jan89:4
Trotter, Thomas, SG8Jan89:3, SG15Jan89:4,
SG2Apr89:3—
"True Federalist, A," FG21Sep89:1
Tryon, William, NCG29Mar86:2, SG6Jul86:3
Tryon County, N.C., NCG29Mar86:2
Tubbs, Capt., SG18Jan87:3
Tucker, Doctor, NCG29Mar86:2
Tugalow, letter from, SG4Dec88:3
Turkey, SG18Dec88:2
attack on Wallachia, WC30Jul88:2
French relations with, WC22Jan89:2
navy of, WC19Nov88:2
news from, WC18Jun88:2
plague in, WC9Jul88:2
politics in, SG5Nov89:1
preparation for war by, WC19Feb89:2
present from ruler of, SG4Dec88:3
proposed war against Russia, FG14Sep89:2
ruler of, WC10Sep88:2, SG13Aug89:3,
SG20Aug89:3, SG3Sep89:2
war of, WC10Sep88:2, WC26Oct88:2,
WC19Nov88:2, WC26Nov88:1, WC3Dec88:2,
WC25Dec88:2, WC22Jan89:2, FG14Sep89:2
Turk's Island, SG1Oct89:3
Turpentine, WC17Sep88:3
Turner, D., SG3Dec89:2
Turner, J., SG3Dec89:3
Turner, James, FG14Sep89:3
Turner, Robert, NCG29Mar86:2
Tuton
See Reilly and Tuton
Tuton, Oliver, NCG9Dec84:4, NCG6Jan85:1
Tuzo, Thomas, SG18Jan87:4
Twenty Pound Law, N.C., NCG15Aug87:2,
SG13Aug89:3
Twining, Nathaniel, SG6Jul86:4, WC16Jul88:3
Tyler, William, SG9Apr89:3
Tylor, Peter, SG9Apr89:3
Tylor, Thomas, SG9Apr89:3
Tyrrell County, N.C., WC26Nov88:3, SG25Dec88:2,
SG30Jul89:3, SG27Aug89:3, FG14Sep89:3
elections in, SG31Dec89:3
letter from, SG30Jul89:3
Tyson, ____, SG3Dec89:3
Tyson, Henry, SG22Oct89:3, SG29Oct89:3,
SG12Nov89:4
Tyson, Thomas, WC20Aug88:2, SG24Sep89:3

U

Unanimity Lodge, SG25Jun89:2, SG24Sep89:3
United Netherlands, representative of, SG28May89:3
United States
accounts of, WC25Jun88:1
act for imposing duties on imports, SG30Jul89:4,
FG24Aug89:3, FG21Sep89:4
act for safekeeping laws, records, and seal of,
SG29Oct89:4
act regulating duties of, FG24Aug89:2, SG1Oct89:3
African trade of, WC17Sep88:1
agriculture of, SG12Jan86:3
Algerian relations of, SG12Jan86:3

Algerian war against, NCG3Nov85:3
allowed to load salt at Turk's Island, WC24Sep88:2
appropriations of, SG12Nov89:4
approval of government of, SG11Dec88:2
army of, SG12Nov89:4
attitude of citizens toward government of, SG29Jan89:2
benefits of government of, SG5Nov89:2
British diplomatic relations with, SG12Jan86:3, WC8Jan89:2
British opinion of government of, SG6Aug89:3, SG8Oct89:2
British protection of shipping of, WC24Sep88:2
British refusal to leave western forts, SG10Nov88:2, WC26Nov88:2
British trade with, WC25Jun88:2, SG11Dec88:1, SG19Nov89:2
budget of, SG13Aug89:4
capital of, WC3Sep88:2, SG22Sep88:2, SG19Feb89:2, WC19Feb89:3, WC5Mar89:2, SG2Apr89:3, SG16Apr89:2, SG23Apr89:3, SG27Aug89:3, SG17Sep89:1, FG21Sep89:3, SG24Sep89:1,4, SG1Oct89:2,3,4, SG8Oct89:3, SG15Oct89:3, SG22Oct89:2,4, SG12Nov89:3
capitol building of, SG27Oct88:3, WC26Nov88:2, SG29Jan89:3, SG19Feb89:3, SG12Mar89:2, SG2Apr89:2,3
caricature of, WC13Aug88:1
characterization of states of, SG12Feb89:3
chief justice of, SG9Apr89:2
China trade of, WC19Nov88:2, WC26Nov88:2
coastal trade of, SG29Nov87:2
coinage of, NCG15Aug87:2
claims against, SG4Oct87:3, SG29Nov87:4
commencement of government of, SG2Apr89:2
commentary on, SG18Jun89:2,3
commentary on government of, SG5Feb89:3, SG26Feb89:2
comparison of to Europe, SG17Nov88:1
comparison of to Russia, SG3Dec89:1
debt of, SG23Feb86:3, SG29Sep88:1,2
debtors of, WC25Jun88:1
delay in collection of tariff duties, SG23Apr89:3
distress in, SG5Nov89:2
District Court judicial appointments, SG15Oct89:3, SG22Oct89:3
East Florida trade of, SG26Mar89:2
economy of, FG24Aug89:3
economic conditions in, SG11Jun89:1,4
emigration to Cartagena, SG23Jul89:3
encouragement of economy by, SG3Sep89:1
encouragement to ship grain to France, SG19Mar89:3
English trade of, WC10Dec88:2
English view of, WC8Jan89:2,3, FG24Aug89:2,3
executive departments of, SG4Jun89:2, SG9Jul89:2, SG16Jul89:1, SG27Aug89:4
executive officers of appointed, SG27Aug88:2, SG17Sep89:1, SG1Oct89:3,4, FG12Oct89:3, SG22Oct89:3, SG29Oct89:3
expense of government of, SG20Aug89:1
facilitation of commerce of, SG10Sep89:4
foreign commerce of, SG16Jul89:3
foreign emissary appointments of, SG22Oct89:3
foreign opinion of, SG29Jan89:2, SG10Dec89:2
foreign relations of, NCGH2Feb86:2

formation of, SG16Apr89:2
French minister to, NCG19Dec87:4
French relations of, SG27Mar88:2,3, SG11Dec88:2, SG1Oct89:3
French trade of, NCG29Jul84:2, WC18Jun88:2, WC5Feb89:2, WC26Feb89:2, SG19Mar89:3, SG6Aug89:4, SG20Aug89:1
future of, EI19Dec87:2, WC17Sep88:2
gazettes in, SG22Jan89:3
government of, SG5Feb89:3, SG26Feb89:2, SG7May89:3
immigration to, NCG2Sep84:2,3
import duties of, SG12Nov89:2
importance of agriculture in, SG11Jun89:1,4
importations from French West Indies, WC5Feb89:2
India trade of, SG11Jun89:3
Indian commissioners of, NCGH2Feb86:2, SG22Jan89:3, SG2Apr89:2,3, SG13Aug89:1, SG24Sep89:2, SG26Nov89:3
Indian relations of, SG8Sep88:2, SG9Apr89:3, SG30Jul89:2,3, SG13Aug89:1,2, SG3Sep89:1,4
Indian trade of, WC12Feb89:1
Indian treaty of, SG13Aug89:1, FG21Sep89:3
Indians negotiations of, NCGH2Feb86:2, WC18Jun88:3
Indians in western territory of, SG26Feb89:3, SG30Apr89:3, SG1Oct89:3,4
inscription on cannon for, SG25Jun89:2
judiciary of, SG30Jul89:3, SG22Oct89:2, SG12Nov89:4
judicial appointments of, SG15Oct89:3
legislation of, SG13Aug89:2, SG12Nov89:4
legislature of, SG6Jul86:1
loans to, NCGH23Feb86:3
Louis XVI communication to, SG22Oct89:4
manufacturing in, SG11Dec88:2, WC29Jan89:2, WC12Feb89:1, SG23Apr89:3
military claims against, NCGH2Feb86:3,4, NCGH16Feb86:4, NCGH23Feb86:4
names in confuse foreigners, SG18Jun89:2
nature of government of, SG6Jul86:1,2, WC10Dec88:4
need for change in government of, SG28May89:3
need for haste in organizing government of, SG15Sep88:1
need for manufacturing in, WC5Nov88:2
need for qualified officers of, SG9Jul89:2
need for revenue, SG4Jun89:3
need to trade with West Indies, SG5Nov89:2
New Hampshire support of, SG23Apr89:2
newspapers in, WC29Jan89:2
North Carolina accounts with, SG18Dec88:2,3, SG31Dec89:3
North Carolina relations with, SG15Sep88:1, SG6Oct88:1, SG20Aug89:3
obedience to laws of, SG27Aug89:3
ode to, WC3Sep88:4, SG17Dec89:4
officeseekers in, SG28May89:3
officials of, SG22Sep88:3, SG17Sep89:1, SG1Oct89:3, SG8Oct89:3, SG29Oct89:2
organization of government of, WC23Jul88:2, SG15Sep88:1, SG22Sep88:2, SG29Sep88:3, SG6Oct88:3, SG4Dec88:2, WC8Jan89:2,3, SG29Jan89:2, SG19Feb89:2, SG2Apr89:2, SG23Apr89:2, SG16Jul89:2, SG6Aug89:3, SG15Oct89:3

Oriental trade of, SG25Jun89:3
paper money in, SG13Oct88:2
payment of government officers of, SG4Jun89:2
pensioners of, SG19Nov89:4
permitted to send coal to French West Indies,
    WC5Feb89:2
politicians to wear homespun cloth, SG5Feb89:2
politics in, SG19Feb89:2
population of, SG30Apr89:3, SG11Jun89:4,
    SG3Sep89:3, SG10Sep89:2
Portuguese trade of, SG30Apr89:2
praise for government of, SG17Nov88:3,
    SG18Jun89:3
president of, SG9Jul89:2
presidential electors of, SG6Oct88:3
prevention of immigration of felons to, SG6Oct88:3
price of British goods in, SG11Dec88:1
privateering of, NCG29Mar86:4
Prussian treaty with, NCG29Mar86:1,
    WC18Jun88:2, WC22Jan89:1
regulation of trade of, NCG29Jul84:2,
    WC17Sep88:1, SG12Nov89:4
removal of government officers, SG13Aug89:2
reputation of, SG17Nov88:3
restrictions on grain exports of, WC26Oct88:2
revenue collection of, SG9Jul89:2
revenue officers of, FG14Sep89:2,3
Rhode Island attitude toward, SG26Feb89:2
risk of shipping in Mediterranean, SG28May89:3
safekeeping of Acts, Records, and Seal of,
    SG29Oct89:4
salaries of officials of, SG13Aug89:2, SG8Oct89:2
settlement of accounts of, WC25Jun88:1
ships bound for, WC27Aug88:3
Spanish minister to, SG5Nov89:2
spending habits of, SG12Jan86:3
supplies needed in 1789 by government of,
    SG13Aug89:4
Supreme Court appointments of, SG15Oct89:3
tariff of, WC16Jul88:2, SG11Jun89:2, FG21Sep89:4,
    SG12Nov89:4
tariff duties compared to those of Europe,
    SG12Nov89:2
taxes of, FG21Sep89:3
trade of, NCG2Sep84:3, NCG9Dec84:2,3,
    NCG3Nov85:3, NCGH23Feb86:2,
    SG29Nov87:2, SG7Feb88:2, WC30Jul88:2,
    SG8Sep88:3, WC10Sep88:2, SG6Oct88:3,
    SG13Oct88:3, SG27Oct88:2, SG10Nov88:2,
    WC3Dec88:3, SG11Dec88:2, SG8Jan89:3,
    WC8Jan89:1, SG22Jan89:3, WC5Feb89:2,
    SG5Mar89:2, SG26Mar89:2, SG4Jun89:3,
    SG11Jun89:3, SG2Jul89:2, SG10Sep89:2,
    FG14Sep89:3
trade restricted by Great Britain, SG27Oct88:2
trade threatened by Barbary pirates,
    NCGH23Feb86:2
Treasury Office examination, NCG23Feb86:3
troops raised by, SG3Sep89:4
vessels registered by, SG12Nov89:4
War Office of, SG26Mar89:3
West Indies trade of, NCGH19Jan86:2,
    SG29Nov87:2, SG5Nov89:2
western territory of, WC18Jun88:1, WC15Jan89:1
    disposition of, SG29Sep89:2
westward migration in, SG18Jun89:3

whaling in, WC6Aug88:2
wheat exports of, WC24Sep88:2
    See also Congress, U.S.
United States Gazette, extract from, SG10Sep89:3
University, federal, SG6Jul86:1
University of Edinburgh, SG24Nov88:2
University of North Carolina
    establishment of, SG3Dec89:3, SG31Dec89:3
    meeting of trustees of, SG31Dec89:3
University of Pennsylvania, SG14May89:2
Urquhart, Henry, WC12Nov88:3, WC19Nov88:4
Urrey, Francis, SG20Oct88:3, SG27Oct88:3
Ussery, Thomas, WC20Aug88:2
Ussory, Mr., SG29Sep88:3

V

Vail, Mr., EI4Jun88:3
Vail, Thomas, SG27Oct88:1, SG8Jan89:3
    trail of, EI9Apr88:2,3
Valteline, SG18Dec88:1
Vance, Capt. John, WC13Aug88:3
Vance, Mary, NCG6Jan85:1
Vance, Samuel, WC2Jul88:3—, WC17Sep88:3,
    WC24Sep88:1
Vance, Samuel, and Company, WC2Jul88:3—
Vancise, Capt., NCG29Jul84:3
Vandeburgh, Henry, NCG6Jan85:1
Vaughn, James, WC20Aug88:2
Vendue sale, WC15Oct88:1
Venice, Republic of
    letter from, WC25Jun88:2, WC5Nov89:2
    politics in, WC10Sep88:2
Vergin, William, SG12Jan86:4
Vermin, destruction of, SG18Jan87:3, SG18Dec88:3,
    WC18Dec88:2
Vermont, SG23Apr89:3
    approval of amendments to federal Constitution,
        SG17Dec89:2
    delegates of to Congress, SG15Nov87:2,
        SG15Sep88:1, WC24Sep88:2
    governor appointed in, SG10Dec89:2
    gubernatorial proclamation of, SG25Dec88:3
    politics in, SG15Sep88:1, WC24Sep88:2,
        SG24Nov88:2, SG25Dec88:3, SG10Dec89:2
    population of, SG10Nov88:2, SG10Sep89:2
    proposed consideration of federal Constitution,
        SG15Nov87:2, WC24Sep88:2
    relations with U.S., SG19Mar89:3, SG16Apr89:2,
        SG23Apr89:3
Vermont Journal, extract from, SG20Aug89:4
Versailles, report from, SG24Sep89:2
Versoul, France, explosion in, SG26Nov89:2
Vessel, William, SG17Sep89:3
Vestal, William, WC20Aug88:2
Vice president, U.S.
    election of, WC27Aug88:3, SG10Nov88:3,
        SG4Dec88:2, WC10Dec88:2,3, SG22Jan89:3,
        SG29Jan89:2, SG5Feb89:2, WCFeb89:2,
        SG12Feb89:2,3, WC12Feb89:1, SG19Feb89:2,3,
        WC19Feb89:2, SG5Mar89:3, SG12Mar89:2,3,
        SG19Mar89:3, SG30Apr89:2, SG19Nov89:2
    salary of considered by Congress, SG2Jul89:1
Vick, ____, SG3Dec89:3
Vienna

insurrection in, WC10Dec88:2
letter from, SG12Feb89:2, SG2Apr89:2,
    SG14May89:1, SG25Jun89:2
news from, NCG9Dec84:3, NCG3Nov85:3,
    NCGH2Feb86:2, NCGH16Feb86:2,
    WC18Jun88:2, WC5Nov88:2, SG8Jan89:2,
    WC22Jan89:2, SG4Jun89:1, SG23Jul89:1,
    SG30Jul89:1, SG19Nov89:1
Vinson, James, WC20Aug88:2
Vipon, Henry, SG27Mar88:3
Virginia, NCG29Mar86:2, SG26Feb89:3
    address to legislature of, SG16Apr89:1
    agriculture of, SG16Jul89:3
    American Revolution in, SG24Nov88:3
    calls for amendments to federal Constitution,
        WC3Dec88:2,3
    congressmen of, SG19Feb89:3
    consideration of federal Constitution, SG11Dec88:2,
        SG1Jan89:2,3
    constitutional convention of, SG15Nov87:2,
        WC3Dec88:2
    crops in, SG3Nov88:2, SG16Jul89:3
    description of, SG28May89:4
    elections in, WC25Jun88:2, WC3Dec88:3,
        WC19Feb89:2, SG5Mar89:3
    electors of, SG12Feb89:3
    Federalist sentiment in, EI4Jun88:1,2
    governor of, SG15Nov87:2, WC15Jan89:3
    letter from, SG12Feb89:3
    loyalists in, NCG9Dec84:3
    newspaper extract from, WC30Jul88:3
    opposition to federal Constitution, in, WC30Jul88:3
    politics in, SG15Nov87:3, SG29Nov87:3,
        EI4Jun88:1, WC25Jun88:2, WC2Jul88:2,
        WC9Jul88:1, WC30Jul88:3, SG17Nov88:3,
        SG24Nov88:3, WC3Dec88:3, SG11Dec88:2,
        SG18Dec88:3, SG1Jan89:2,3, SG12Feb89:2,3,
        SG19Feb89:3, WC19Feb89:2, SG9Apr89:2,
        SG5Mar89:3, SG5Nov89:3, SG17Dec89:2
    Patowmack Canal in, SG10Sep89:2
    proceedings of legislature in, SG3Nov88:2,
        WC3Dec88:2,3, SG9Apr89:3
    public securities in, SG6Oct88:3
    resolutions of legislature in, WC3Dec88:2,3
    state constitutional convention of, WC25Jun88:2
    storm in, WC20Aug88:3
    support for federal Constitution in, WC9Jul88:1,2,3
    trade of, WC24Sep88:1
Virginia Gazette, extract from, WC9Jul88:2
Virginia Independent Chronicle, extract from, SG30Jul89:4
"Virginian, A," SG23Apr89:1
Virtue
    lack of, NCG23Feb86:3
    praise for, NCG2Sep84:1
Volentine, Josiah, SG20Oct88:3, SG27Oct88:3
Vollintine
    See Watson and Vollintine
Vollintine, J., EI9Apr88:4, EI4Jun88:4
"Voter, A," NCG11Jul87:1

                        W

Waddell, Edmund, WC20Aug88:2
Waddell, General, WC23Jul88:3—
Waddell, Hugh, WC23Jul88:3—

Waddell, John B., WC23Jul88:3—
Wade, Thomas, WC20Aug88:2, SG24Sep89:3
Wadlor, William, NCG6Jan85:1
Wager, SG20Aug89:1
Waite, William, NCG9Dec84:4
Wake County, N.C., NCGH19Jan86:3, SG18Jan87:2,
    NCG15Aug87:4, WC13Aug88:3, SG8Sep88:3,
    SG29Sep88:3, WC26Nov88:3, SG25Dec88:2,
    SG17Sep89:3, SG3Dec89:3
Wake Court House, WC6Aug88:3
Walke, Anthony, SG22Oct89:3, SG29Oct89:3,
    SG12Nov89:4
Walker, Ann, WC13Aug88:3
Walker, Arthur, SG20Oct88:3, SG27Oct88:3
Walker, James, WC25Jun88:3, WC8Jan89:3,
    WC19Feb89:3, WC26Feb89:1
Walker, John, WC13Aug88:3, WC19Feb89:3,
    WC26Feb89:1
Walker, Major, WC16Jul88:2, WC23Jul88:1
Walker & Younger, WC3Dec88:3—
Wallace, J., SG3Dec89:2
Wallace, John, SG12Jan86:4, NCG29Mar86:2,
    SG24Sep89:3
Wallace, Michael, SG12Jan86:4, NCG29Mar86:2
Wallace, T., SG3Dec89:3
Waller and Bregen, NCG29Mar86:2
Wamock, ____, SG17Sep89:3
Ward, Charles, WC20Aug88:2, SG22Sep88:3
Ward, Edward, SG10Sep89:3
Ward, Mr., SG29Sep88:3
Ward, Richard, SG18Jan87:3
Ward, T., SG19Mar89:3—
Wardens of the Poor, WC18Dec88:3, SG31Dec89:3
Warehouse, SG6Jul86:4, WC5Feb89:3, WC12Feb89:4
    breaking into, SG25Dec88:3
    inspectors for, WC18Dec88:3
Warford, truce arranged at with Cherokee Indians,
    SG26Nov89:3
Warrants, military bounty, SG30Apr89:4
Warren County, N.C., SG18Jan87:3, NCG1Aug87:3,
    SG25Dec88:2, SG24Sep89:3
Warrenton, N.C., NCG11Jul87:4, NCG15Aug87:4,
    EI19Dec87:2, SG8Sep88:2,3, SG15Sep88:4—,
    WC26Nov88:3, SG4Dec88:3, SG3Dec89:3
    academy in, SG18Jan87:3
Warrenton Academy, SG8Sep88:3—
    meeting of trustees of, SG22Oct89:3
Warrington, John, SG12Jan86:2
Warsaw, Poland
    letter from, SG27Oct88:2, WC5Feb:1,2
    news from, NCG29Jul84:1, NCG2Sep84:2,
        WC9Jul88:2, WC30Jul88:2, SG17Dec89:1
Warwick County, England, murder in, SG11Dec88:3
Washington, ____, SG27Mar88:2, SG29Jan89:2
Washington, General, SG20Oct88:3
Washington, George, WC20Aug88:4, SG9Apr89:3,
    SG23Apr89:1, SG11Jun89:3, SG22Oct89:4
    address to SG14May89:2, SG21May89:2,
        SG9Jul89:2,3, FG24Aug89:1, SG29Oct89:2,
        SG19Nov89:4, SG10Dec89:4
    address to Congress by, SG21May89:2
    arrival of in Boston, SG10Dec89:2
    birthday celebration of, WC12Feb89:2,3,
        SG19Feb89:2, WC5Mar89:2
    character of, WC10Sep88:1, WC22Sep88:4,
        SG15Jan89:2, SG20Aug89:2

escort for as President, SG7May89:3, SG14May89:3
estate of, SG13Aug89:2, FG24Aug89:2
gift to, NCG3Nov85:3
inauguration of, SG21May89:1,2
inscription for tombstone of, SG26Feb89:4
letter by, NCG9Dec84:3, WC16Jul88:3,
    SG20Aug89:2
levee given by, SG8Oct89:2
mother of, SG8Oct89:2
ode to, WC24Sep88:2
reception of in N.Y., SG21May89:2,3
resignation of, NCGH19Jan86:4
response to addresses to, SG14May89:2,
    SG21May89:2,3, SG11Jun89:3, SG9Jul89:3,
    SG29Oct89:2, SG19Nov89:4, SG10Dec89:4
sonata to, SG21May89:4
speech of, SG21May89:2
tour of, SG23Apr89:2, SG30Apr89:3, SG7May89:3,
    SG14May89:2, SG17Sep89:3, SG19Nov89:2,4,
    SG26Nov89:1,2
Washington, Mary, death of, SG10Sep89:3
Washington, Mrs., reception for in N.J., SG25Jun89:2
Washington, N.C., NCG2Sep84:3,4, NCG9Dec84:4,
    NCG3Nov85:1, NCG29Mar86:1, SG6Jul86:3,4,
    NCG19Dec87:4, SG7Feb88:3, SG27Mar88:4,
    SG8Sep88:4, SG22Sep88:4—, SG27Oct88:3,4,
    SG17Nov88:4, SG8Jan89:3, SG3Dec89:3,
    SG17Dec89:2
Washington, Pa., letter from, SG29Nov87:2
Washington County, N.C., SG18Jan87:2,
    SG18Dec88:3, WC18Dec88:2,3, SG25Dec88:2,
    SG15Jan89:4—, SG16Apr89:3
court of, SG18Jan87:2
letter from, SG26Feb89:3, WC5Mar89:2
Washington County, Pa., letter from, SG15Jan89:2
Washington District, N.C., SG25Dec88:4
Watch, stolen, SG7Feb88:2
Watchmaker, SG18Jun89:1,2
Watercraft, horse-propelled, NCG2Sep84:2
Waterford, Ireland
letter from, WC10Dec88:2
shipping to, WC10Dec88:2
Waters, Col., WC3Nov88:3
Watertown, quilting by woman in vicinity of,
    WC17Sep88:2
Watkins, SG3Dec89:3
Watkins, Levi, SG17Sep89:3
Watson, Alex., SG3Dec89:3
Watson, Alexander, SG24Sep89:3
Watson, Daniel, SG20Oct88:3, SG27Oct88:3
Watson, Elka., SG27Mar88:3
Watson, Elkanah, EI4Jun88:4
Watson, George, SG27Mar88:3
Watson, J., SG3Dec89:3
Watson, James, SG27Mar88:3, SG3Sep89:3
Watson, Ralph, SG20Oct88:3, SG27Oct88:3,
    SG8Jan89:3, SG15Jan89:4
Watson, William, WC13Aug88:3
Watson and Vollintine, EI4Jun88:4
Watters, W., WC18Jun88:4—, SG10Dec89:3
Watts, John, SG11Dec88:2
Waxworks, WC26Oct88:3
exhibit of, WC10Dec88:3
Wayne County, N.C., NCG2Sep84:3, SG18Jan87:2,
    SG25Dec88:2, SG3Sep89:3
Weakley, Robert, WC20Aug88:2

Weather, variability of, SG11Dec88:3
Webb, Robert, SG24Sep89:3
Webber, Thomas, NCG6Jan85:1
Webster, Noah, marriage of, SG26Nov89:3
Wench, Negro, wanted, NCGH19Jan86:3,
    NCGH2Feb86:3, WC19Nov88:3, WC26Nov88:4
Wescot, John, letter from, SG23Apr89:3
West Indies, NCG29Mar86:1, SG25Dec88:3,
    WC25Dec88:2, WC8Jan89:4, WC22Jan89:2,
    SG16Apr89:3, SG24Sep89:2
British exportation of rum and spirits to U.S.,
    WC8Jan89:1
commerce in, SG27Mar88:3, WC8Jan89:1,
    SG28May89:3, FG24Aug89:3, SG8Oct89:2,
    SG22Oct89:2
crime in, SG20Oct88:2
exchange of islands by France and Spain,
    SG16Apr89:3
export of sugar from, WC25Dec88:2
French attacks on, NCG19Dec87:2
French islands in, SG5Nov89:3
French military movements in, SG3Dec89:1
French trade in, SG29Oct89:2
news from, WC15Jan89:2, WC29Jan89:2
regulation of trade to French islands in,
    SG27Mar88:3
regulation of U.S. imports, WC25Jun88:2
sale of goods from, FG24Aug89:3
slaves in, SG25Jun89:2
U.S. trade with, WC6Aug88:2, SG27Oct88:2,
    SG18Dec88:3
warships in, SG29Oct89:2,3
Western territory (western settlements), U.S.,
    NCG2Sep84:2, SG29Nov87:2, WC18Jun88:1,
    WC17Sep88:3, WC24Sep88:2, SG29Sep88:1,
    SG6Oct88:3, SG20Oct88:1, SG26Feb89:2,
    SG24Sep89:2, SG1Oct89:3, SG8Oct89:3,
    SG15Oct89:3, SG22Oct89:4, SG12Nov89:2
agriculture in, FG12Oct89:3
banditti in, SG24Sep89:3
bill for land office in, SG2Jul89:1
British presence in, EI4Jun88:2, WC26Nov88:2,
    SG22Oct89:2, SG17Dec89:2
description of, SG12Jan86:2,3
forts in, SG10Nov88:2, WC26Nov88:2
future of, SG29Sep88:2
governor, WC17Sep88:2,3
immigrants to, SG3Sep89:2,3
Indians in, SG8Sep88:2,3, SG22Sep88:3,
    SG24Nov88:3, SG24Sep89:3, SG15Oct89:3,
    SG5Nov89:3
land office for, SG2Jul89:1
protection for, WC17Sep88:2, SG18Dec88:3
report of governor of, SG15Oct89:3
Spanish involvement in, SG29Nov87:2,
    SG20Oct88:2, SG6Aug89:1, SG10Sep89:3,
    SG24Sep89:2,3
U.S. governance of, SG29Sep88:2
Westfields, NCG15Aug87:2
Westmore
    See Savage & Westmore
Wet nurse, WC26Nov88:1
Whale oil, SG12Jan86:2
Whaling, SG12Jan86:2, WC6Aug88:2, SG12Mar89:2,
    SG5Nov89:2
Wharf, WC12Nov88:3, WC19Nov88:3

Campbell's, WC19Feb89:3
county, SG18Jan87:4
market, WC19Feb89:3, WC26Feb89:1
Maxwell's, WC12Feb89:3, WC19Feb89:4
Potts, WC19Feb89:3, WC26Feb89:1
Quince's, WC3Dec88:3—
sale of, WC12Nov88:3, WC19Nov88:3
Wheaton, William, SG20Oct88:3, SG27Oct88:3
Wheeler, John, SG9Jul89:3—
Whiston, Joseph, WC20Aug88:2
Whitaker, ____, SG3Dec89:3
Whitaker, John, SG24Sep89:3
White, ____, SG3Dec89:3
White, Adam, SG22Oct89:3, SG29Oct89:3,
SG12Nov89:4
White, Capt., SG11Dec88:3
White, Dr., SG27Mar88:3
White, Henry, SG18Jan87:3
White, J., SG3Dec89:3
White, James, SG6Jul86:3, SG7Feb88:3, SG9Apr89:3,
SG17Dec89:3, SG31Dec89:2,3
White, Thomas, EI9Apr88:1, SG20Oct88:3,
SG27Oct88:3, SG9Jul89:3—
Whitehall, news from, WC10Sep88:2, SG27Aug89:2
Whiteman, Mathew, Sr., SG9Apr89:3—
Whiteside, James, WC20Aug88:2
Whitney, Capt., NCG29Jul84:3
Whitney, John M., NCGH19Jan86:4, NCGH2Feb86:3
Whitney, Myrick, SG27Mar88:3
Whitty, ____, SG3Dec89:3
Whitty, E., WC20Aug88:2
Whitty, Edward, SG3Sep89:3
Widows
anecdote about, SG25Jun89:4
provision for, SG31Dec89:3
Wife
elopement of, NCG2Sep84:4, SG29Nov87:4,
WC2Jul88:3, WC19Nov88:3
infidelity of, SG20Oct88:2
sale of, WC26Nov88:2
Wigan, England, christenings in, WC18Dec88:3
Wilcox, John, WC18Jun88:4—
Wilkes, Mr., anecdote from, NCGH23Feb86:1
Wilkes County, N.C., SG25Dec88:2, FG14Sep89:3,
SG31Dec89:3
Wilkie, Malcom, WC3Dec88:3—
Wilkie, Mr., NCGH23Feb86:1
Wilkings, M. R., SG7Feb88:2
Wilkings, Mar. R., WC3Sep88:3, WC10Sep88:4,
WC17Sep88:3,4, WC24Sep88:1, WC8Jan89:3
Wilkings, Robert, WC5Feb89:3
Wilkinson, Frances, NCGH16Feb86:4,
NCGH23Feb86:4
Will (slave), WC29Jan89:3, SG25Jun89:3—,
SG23Jul89:4
Williams, B., SG3Dec89:3
Williams, Benjamin, NCG29Jul84:3, SG29Nov87:4,
WC13Aug88:3, WC20Aug88:2, SG31Dec89:3
Williams, Charles, SG29Nov87:4
Williams, E., SG24Sep89:3, SG3Dec89:3
Williams, Edward, WC20Aug88:2
Williams, Elizabeth, SG18Jan87:3
Williams, Jacob, WC13Aug88:3
Williams, James, SG23Feb86:4
Williams, John, NCG19Dec87:4, SG17Dec89:3
Williams, John P., SG22Sep88:3, WC12Feb89:3—,

SG10Sep89:3
Williams, John Pugh, WC20Aug88:2,3
Williams, Joseph, NCG29Jul84:3
Williams, Robert, SG29Nov87:4, WC20Aug88:2,
SG10Sep89:4, SG17Sep89:4
Williams, S., EI4Jun88:3
Williams, Samuel, NCG29Mar86:2
Williams, T. P., SG3Dec89:2,3
Williams, Thomas, NCG3Nov85:4, SG7Feb88:3,
SG3Sep89:3
Williams, W., SG3Dec89:3
Williams, William, NCG6Jan85:1, SG27Mar88:3,
SG3Sep89:3
Williamsborough, N.C., SG10Nov88:3, SG31Dec89:2,4
Williamsborough Seminary, SG24Sep89:3,
SG31Dec89:4
Williamsburg, Va., Grammar School, SG23Feb86:4
Williamsburgh, Va., SG23Feb86:4
letter from, SG19Feb89:2
Williamson, ____, SG27Mar88:2, SG3Dec89:2
Williamson, Dr., SG29Nov87:2
Williamson, Francis, NCG29Mar86:2
Williamson, H., SG3Dec89:3
Williamson, Henry, SG20Oct88:3, SG27Oct88:3
Williamson, Hugh, SG7Feb88:3, SG27Mar88:3,
SG22Jan89:3, WC5Feb89:2, SG27Aug89:3,
FG14Sep89:3, SG1Oct89:3, SG31Dec89:3
letter from, SG24Dec89:4
Williamson, Jacob, SG8Jan89:3, SG15Jan89:4
Williamson, John, SG27Mar88:3
Williamson, Mr., FG12Oct89:3
Willis, A., SG22Jan89:3
Willis, Augustine, SG27Mar88:3
Willis, John, WC20Aug88:2, SG22Sep88:3,
SG17Sep89:3
Willis, Mildred, NCG11Jul87:4
Wills
See Hodge & Wills
Wills
execution of, SG31Dec89:3
proving of, SG3Dec89:3, SG31Dec89:3
Willson, James, SG9Jul89:3—
Willson, Joshua, SG22Oct89:3, SG29Oct89:3,
SG12Nov89:4
Wilson, ____, SG3Dec89:3
Wilson, Andrew, NCG5Jan85:1
Wilson, D., SG3Dec89:3
Wilson, Hezekiah, SG17Sep89:3
Wilson, James, SG18Jan87:3, WC20Aug88:2,
SG20Oct88:3, SG27Oct88:3, WC29Jan89:3,
WC5Feb89:1, SG9Apr89:2
Wilson, Doctor Lewis F., WC13Aug88:3
Wilson, Z., SG3Dec89:3
Wilson, Zachias, WC20Aug88:2
Wilton, Robert, SG27Mar88:3
Wilmington, Del., WC8Jan89:2
news from, SG19Feb89:2, SG10Sep89:2
storm in, WC8Jan89:2
Wilmington, N.C., NCG29Jul84:2, NCG9Dec84:2,
NCGH19Jan86:4, NCGH2Feb86:3, SG23Feb86:2,
NCG29Mar86:2, SG6Jul86:3,4, SG4Oct87:4,
SG29Nov87:4, SG7Feb88:2, WC18Jun88:1,3,4,
WC25Jun88:3,4, WC2Jul88:3,4, WC9Jul88:3,4,
WC16Jul88:2,3,4, WC23Jul88:1,3,4,
WC30Jul88:1,3,4, WC6Aug88:1,3,4,
WC13Aug88:4, WC20Aug88:3,4, WC27Aug88:3,4,

WC3Sep88:3,4, SG8Sep88:4, WC10Sep88:3,4,
SG15Sep88:4, WC17Sep88:3,4, SG22Sep88:3,
WC24Sep88:1, SG29Sep88:4, SG6Oct88:4,
SG13Oct88:4, WC15Oct88:1,2, SG20Oct88:4,
WC26Oct88:3,4, SG27Oct88:4, SG2Nov88:3,
WC5Nov88:3,4, SG10Nov88:3, WC12Nov88:1,3,4,
SG17Nov88:4, WC19Nov88:3,4, WC26Nov88:3,4,
WC3Dec88:1,3, WC8Jan89:3, WC15Jan89:3,4,
WC22Jan89:3,4, WC29Jan89:2,3,4, WC5Feb89:3,4,
WC12Feb89:4, WC19Feb89:1,3,4,
WC26Feb89:1,3,4, WC5Mar89:1, SG10Sep89:3,
SG3Dec89:3, SG17Dec89:3, SG31Dec89:3
accident to shipping of, WC29Jan89:2
celebration of George Washington's birthday in,
    WC12Feb89:1,2
celebration of Virginia's ratification, WC16Jul88:2
cemetery in, WC29Jan89:2
clerk of the market in, WC12Feb89:2
commissioners of, WC5Feb89:2
disorderly sailors in, WC12Feb89:3
drowning in, WC26Oct88:3
elections in, WC16Jul88:2, WC6Aug88:2,
    WC13Aug88:2, WC3Sep88:3, WC8Jan89:3
exports from, SG14May89:3
fire in, WC10Sep88:3
fire fighting in, WC5Feb89:3
government of, WC5Feb89:2,3, WC12Feb89:3,
    WC19Feb89:3, WC26Feb89:1
lack of jail in, WC18Jun88:3
law regulating town of, SG31Dec89:3
letter from, SG23Feb86:3, SG29Sep88:3,
    SG29Jan89:2, SG24Sep89:3
mercantile intelligence office in, WC18Dec88:3
news from, WC18Jun88:3, WC25Jun88:2,
    WC2Jul88:2, WC9Jul88:2, WC16Jul88:3,
    WC23Jul88:2,3, WC30Jul88:3, WC6Aug88:2,
    WC13Aug88:3, WC20Aug88:3, WC3Sep88:2,
    WC10Sep88:3, WC17Sep88:3, WC24Sep88:2,
    SG29Sep88:3, WC1Oct88:1, WC26Oct88:3,
    SG27Oct88:2, WC5Nov88:2,3, WC12Nov88:3,
    WC19Nov88:3, WC26Nov88:3, WC3Dec88:3,
    WC10Dec88:3, WC18Dec88:2, WC25Dec88:3,
    WC8Jan89:3, WC15Jan89:3, WC22Jan89:3,
    WC29Jan89:2, WC5Feb89:2, WC12Feb89:2,3,
    WC19Feb89:3, WC26Feb89:2,3,
    SG26Mar89:2,3, SG2Apr89:2,3, SG14May89:3,
    SG24Sep89:3
receipts and expenditures of town commissioner of,
    WC19Feb89:3, WC26Feb89:1
regulation of market house of, WC12Feb89:3
robbery, WC2Jul88:2
rubbish disposed in, WC5Feb89:3
runaway slaves from, WC9Jul88:3
shipping of, WC18Jun88:2, WC5Nov88:3,
    WC3Dec88:3, WC19Feb89:3
slave curfew in, WC5Feb89:3
spurious meat brought to market in, WC18Jun88:3
theater in, WC26Feb89:3
town politics of, WC16Jul88:2, WC23Jul88:1,2
trade of, WC15Jan89:3
Wilmington Centinel, publication schedule of,
    WC15Oct88:1, WC18Dec88:3
Wilmington District, SG25Dec88:4
    Superior Court session in adjourned, WC18Dec88:3
Wilmington Hunting Club, SG23Feb86:3
Wilmington packet, WC25Dec88:3

Wimble, James, WC29Jan89:4—
Wimble, William, WC29Jan89:4—
Winchester, James, WC20Aug88:2
Winchester, Va., news from, SG6Oct88:3,
    SG13Oct88:4, WC10Dec88:2, SG16Jul89:3,
    SG30Jul89:2, SG10Sep89:3, SG12Nov89:3
Windsor, England, letter from, SG25Jun89:2
Windsor, N.C., SG18Jan87:2, SG15Jan89:3,
    SG22Jan89:3,4, SG29Jan89:3—, SG26Feb89:3,
    SG12Mar89:4, SG2Apr89:3, SG9Apr89:4,
    SG23Apr89:3—, SG18Jun89:4, SG25Jun89:4,
    SG9Jul89:4, SG23Jul89:4—, SG17Sep89:3,4,
    SG24Sep89:4—, SG22Oct89:4—
    letter from, SG25Jun89:2
    regulation of, SG18Jan87:2
Windward Islands, arrival of Prince William Henry in,
    WC25Jun88:2
Wine, sale of, WC18Jun88:3, WC2Jul88:1—,
    WC26Feb89:1, SG6Aug89:3—
Winslow, Caleb, SG8Jan89:3
Winslow, NCGH6Oct85:4
Winston, J., SG3Dec89:3
Winston, Joseph, SG24Sep89:3
Winton, N.C., SG12Jan86:4, SG30Apr89:3—,
    SG13Aug89:3—
Witherspoon, David, SG20Oct88:3
Witherspoon, Elizabeth, death of, SG5Nov89:3
Wodkin, John, NCGH19Jan86:3, NCGH2Feb86:3
Wodkins, Mr., SG20Oct88:3, SG27Oct88:3
Womack, ____, SG3Dec89:3
Womack, John, WC20Aug88:2
Woman
    adventure of in France, SG19Feb89:3
    brittle bones of, NCGH16Feb86:2
Women
    advice on reading for, NCG29Jul84:1
    appreciation for, NCGH6Oct85:1
    consequences of political involvement of,
        SG3Dec89:2
    dress of, SG12Jan86:3
    fashions of, SG18Jun89:3
    hints for the married, WC18Jun88:1
    novel to promote education of, WC12Feb89:1
    problems of in traveling, SG23Feb86:2
    qualification to hold public office, SG29Sep88:2
    unmarried, WC13Aug88:4
Wood, James, SG29Nov87:1
Wood, Mr., SG29Sep88:3
Wood, R., SG3Dec89:3
Wood, Reuben, FG14Sep89:3
Wood, William, SG24Sep89:3
Wood, Z., SG3Dec89:3
Wood, Zebeda, WC20Aug88:2
Wood, Zebulon, FG14Sep89:3
Wood, preservation of, WC10Sep88:1
Woodburn, Thomas, NCG6Jan85:1
Woods, Bob, ran away, FG12Oct89:4
Woods, T., SG3Dec89:3
Woods, W., SG3Dec89:3
Woodstock, N.C., NCG2Sep84:3
Wootten, William, WC20Aug88:2
Worcester, Mass.
    cod fish industry in, SG19Mar89:2
    manufacturing in, SG19Mar89:2
    news from, SG1Jan89:2, SG19Mar89:2,
        SG23Apr89:2, SG28May89:3

nomination of sheriff for, WC15Jan89:3
supreme court meeting in, SG28May89:3
Words, improper use of, SG25Dec88:2
Worsley, James SG9Apr89:3
Worsley, John, SG9Apr89:3
Worsley, Petman, SG9Apr89:3
Wounded persons, relief of, SG31Dec89:3
Wrapping paper, WC15Oct88:2
Wright, David, SG20Oct88:3, SG27Oct88:3,
SG8Jan89:3, SG15Jan89:4
Wright, Dr., SG12Jan86:4
Wright, James, SG22Oct89:3, SG29Oct89:3,
SG12Nov89:4
Wright, Mr., WC18Jun88:4, WC25Jun88:4
Wright, Mrs., WC5Nov88:3
Wright, Sheriff, WC18Jun88:4
Wright, Thomas, SG12Jan86:4, SG7Feb88:2,
WC16Jul88:3—
Writing paper, WC18Jun88:4—
Writing supplies, SG19Feb89:3, SG12Mar89:3—
Wynes, Thomas, WC20Aug88:2
Wynns, T., SG3Dec89:3
Wynns, Thomas, SG27Aug89:3, FG14Sep89:3
Wyns, George, WC20Aug88:2
Wythe, George, SG23Feb86:4

Y

"Y," WC10Sep88:1
Yancey, ____, SG3Dec89:3
Yancey, T., SG17Sep89:3
Yancey, Thornton, WC20Aug88:2
Yates, ____, SG22Sep88:3
Yates, Daniel, WC20Aug88:2, SG10Sep89:3
Yeargan, Samuel, SG18Jan87:3
"Yeoman, A," NCG15Aug87:2
Yonkers, N.Y., fire in, SG26Feb89:2
York, England, death of girl in, SG19Feb89:1
York, Pa., news from, SG5Mar89:3
Yorktown, Pa., politics in, WC10Sep88:1
Young, ____, NCGH16Feb86:3
Young, James, NCG6Jan85:1
Young, Miller, and Co., NCGH2Feb86:3,
NCGH23Feb86:3
Younger
See Walker & Younger

Z

Zoffany, ____, death of, SG6Aug89:3
Zollicoffer, George, SG20Oct88:3, SG27Oct88:3,
SG9Jul89:3—

APPENDIX 1
Advertisements in North Carolina Newspapers, 1784-1789

	STATE GAZETTE OF NORTH CAROLINA[a] (New Bern and Edenton)	THE WILMINTON CENTINEL, AND GENERAL ADVERTISER[b]	NORTH CAROLINA GAZETTE, OR IMPARTIAL INTELLIGENCER AND WEEKLY ADVERTISER[b] (New Bern)	MARTIN'S NORTH CAROLINA GAZETTE[b] (New Bern)	FAYETTEVILLE GAZETTE[b]	THE NORTH CAROLINA GAZETTE; OR THE EDENTON INTELLIGENCER[b]	NORTH CAROLINA GAZETTE (Hillsborough)	TOTAL
	N=20	N=9	N=2	N=5	N=4	N=3	N=5	48
Land, Houses, Lots for sale	15	14	1	2			16	48
Land, Houses, Lots for rent	5	7	2	1				15
Slaves for sale or hire	6	1			2		5	14
Slaves-runaways or captured	11	7	5	2	1	1		27
Business Notices– openings or dissolutions	8	2		2	1	3	4	20
Merchandise for sale	19	19	5	6	6	2	7	64
Positions wanted	3	1		1	1	1	1	8
Merchandise wanted		8		1			4	13
Ships—sailing, for sale, for hire	1	6		1		1		9
Schools Opening	8	3		2				13
Public Entertainments	4	2	1		1			8
Lost, Found, and Stolen Goods	5	1	1	1	3	1		12
Administrator and Executor Notices	4	15	6		1		1	27
Other	45	12	5	6	5	5	25	103
Total	134	98	26	25	21	14	53	371
Average	6.7	10.9	13	5	5.3	4.7	10.6	7.7

N—Number of issues sampled
[a]Represents samples of the newspaper taken from the first extant issue of each available month.
[b]Represents the total extant issues of the newspaper.

APPENDIX 2

The Speed with Which News Was Reported in North Carolina Newspapers, 1784-1789

(N=number of datelines; R=range in days between the fastest and slowest reports;
A=average time of transit and reporting.)

ORIGIN OF DATELINES		STATE GAZETTE OF NORTH CAROLINA (New Bern and Edenton)	THE WILMINGTON CENTINEL, AND GENERAL ADVERTISER	MARTIN'S NORTH CAROLINA GAZETTE (New Bern)	FAYETTEVILLE GAZETTE	THE NORTH CAROLINA GAZETTE, OR IMPARTIAL INTELLIGENCER AND WEEKLY GENERAL ADVERTISER (New Bern)	THE NORTH CAROLINA GAZETTE; OR THE EDENTON INTELLIGENCER	NORTH CAROLINA GAZETTE (Hillsborough)
British Isles	N	13	9	2	3	2	1	5
	R	67/125	72/102	70/75	95/114	114/117	91	91/131
	A	94	90	73	101	116	91	108
Continental Europe	N	3	7	2		5		
	R	67/173	95/129	76/112		123/142		
	A	123	108	94		130		
Massachusetts	N	9	3	2			1	
	R	17/52	34/36	21/46			32	
	A	38	35	34			32	
Connecticut	N	1	1					
	R	52	40					
	A	52	40					
Rhode Island	N	2	1					
	R	21/28	60					
	A	25	60					
New York	N	17	6	2	1			2
	R	14/41	18/42	26/47	23			45/59
	A	27	30	37	23			52
Pennsylvania	N	15	3	2	1	2	1	1
	R	18/37	28/34	19/20	47	40/40	16	73
	A	26	32	20	47	40	16	73
Maryland	N	6	2	2	1	1		
	R	16/34	27/30	15/25	48	30		
	A	23	29	20	48	30		
Virginia	N	7	2			3		1
	R	5/26	20/27			26/27		48
	A	15	24			26		48
North Carolina	N	3	1		1		1	
	R	14/27	13		25		37	
	A	21	13		25		37	
South Carolina	N	4	3		1			1
	R	17/50	6/13		42			49
	A	40	10		42			49
Georgia	N	1	1					
	R	35	75					
	A	35	75					
West Indies	N	2						1
	R	37/75						99
	A	56						99